ESSENTIALS OF
BREAKFAST
& BRUNCH

WILLIAMS-SONOMA

ESSENTIALS OF
BREAKFAST
& BRUNCH

RECIPES, MENUS, AND IDEAS FOR DELICIOUS MORNING MEALS

GENERAL EDITOR
CHUCK WILLIAMS

PHOTOGRAPHY
TUCKER + HOSSLER

RECIPES
GEORGEANNE BRENNAN
ELINOR KLIVANS
JORDAN MACKAY
CHARLES PIERCE

Contents

A satisfying morning meal can set the tone for the rest of the day. Even on a busy weekday, I like to start off with a satisfying breakfast. If you're not in the habit of cooking for yourself or your family in the morning, you're guaranteed to be tempted to change your ways by the recipes in this book, many of them easy to prepare. On a leisurely weekend or for a special occasion or holiday celebration, hosting a brunch is an ever-popular way to entertain.

You may be accustomed to thinking that eggs, cereals, and pancakes are the fundamentals of a breakfast or brunch menu. On the following pages, you will discover dozens of recipes that you may never have considered serving at a morning meal. Brunch lends itself to main dishes like crab cakes and pasta, sandwiches of grilled chicken or vegetables, and salads with seafood and fruit. If your tastes lean toward breakfast and brunch classics, you'll find plenty of these, too, including waffles, pancakes, potato side dishes, and a host of delicious preparations for eggs. An entire chapter is devoted to baking breads and pastries, everyone's favorites at the morning table. Rounding out the recipes is a selection of drinks. With these numerous and versatile choices, you'll be able to create a breakfast or brunch menu for any occasion.

Whether your time in the kitchen is limited or generous, *Essentials of Breakfast & Brunch* gives you a wealth of information for planning ahead. Detailed information on ingredients will help you stock your pantry and refrigerator, cook with fresh produce in season, and make sure you have the right equipment on hand. Tips are provided for sending invitations, planning a menu, organizing a buffet, and setting an attractive table. Each chapter describes techniques that will allow you to learn key culinary skills when you prepare the recipes, from working with a yeast dough and beating egg whites for a soufflé to cooking perfect pancakes.

Essentials of Breakfast & Brunch shows how versatile the morning meal can be. After making these recipes, a homemade breakfast may become routine at your house, and brunch may be one of your favorite meals for entertaining family and friends.

Chuck Williams

The First Meal of the Day

Throughout much of history, breakfast was a practical necessity for launching the workday. With the rising popularity of brunch, both of these first meals of the day are the perfect opportunity for celebrating a special occasion or just enjoying good food in the company of friends and family.

THE EVOLUTION OF BREAKFAST AND BRUNCH

Breakfast in many forms, depending on the culture, has been part of the daily routine for centuries. The word itself reveals the meal's purpose: to break the fast after a night's rest. Brunch has become a more recent addition to the culinary vocabulary. Food historians have various theories about its origin, but many reliable sources agree that the first reference to brunch appeared in England in the 1890s.

The name, a contraction of the words "breakfast" and "lunch," described a meal that was leisurely and sociable. It was often served later in the morning than breakfast and lacked breakfast's time constraints, and the menu could be more substantial and adventurous. Nowadays, brunch implies an occasion for entertaining and is considered a meal made for lingering in the company of friends and family, or for spending a lazy Sunday morning reading the newspaper.

At the brunch table, longtime favorites like eggs Benedict, Belgian waffles, and quiche remain popular. Foods that were once regional specialities, such as bagels and lox in New York City and polenta and focaccia in Italy, have spread far beyond their places of origin and are at home on a brunch menu. As this book shows, brunch also embraces risotto, panini, seafood salads, and other dishes associated with lunch or even dinner.

Breakfasts, too, have evolved. Classic fare such as ham, eggs, toast, and home fries, perhaps with griddle cakes and syrup—used to be the morning standard from rural home kitchens and whistle-stop cafés to city coffee shops. As workers traded in physical labor for office work, breakfast slimmed down, and such hefty spreads were relegated to special events, in favor of foods that could be prepared and consumed quickly.

Nowadays, the morning meal, by whatever name you give it, can vary based on the time, the occasion, and the preferences of the cook and guests. You can start the day with old-fashioned oatmeal or an omelet, or a crab salad or a breakfast pizza, all of which you will find in these pages.

BENEFITS OF THE FIRST MEAL

Nutritionists champion the importance of breakfast for good reason. It stimulates the body's metabolism, it boosts energy and alertness, and it helps both adults and children stay focused and productive throughout most of the day. Eating well in the morning also helps stave off unwelcome midday energy slumps caused by low blood sugar.

A wholesome breakfast should provide a balance of protein, complex carbohydrates, and healthy fats. Recipes that meet these requirements do not have to be time-consuming to prepare, and sometimes they can be assembled ahead, all or in part. Quick weekday favorites include a parfait of made-ahead granola layered with fresh fruit or a bowl of oatmeal with a fruit topping.

If you are allowing more time to make brunch for guests, you have a broader range of options, such as planning a menu with a main dish using eggs or another protein such as bacon or sausage, or with hearty

A simple meal such as scrambled eggs, bacon, and toast is perfect morning fare.

pancakes or waffles accompanied by a side dish of fruits. Baked treats, such as muffins or other quick breads, are possibilities, too.

A REASON TO COME TOGETHER

Birthdays, anniversaries, engagements, graduations, bridal and baby showers, and other important events in the lives of your family and friends are ideal times to celebrate with a festive breakfast or brunch. However, you don't need a landmark occasion to bring together and treat the people you care about to a special morning meal.

With flexible menu options and timing, a weekend breakfast or brunch can allow for a range of schedules, especially during busy times of the year such as the holiday season. It can also be a casual, yet elegant meal that doesn't require the planning and timing of a formal sit-down dinner. For example, you can set up a buffet in the living room, garden, or even on a kitchen counter, so guests can help themselves as they mingle.

KEEPING IT SIMPLE

You don't have to be a restaurant chef to serve a delicious breakfast or brunch. Geared toward today's busy lifestyles, most of the recipes in this book are easy to prepare, and many can be made partially or wholly in advance.

If you feel challenged by preparing a large menu, plan on making only one dish requiring last-minute preparation. Instead of pancakes and scrambled eggs, for example, prepare an egg dish the day of the party and accompany it with muffins, scones, or coffee cake baked the day before. Or, offer guests hot pancakes, French toast, or waffles and a salad of fruit in season that can be assembled in advance.

You can also create a juice bar (page 34) or a smoothie station (page 35), or you can lay out a bagel bar (page 98). Not only will one of these options ease your work as host and allow you more time to socialize, but it will give guests an opportunity to create their own drinks as well as assemble bagels to suit their own taste.

GETTING ORGANIZED

Here are some suggestions for planning your menu and easing your meal preparation.

■ Choose a variety of recipes that can be made ahead and some that can be prepared the day of the event.

■ Balance a rich main course with a fruit or vegetable salad or another light side dish.

■ For a large gathering, consider doubling a make-ahead recipe, such as a *strata* (page 187) or individual quiches (page 61).

■ If your main course features meat, chicken, or seafood, be sure to offer a vegetarian option, especially for larger gatherings.

■ For recipes that cannot be made entirely in advance, wash, peel, and chop raw ingredients the night before and store them in separate airtight containers in the refrigerator.

■ When writing your shopping list, check that you have plenty of ice in your freezer for drinks and, if necessary, purchase a bag or two to have on hand.

■ Assemble as much tableware as you can the night before. Set the table or buffet with plates, utensils, and napkins. If you are serving the meal outdoors, organize the tableware on trays so it's ready to go. Pick out the serving dishes, serving utensils, and platters you'll use to present the food on your menu.

■ If you are hosting an outdoor event, have a backup plan in case the weather changes.

Fill a pitcher with fresh orange juice or another fruit or vegetable juice and let guests pour their own glass.

Breakfast and Brunch Ingredients

Preparing the morning meal begins with the best-quality ingredients, from the most flavorful grains to the freshest fruits and vegetables in season. Follow the guidelines here for stocking your pantry and refrigerator and for making sure you have the right cooking equipment on hand.

EGGS

Scrambled or fried, made into an omelet or a quiche, or used to add moisture and texture to baked goods, eggs are a versatile mainstay of the morning menu. You'll get the best results by purchasing fresh eggs and storing them properly in the refrigerator.

Look for grade AA eggs, sold in most markets. These eggs, which are the highest quality, will have a firm, rounded yolk and a thick, gelatinous white.

Freshness is another indication of quality. Check the sell-by date on the carton and don't buy the eggs if this date is approaching.

Eggs are sold by size. Most of the recipes in this book, especially for baking, use large eggs.

When possible, buy eggs labeled "free range," which means the hens were allowed to roam outdoors. The less-regulated "cage free" label promises some access to the outside, though it is often highly limited.

Store eggs in the refrigerator where the temperature is below 40°F (4°C). Keep them in their carton, rather than storing them in the open, so they don't absorb other flavors.

DAIRY

Dairy products could not be more essential to breakfast and brunch. Yogurt enriches smoothies, cheese of all kinds fills omelets, sour cream garnishes potatoes, and milk is indispensable for baked goods and for serving with cereal and coffee.

When you purchase dairy products, apply the same criteria as you would for selecting eggs. Milk, cream, butter, and other items should be fresh, so look carefully at the sell-by dates on cartons and packages.

Store dairy products in the coldest area of the refrigerator. Cheeses should be wrapped tightly in plastic wrap to prevent them from drying out and spoiling.

Dairy products that were once hard to find are now stocked in many markets. Greek-style yogurt is made by straining the yogurt to remove excess liquid. Thick, creamy, and tangy, it can be used in place of milk on granola and is a delicious garnish. Crème fraîche, a rich, velvety cultured cream, makes an incomparable garnish for crepes, fruit salads, and a host of other dishes.

GRAINS AND CEREALS

Like eggs, grains and cereals have long been staples at the breakfast and brunch table. Given their popularity, an entire chapter of this book is devoted to recipes for oatmeal, granola, polenta, and grits.

Packaged grains and cereals are readily available, but for the best quality, look for these ingredients sold in bulk at natural-foods stores or other well-stocked markets with a high turnover, which helps guarantee freshness. You'll also find grains marketed in vacuum-sealed packages that maintain freshness while the products are on the store shelves. Keep in mind that once a package is opened, the contents need to be transferred to a tightly sealed container. If you store all grains and cereals this way in a cool, dry place, they will last for up to 1 year.

Oatmeal, polenta, and grits are processed into fast-cooking forms. Despite the ease of these products, they lack the flavor and texture of the standard versions. Old-fashioned rolled oats, for instance, are more robust than the instant and quick-cooking varieties, and they take only 5 minutes to prepare. Also, there is no substitute for rolled oats when making homemade granola.

Grits and polenta need to cook about 15 minutes longer than the quick-cooking products, but the results are well worth the extra time you spend at the stove.

DRY INGREDIENTS

When you keep your pantry stocked with dry ingredients such as flour, baking powder, baking soda (bicarbonate of soda), sugar, and a selection of spices, nuts, and dried fruits, you'll have most of the ingredients you need for making delicious breakfast treats such as pancakes, waffles, and baked goods like muffins and quick breads.

Many of these ingredients can be purchased in bulk at a store where the supply sells quickly and is replenished often. If you buy packaged flours, and especially when you select baking powder and baking soda, avoid items that are nearing their expiration dates.

As for keeping grains and cereals, the major concern when storing them is preventing rancidity. Try to purchase both flour and nuts in amounts that you can use within a few months. Flour also readily absorbs odors. Transfer flour to an airtight container, put in a cool, dry place, and use within 4 to 6 months.

Store nuts in airtight containers or plastic bags in a cool, dry place for 1 to 2 months. For longer storage, place them in the refrigerator or freezer, which will extend their shelf life up to 6 months. To save time, nuts can be toasted in advance and stored until they are needed.

SEASONAL FRUITS AND VEGETABLES

Always choose fresh fruits and vegetables in season for the best flavor and value. Here is a chart to help get you thinking seasonally.

SEASON	FRUITS	VEGETABLES
Spring	cherries, grapefruits, limes, mandarins, pomelos, raspberries, rhubarb, strawberries	artichokes, arugula (rocket), asparagus, celery, fava (broad) beans, peas, potatoes
Summer	apricots, blackberries, blueberries, boysenberries, cherries, figs, melons, nectarines, peaches, plums, raspberries, rhubarb, strawberries	arugula (rocket), bell peppers (capsicums), corn, cucumbers, eggplants (aubergines), peas, shallots, summer squashes, tomatoes
Fall	apples, figs, grapes, kiwifruits, melons, pears, pomegranates, rhubarb	arugula (rocket), bell peppers (capsicums), celery, corn, cucumbers, eggplants (aubergines), rhubarb, shallots, tomatoes, turnips
Winter	dates, grapefruits, grapes, kiwifruits, limes, pears, pomegranates, pomelos, quinces, tangerines	Brussels sprouts, cauliflower, celery, parsnips, sweet potatoes, turnips
Year-round	bananas, lemons, oranges	avocados, Belgian endive (chicory/witloof), beets, broccoli, carrots, chard, fennel, garlic, green (spring) onions, herbs, leeks, mushrooms, onions, potatoes, radishes, scallions

FRUITS

Mimosas with freshly squeezed tangerine juice; granola layered with strawberries, nectarines, and yogurt; and plump fresh figs partnered with crisp, golden French toast are just some of the ways that fruits are integral to breakfast and brunch dishes.

Fruits benefit from special handling to preserve their flavor. When you bring fruit home from the market, do not wash it before storing. Wet or damp fruit can easily develop a layer of mold.

Take special care when storing delicate berries. Line a shallow glass or plastic container with a paper towel or two, spread the berries in a single layer, cover, and refrigerate for up to 3 days.

Many fruits, in contrast, should be stored at room temperature to preserve their flavor and aroma. Set bananas, peaches, nectarines, plums, mangoes, and citrus on a counter until ready to use. They will also ripen faster if set out at room temperature.

Raisins, currants, and other dried fruits retain moisture that is important to their flavor and texture. To prevent them from drying out, store in tightly sealed containers at room temperature for up to 1 month or in the refrigerator or freezer for up to 6 months.

VEGETABLES

When you think of vegetables as part of the morning menu, potatoes may first come to mind, but in this book you'll discover recipes for salads, soups, and even sandwiches that show how vegetables of many varieties enhance a breakfast or brunch menu.

As with fruit, proper handling and storage of vegetables help guarantee the best flavor and allow you to purchase some vegetables well in advance of preparation.

Lettuce, arugula (rocket), and other greens should be wrapped loosely in paper towels and stored in a resealable plastic bag in the refrigerator. They will keep for up to 1 week.

Most vegetables, such as artichokes, asparagus, beets, bell peppers (capsicums), carrots, and fennel, should be refrigerated in a plastic bag. They will keep for up to 1 week.

Other produce should be set out at room temperature. Tomatoes and eggplants (aubergines) will stay fresh for 2 to 3 days.

Enclose potatoes in a paper bag to shield them from direct light and use them within 2 to 3 weeks. Onions and garlic should be kept separately from potatoes. Put them in a cool, dry place away from direct light, which can cause sprouting.

MEAT, POULTRY, AND FISH

Bacon, ham, and sausages of many types and flavors contribute protein to the breakfast or brunch plate. Chicken can be cooked into such hearty dishes as hash or potpies. Lobster, smoked trout, or crab salad always makes a much appreciated as well as elegant main course for brunch.

When preparing meat, poultry, and fish, make sure to follow several food-safety practices and guidelines.

Prepackaged meats should be used in advance of the sell-by date indicated on the package. If you buy meat or poultry directly from a butcher, use within 2 days.

Fresh fish and shellfish should ideally be served on the day of purchase or at most within 1 day of purchase.

To prevent cross-contamination with other foods, consider reserving a cutting board for the exclusive use of preparing raw meat, poultry, and fish. These raw items should never be left at room temperature for more than 1 hour.

Especially when serving buffet style, keep in mind that cooked meat, poultry, and fish should not be allowed to stand at room temperature for more than 1 to 2 hours. In hot weather, reduce the time to 1 hour.

Breakfast and Brunch Entertaining

As experienced hosts know, planning ahead is the key to a successful party. After you pick an occasion and send the invitations, you can decide where and how to serve the food and choose the servingware that will make the most attractive and practical presentation.

THE OCCASION

You can host a breakfast or brunch to suit any occasion, whether it's formal or informal, large or small. Inviting guests for a morning or midday meal is also a great way to entertain during daylight hours, especially when serving outdoors—in the garden, on the patio, terrace, or deck—is an option.

A breakfast or brunch is traditionally held before a wedding to welcome family and guests from out of town. A festive morning meal is also a good choice when a bridal or baby shower is on the calendar. Nearly any occasion can be suited to celebrating with a brunch: engagement, housewarming, birthday, anniversary, graduation, retirement, or reunion, just to name a few.

Mimosas are the signature cocktail for any breakfast and brunch gathering.

If you belong to a book club, knitting circle, softball team, or hiking group, you can invite members for breakfast or brunch as a change from your regular meeting schedule, or enjoy a meal before or after a game or outing.

Breakfast is an ideal time to entertain colleagues and to socialize with a small group of friends, especially when schedules might preclude evening get-togethers.

WHERE AND WHEN

Once you have chosen the occasion and made a guest list, think about how you want to use the space in your home for preparation, serving, and socializing.

If you are inviting a small group of friends for an informal breakfast and you have an eat-in kitchen, guests can keep you company while you cook—or even lend a hand—and everyone can eat at a kitchen counter or table.

For a more formal brunch, decide if you want to seat everyone at your dining room table and prearrange the seating with place cards. Or, if you're hosting a large group, you may want to set up a buffet or multiple stations for food and drinks, and allow casual seating so guests can circulate as they wish.

In general, unless you are working around another event, specify starting and ending times for your party. Breakfast usually ranges from 9 a.m. to 10:30 a.m., though you can certainly start earlier. Brunch can go from 10 a.m. to noon, or from 11 a.m. to 1 p.m. Times are not hard and fast, as guests may linger after the hour stated on your invitation.

Place cards, handwritten or printed, are an elegant touch for a sit-down breakfast or brunch.

INVITATIONS

Thanks to the prevalence of Web-based invitation services, e-mail is a common way to send invitations, keep track of guest lists, and disseminate useful information like driving directions and maps.

If you're planning a casual event for friends, arrangements can be made by e-mail or by phone. Even if you've called guests, a follow-up e-mail is a helpful reminder.

For a more formal party that celebrates a milestone for a guest of honor or marks a special event like an engagement, invitations should be sent in the mail and should give guests two to three weeks advance notice.

In the invitation, be sure to ask for an RSVP and include your phone number for responses. Add any other details, such as directions for guests who have never been to your home. If children are welcome, be sure to note this on the invitation. But if the occasion is appropriate for adults only, let the parents on your list know so they can make arrangements.

The breakfast and brunch table can be set as formally—white porcelain plates, white linen napkins—or informally—casual plates, colorful cotton napkins—as you like.

SERVING STYLES

You'll want to match the serving style to the size and nature of your event. Two popular ways to enjoy breakfast and brunch are a buffet and a sit-down meal served family style. If you have a suitable outdoor space and weather permitting, guests can dine alfresco.

Buffet

For a buffet, all of the food is laid out on a kitchen counter or one or two tables elsewhere in your home. Arrange the food in the order it will be eaten. Guests each pick up a plate and help themselves from the variety of dishes. Items like condiments, flatware, and napkins are arranged at the end of the line or in a separate location close to the food.

Buffets are convenient for large gatherings, especially open houses where guests come and go over a span of time. You can avoid traffic jams around the buffet by setting up dedicated tables for such items as drinks and baked goods.

Family Style

A family-style meal is a casual and congenial variation of a sit-down party. The food is presented on platters and in serving bowls. Guests gather at the same table and pass the food. Condiments like butter, jam, and maple syrup can be arranged on the table within easy reach of everyone.

Outdoors

Entertaining outdoors is a wonderful option if you have a terrace, deck, patio, or backyard. Depending on the space available, guests can help themselves to food inside and then proceed outdoors to eat. Or, you can set up an outdoor buffet, preferably in a shady spot protected from direct sunlight.

PLANNING AHEAD

For a stress-free breakfast or brunch, the best approach is to divide the work into tasks that are manageable and establish a time frame. Starting a few days ahead—or even longer for a large party—make a game plan that details the shopping, preparation, and setup.

A few days prior to the event, wash and iron table linens. The day or two before, clean the house and do any last-minute shopping. Buy flowers in advance and arrange them so the blooms will have time to open. Setting out dishes, flatware, glasses, and serving platters a day ahead will ease your work in the morning.

For most morning get-togethers, a table set with attractive everyday dishes, drinkware, and flatware is a good choice.

SETTING THE TABLE OR BUFFET

Serving food buffet style gives you a lot of flexibility. Any table can be turned into the location for a buffet, or one or more tables can be set up in attractive spaces in your home.

When arranging a buffet, consider the circulation. Guests should be able to help themselves to food without blocking the entrance to the kitchen or other rooms that need to remain accessible. If your gathering will be a large one, have guests pick up their coffee or tea, wine or cocktails, in the kitchen. Separate stations might also be desirable for juice (page 34) or smoothies (page 35).

If you are having a sit-down breakfast or brunch, you may want to determine the seating arrangements with place cards. For a buffet, some hosts write the name of each dish and its ingredients on a card.

Choosing the table decorations is another task that you can do in advance. For a sit-down meal, create a single flower arrangement or feature a bowl of seasonal fresh fruit. Just make sure that the centerpiece does not block guests' sight lines. A buffet table can easily accommodate a larger floral or other type of decorative arrangement placed towards the back of the table, behind the food.

Table Linens

Whether you are serving your menu family style or buffet style, using a tablecloth will both protect the table and add a decorative element. It should hang over the tabletop by about 18 inches (45 cm). If servingware will contain hot food, you'll want to use a pad or liner underneath the tablecloth or set out trivets.

For a sit-down dinner, you can arrange each guest's place setting and other items directly on the tablecloth or on place mats of a compatible color and design. Always use cloth napkins, which can match or contrast harmoniously with the tablecloth. The napkins should be generously sized, no less than 20 inches (50 cm) per side.

A more casual breakfast or brunch lends itself to mixing a variety of linens, such as patterned napkins with a plain tablecloth. Or, you can eliminate the tablecloth and use place mats alone.

Flatware

Begin by thinking about the various dishes on your menu, then choose the flatware guests will need, whether you are serving buffet style or family style. For a buffet, have extra flatware on hand for guests who return for seconds.

Reserve one end of the buffet table for the flatware. You can organize like items in napkin-lined baskets, next to a stack of napkins, so guests can help themselves after they have chosen their food.

If you're creating individual place settings for a family-style meal, include enough pieces for each course, such as soupspoons and salad forks, as well as extras like butter knives.

Plates & Bowls

Referring again to your menu, provide plenty of plates and bowls for every course. On a buffet, stack dinner plates next to the area where you will be putting the main dishes and their accompaniments.

Have on hand small plates and bowls if your menu includes salads, in case guests prefer salad after their main course, or if some just want a muffin and jam.

Drinkware

Have a generous supply of mugs or cups and saucers for coffee and tea, as well as glasses for juices and water.

When offering wine or cocktails, establish an area where you can pour drinks for guests or where guests can conveniently serve themselves. Set out glasses for red and white wine and highball, old-fashioned, Champagne, or other glasses appropriate for the cocktails you'll be making.

Servingware

Select the platters, bowls, and other items for presenting the food on your menu. If you don't have enough servingware, put baked goods such as muffins in a napkin-lined basket, or combine two or more dishes, such as deviled eggs and squares of corn bread, on an attractive tray.

Platters and Plates

When choosing platters, be mindful of their size and weight. For a family-style breakfast or brunch, guests will be passing food at the table and should easily be able to lift and pass platters to their neighbors. If necessary, divide a dish between two smaller platters or two dinner plates.

Dividing a dish between two platters may be a practical strategy for the buffet table too, especially if you are hosting a large gathering.

You may want to reserve a heatproof platter or two for foods that need to be kept warm before serving. Setting aside a platter for this purpose allows you to bring the food directly from the oven to the table.

Don't forget small plates for condiments such as cream cheese or butter.

Serving Bowls

Large, shallow serving bowls are easy to use and can be passed at the table for a sit-down breakfast or brunch.

If necessary, set aside heatproof bowls for keeping food warm in the oven before bringing it to the table.

Don't forget small bowls for accompaniments, such as compotes, jams, and applesauce.

Utensils

Put out enough utensils for all the serving platters and bowls, either on the table or on the buffet table.

Remember to provide enough butter knives and small spoons for serving condiments.

Pitchers and Carafes

To keep water cold or drinks like fruit juice chilled without diluting them, you may want to purchase a pitcher or two that include an insert for ice. Alternatively, briefly chill a pitcher in the freezer before use.

Glass carafes are ideal for holding juice, water, wine, or other beverages.

For maintaining the temperature of hot beverages or for holding hot water for tea, use an insulated thermos with a pouring spout. A high-quality thermos can keep beverages hot (or chilled) for hours.

SEASONAL FLOWERS

Creating your own flower arrangements is easy to do. First, select one vase for the center of the table, or two or more vases for smaller bouquets evenly spaced down the center. Choose low, unobtrusive vases to avoid blocking your guests' sight lines. Stand the flowers next to the vase(s) to judge the best height, then trim the stems on the diagonal and strip off any leaves that would be submerged in the water. Arrange the flowers the day before your get-together so they are fully opened the next morning.

SEASON	FLOWERS
Spring	daffodils, forsythias, irises, lilacs, lilies, narcissi, peonies, ranunculus, sweet peas, violets
Summer	chrysanthemums, cornflowers, daisies, forget-me-nots, Gerber daisies, lavender, roses, sunflowers, zinnias
Fall	chrysanthemums, cosmos, dahlias, gladioli, hyacinths, marigolds
Winter	daffodils, narcissi, poinsettias
Year-round	carnations, gardenias, hydrangeas, orchids, roses, tulips

The Breakfast and Brunch Menu

As tempted as you are by the many delicious recipes in this book, you do not need an extensive menu. Along with considering the occasion, the serving style, and your guests' tastes, take into account how much time you will be able to spend in the kitchen preparing the dishes.

PLANNING THE MENU

As you create your menu, select recipes such as breads and pastries or salads and compotes that can be made in advance. With some of the cooking completed ahead, you can prepare eggs, pancakes, or waffles in the morning just before guests arrive.

Remember to build your menu around the seasons. In spring, for instance, select recipes that showcase asparagus and strawberries. Summer is the time for taking advantage of sun-ripened tomatoes and stone fruits like nectarines and peaches.

For a formal brunch, you may prefer elegant dishes, such as lobster salad, crepes, gravlax, or tea cakes. A casual breakfast with friends may be just the right occasion for *chilaquiles,* pulled pork sandwiches, or French toast.

What to Drink

Coffee, tea, and juice are the standard beverages on any breakfast or brunch menu. You may want to make a special drink such as Bittersweet Café Mocha (page 26) or Chai Latte (page 29), or let guests choose freshly squeezed juice on its own or made into spritzers (page 33).

Lighter white, red, or rosé wines may complement your menu. Or, if you want to serve a cocktail, choose a signature morning drink also on the lighter side, such as a mimosa, a mixture of sparkling wine and orange juice, or a Bloody Mary, a mixture of vegetable juice and vodka.

MENUS

SUMMERTIME BREAKFAST

Raspberry-Mint Agua Fresca

Ginger Lemonade

•

Raspberry-Lemon Muffins

Fennel, Sausage, and Egg Tartlets

Summer Fruit Salad with Lime-Mint Sugar

LAZY SUNDAY MORNING

Fresh Citrus Spritzers

Blackberry Champagne Cocktail

•

Baked Eggs with Tomatoes, Herbs, and Cream

Lemon-Ricotta Pancakes

Cider-Glazed Sausage

HEARTY FAMILY BREAKFAST

Bittersweet Café Mocha

Chai Latte

•

Oatmeal with Blueberries and Cream

Buttermilk Belgian Waffles with Orange Blossom Maple Syrup

Herbed Sausage with Spicy Mustard

BRUNCH WITH FRIENDS

Balsamic Bloody Mary

•

Eggs Blackstone with Meyer Lemon
Hollandaise

Polenta with Mascarpone, Maple Syrup,
and Toasted Pecans

Poppy Seed Bread with Lemon Curd

Crab Salad with Tarragon Vinaigrette

HOLIDAY BRUNCH BUFFET

Spicy Hot Cocoa

Tangerine Mimosa

•

Scrambled Eggs with Chives

Almond Breakfast Cake

Sweet Crepes with Banana Cream

Herb-Roasted Red Potatoes

Bacon with Brown Sugar and Cardamom

TEATIME BRUNCH

Lemon Verbena and Mint Tisane

•

Scones with Currants and Lemon Zest

Blueberry Tea Cake

Ham, Leek, and Gruyère Quiches

Deviled Eggs with Lemon Zest,
Chives, and Capers

Tea Sandwiches

LIGHT AND HEALTHY BRUNCH

Three-Berry Smoothies

•

Soft-Boiled Egg with Rosemary-Chili Salt

Granola and Ricotta Cream Parfait

Peas with Pancetta,
Mint, and Ricotta Salata

Turkey, Smoked Mozzarella,
and Arugula Panini

NEW YEAR'S BRUNCH BUFFET

Mango Bellini

Ramos Gin Fizz

•

Cheese Blintzes with Berry Jam

Lobster Salad with
Grapefruit and Avocado

Sausage Strata with Cheddar Cheese
and Sun-Dried Tomatoes

Drinks

About the Perfect Cup of Coffee

If you don't usually prepare coffee from freshly ground beans, hosting a breakfast or brunch is a good time to start. The perfect cup begins with selecting whole beans that you can grind and brew just as your guests walk in the door.

SELECTING BEANS

Whole beans are now readily available from specialized coffee merchants and at many large markets. You want to be sure that the merchant has a good turnover so you know the beans are fresh.

If you don't already have a coffee preference, you can try a couple of varieties to see what suits your taste. The finest coffees are made from arabica beans. Grown at high altitudes, these come from various countries around the world: Kenya, Ethiopia, Sumatra, New Guinea, Costa Rica, and Guatemala, to name a handful. Each has its own character.

Because coffee beans need to be roasted to bring out their flavor, beans are also described by type of roast. Dark-roasted beans, customarily French roast or Italian roast, are brewed into an intensely flavored cup. If your guests prefer a less full-bodied brew, you can choose a medium-dark roast such as Viennese.

Store beans and ground coffee in airtight containers in a cool place for up to 2 weeks or in the refrigerator for up to 1 month.

BREWING

Although you can purchase already ground beans, grinding the beans yourself, as they are needed, offers the freshest results. Home grinders are widely available and easy to use. To extract the most flavor from the beans, they need to be ground to the texture that is most appropriate for your brewing method. Always have decaffeinated beans on hand for guests who prefer to drink coffee without caffeine.

Whether you prefer an electric drip pot, a French press, or a filter-lined cone set over a drip pot, always use the correct proportion of ground coffee to water—typically 2 tablespoons coffee to 1 cup (8 fl oz/250 ml) hot water just off the boil.

For example, the popular drip method calls for a medium-fine grind, while the excellent French-press method calls for a coarse grind. For the latter, ground coffee is steeped in hot water, then a snug-fitting plunger is pushed through the pot to separate the brewed coffee from the grounds.

FINISHING TOUCHES

Give guests a choice of accompaniments. Set out a pitcher of warm whole milk or half-and-half (half cream) alongside a bowl of sugar. Sugar cubes make a particularly elegant touch.

About the Perfect Cup of Tea

For some people, their morning ritual begins with a hot cup of tea rather than a steaming mug of coffee. You can treat guests to a choice of black and green teas. Making the perfect pot is a matter of following a few simple steps.

SELECTING TEA

For the best cup of tea, begin with loose tea leaves rather than tea bags. If you are accustomed to using tea bags, you'll enjoy exploring the wide variety of teas sold by specialty stores, some of which also carry coffee beans by the pound.

Your two basic choices are black tea and green tea. Both types come from the same plants. What distinguishes them is where the plant was grown and how the leaves are processed. The highest-quality teas are from plants grown at high altitudes whose newest leaves and unopened buds are harvested by hand. Whereas black tea leaves are fermented, heated, and then dried, green tea leaves are steamed and dried without undergoing fermentation. Oolong (Chinese for "black dragon"), a third category, is partially fermented and is more reminiscent of green tea than black. Black tea leaves, when brewed, produce a full-flavored beverage. Green tea leaves yield a much more delicate flavor. Within these two categories, there are wide variations in taste as well.

When you peruse the offerings of a tea merchant, you'll find teas from countries such as China, England, and Japan, and blends that combine both green and black teas.

You should also have on hand one or two herbal teas, which are made from herbs and other flavorings and are caffeine-free because they contain no leaves.

BREWING AND SERVING TEA

You can make tea by the cup using individual tea balls or infusers, but for the best results, brew loose tea in a pot, which allows the hot water to circulate around the leaves and extract the most flavor.

Use a heatproof glass or ceramic teapot and preheat it by filling it with hot water, letting it stand for about 1 minute, and pouring out the water. For each cup of tea, put 1 teaspoon leaves and 1 cup (8 fl oz/250 ml) water into the pot. Use boiling water for black tea and water off the boil for green tea. Let green tea steep for 1–3 minutes, black tea for 3–6 minutes, and herbal tea for 8–12 minutes. Stir the leaves briefly, then pour the tea through a small strainer into warmed cups.

If any tea remains in the pot, cover it with a tea cozy or wrap it with a clean kitchen towel to keep the tea warm.

FINISHING TOUCHES

Tea purists might insist that certain varieties be sipped straight, but when entertaining guests, offer warm whole milk or half-and-half (half cream), lemon slices, and sugar or sugar cubes and/or honey for guests to flavor their tea as they like. Many tea drinkers favor turbinado, a mild, blond-colored, partially processed sugar, or Demerara, large molasses-coated, golden sugar crystals, for sweetening their tea.

Vanilla Bean Iced Coffee

Cold-brewed iced coffee retains more nuanced flavor than coffee brewed hot and allowed to cool. Make the coffee a day before serving so it can brew for at least 12 hours. For the best flavor, use freshly ground coffee. Dark-roasted beans, such as French or Viennese roast, will produce a full-bodied flavor, while medium-roasted beans, such as breakfast or American roast, will yield a less intense flavor.

In a pitcher, stir the ground coffee into 4 cups (32 fl oz/1 l) water. Cover and let rest at room temperature overnight or for at least 12 hours.

In a saucepan over medium heat, combine the vanilla beans, milk, and sugar. Bring the mixture to a simmer and immediately remove from the heat. Allow to steep for about 20 minutes.

Select 4 tumblers. Strain the coffee through a fine-mesh sieve into a large bowl. Strain again through a coffee filter into a large, clean pitcher. Fill the glasses with ice cubes. Pour the coffee into the glasses, filling them to within 1 inch (2.5 cm) of the rim. Top each glass with ¼ cup (2 fl oz/60 ml) of the vanilla-flavored milk.

Garnish each drink with a vanilla bean pod and serve immediately.

1 cup (7 oz/210 g) ground coffee

4 vanilla beans, split lengthwise (save the pods for garnish)

1 cup (8 fl oz/250 ml) milk

¼ cup (2 oz/60 g) sugar

Ice cubes

Spicy Hot Cocoa

2 dried red chiles

6 tablespoons (1 oz/30 g) unsweetened cocoa powder

2 tablespoons sugar

1½-inch (4-cm) cinnamon stick, plus extra for garnish

2½ cups (20 fl oz/625 ml) whole milk

Whipped cream for garnish, page 276 (optional)

Select 4 mugs. Open the chiles over a saucepan and release the seeds. Add the chiles, cocoa powder, sugar, and ⅓ cup (3 fl oz/80 ml) water. Place over low heat and cook, stirring, until the mixture forms a smooth paste, 3–5 minutes.

Add the cinnamon stick, pour in the milk, and stir until the paste is completely dissolved. Cook until hot, about 5 minutes. Do not allow the milk to boil. Strain the hot cocoa into the mugs and garnish each with a cinnamon stick or a dollop of the whipped cream, if desired. Serve at once.

This recipe mimics the hot cocoa reputedly made by the Aztecs and is still found in parts of southern Mexico, such as the state of Oaxaca. There, however, the drink is made with water, resulting in a thinner, less rich beverage.

Bittersweet Café Mocha

1 tablespoon unsweetened cocoa powder

1½ teaspoons sugar

½ cup (4 fl oz/125 ml) brewed double-strength coffee

Dash of vanilla extract

1 cup (8 fl oz/250 ml) whole milk

Select 1 large mug. In a saucepan over medium heat, combine the cocoa powder, sugar, and coffee, and heat until hot and steaming, about 5 minutes. Remove from the heat and add the vanilla. Pour into the mug.

If you have an espresso machine, steam and froth the milk according to the manufacturer's instructions. Pour the hot milk into the mug and top with milk foam. Alternatively, in a saucepan over medium-high heat, warm the milk until small bubbles appear around the edge of the pan. Do not allow the milk to boil. Pour the hot milk into the mug and stir to combine. Serve at once.

One of the keys to making this drink is using a good-quality Dutch-process or natural cocoa powder. For a particularly full-flavored drink, use dark-roasted coffee, such as a French or Italian roast.

Lemon Verbena and Mint Tisane

Lemon verbena is a lemon-scented herb that can usually be found at farmers' markets during the summer months. If it is unavailable, substitute the peel from 1 or 2 lemons or 1 stalk lemongrass, cut into pieces.

Select 2 mugs. Rinse the herbs. If desired, set aside 2 lemon verbena sprigs for garnish. Put the remaining lemon verbena sprigs and the mint in a teapot. In a saucepan over high heat, bring 3 cups (24 fl oz/750 ml) water to a boil. Remove from the heat, pour into the teapot, and let the tisane steep until the desired strength is reached, usually 3–5 minutes. Pour through a tea strainer or fine-mesh sieve into the mugs, dividing it evenly. Slip a lemon verbena sprig into each mug. Serve at once, passing the sugar at the table, if desired.

1 bunch fresh lemon verbena sprigs

1 bunch fresh mint

Sugar for serving (optional)

Chai Latte

Chai mixes are available in many markets, but the spiced tea is easy to prepare from scratch once you have the ingredients on hand. The added benefit is that you can tailor the recipe to suit your taste by including more ginger, cinnamon, or another favorite seasoning. The black cardamom pods used here add a slightly smoky accent. If they are unavailable, double the number of green cardamom pods.

Select 2 mugs. In a saucepan, combine the cinnamon, cardamom pods, cloves, peppercorns, ginger slices, and 1 1/2 cups (12 fl oz/375 ml) water. Bring to a boil over medium heat, cover, reduce the heat to low, and simmer until the liquid becomes aromatic, about 10 minutes.

Add the milk and sugar and bring to a simmer over medium heat. Stir in the tea leaves, remove from the heat, cover, and let steep until the chai is the desired strength, 3–5 minutes.

If you have an espresso machine, steam and froth half of the chai according to the manufacturer's instructions. Return the chai to the pan. Pour the chai through a tea strainer or fine-mesh sieve into the mugs, dividing it evenly, and top with the foam. Alternatively, reheat the chai over medium heat and pour into the mugs. Serve at once.

1 1/2-inch (4-cm) cinnamon stick

4 green cardamom pods

4 black cardamom pods

10 whole cloves

2 peppercorns

5 thin slices fresh ginger

2/3 cup (5 fl oz/100 ml) whole milk

2 tablespoons sugar

4 teaspoons Darjeeling tea leaves

Raspberry-Mint Agua Fresca

½ cup (3½ oz/105 g) superfine (caster) sugar

22 raspberries

22 fresh mint leaves, plus 4 sprigs for garnish

Ice cubes

Select 4 tumblers. In a saucepan, combine the sugar and ½ cup (4 fl oz/125 ml) water. Bring to a simmer over medium-low heat, stirring to dissolve the sugar. Remove the sugar syrup from the heat and let cool.

In a blender, combine 18 of the raspberries, the mint leaves, and the sugar syrup and process until a smooth purée forms. Strain the purée through a fine-mesh sieve into a pitcher. You should have about ⅔ cup (5 fl oz/160 ml). Add 1⅓ cups (11 fl oz/340 ml) water. Fill the glasses with ice and divide the raspberry mixture among the glasses. Garnish with mint sprigs and remaining raspberries speared on a cocktail pick. Serve at once.

Aguas frescas, cool, refreshing drinks typically made from fruits, grains, and/or herbs mixed with sugar and water, are a specialty of Mexico, where they counter the heat of both the noonday sun and the chile-laced cuisine.

Ginger Lemonade

1 cup (7 oz/210 g) superfine (caster) sugar

8 thin slices fresh ginger

Juice of 3 lemons

Ice cubes

4 candied ginger slices for garnish (optional)

Select 4 tumblers. In a saucepan, combine the sugar and 1 cup (8 fl oz/250 ml) water. Bring to a simmer over low heat, stirring to dissolve the sugar. Add the ginger slices and cook until the syrup is strongly infused with ginger flavor, 20–30 minutes. Remove the ginger from the syrup and set aside.

In a pitcher, combine the lemon juice and ginger syrup. Add 1¾ cups (14 fl oz/430 ml) water and stir to combine. Fill the glasses with ice cubes and pour in the lemonade, dividing it evenly. Garnish each glass with a candied ginger slice (if using) and serve at once.

Ginger adds a refreshing note to this lemonade. For a tart version, use Eureka or Lisbon lemons, and for a sweet version, try Meyer lemons.

Fresh Citrus Spritzers

Be sure to keep the fruits at room temperature before preparing the spritzers, as they will yield more juice than if stored in the refrigerator.

Select 4 tall glasses. In a saucepan, combine the sugar and 1/3 cup (3 fl oz/80 ml) water. Bring to a simmer over medium heat, stirring to dissolve the sugar. Remove the sugar syrup from the heat and let cool.

In a pitcher, stir together the sugar syrup and the juices of the orange, lemon, and limes. Fill the glasses with ice. Divide the citrus mixture among the glasses and top with sparkling water. Garnish with the lemon peel strips and serve at once.

1/3 cup (2 1/2 oz/75 g) superfine (caster) sugar

Juice of 1 orange

Juice of 1 lemon

Juice of 2 limes

Ice cubes

1 bottle (24 fl oz/750 ml) sparkling water, chilled

4 lemon peel strips for garnish

Cucumber-Lime Cooler

Cucumber and lime are a refreshing combination. Choose cucumbers that are dark and don't show signs of yellowing or shriveling. Buy limes with a glossy, dark green rind.

Select 4 tall glasses. In a saucepan, combine the sugar and 1/3 cup (3 fl oz/80 ml) water. Bring to a simmer over medium heat, stirring to dissolve the sugar. Remove the sugar syrup from the heat and let cool.

Cut the cucumber crosswise into 1-inch (2.5-cm) pieces. Place in a blender with 1/4 cup (2 fl oz/60 ml) water and process until a smooth purée forms. Strain the purée through a fine-mesh sieve into a bowl.

Return the cucumber purée to the blender. Add the sugar syrup, lime juice, and about two-thirds of the ice cubes. Process until the mixture is slushy, adding more ice cubes if it is too thin or a little water if it is too thick. Divide the cucumber mixture among the glasses. Garnish with the cucumber peels and serve at once.

1/3 cup (2 1/2 oz/75 g) superfine (caster) sugar

1 cucumber, peeled, halved, and seeded, reserving 4 peels for garnish

Juice of 1 lime

2–3 cups (16–24 oz/ 500–750 g) ice cubes

Setting Up a Juice Bar

Juices make a refreshing complement to every breakfast or brunch menu. Setting up a juice bar allows guests to squeeze their own citrus juices to order and to prepare a variety of other beverages. If you provide the correct ingredients, guests can also make citrus spritzers.

GATHERING THE INGREDIENTS
Depending on your menu and the number of guests you are serving, offer a selection of juices with contrasting tart and sweet flavors. For citrus juice, a morning standard, you can let guests squeeze their own from navel, Valencia, or blood oranges; tangerines; or white or pink grapefruits. Also provide limes and lemons, as well as mint sprigs, for flavoring the drinks.

Purchased juices can include apple, carrot, cranberry, pomegranate, mango, tomato, or blends like apple-cranberry or mango-peach. Avoid juices that contain added sweeteners and a low percentage of pure juice. Chill the juice overnight in the refrigerator and, if possible, chill pitchers to hold the juice. For guests who might like citrus spritzers (page 33), chill bottles of sparkling water.

ARRANGING THE BAR
Set up the ingredients and other items on a table or counter that gives guests plenty of work space. Cut the citrus fruits in half and put each variety in a separate bowl. Place a citrus juicer near the bowls of fruit, then postion an empty bowl next to the juicer for guests to dispose of the spent rinds.

Pour any chilled purchased juices into pitchers, and place them in a convenient spot where guests can reach them without crowding others who are making their own juice. You might want to identify the juices by tying labels on the handles of the pitchers or by puttting a place card in front of each.

Cut some lemons and limes in half for juicing, but cut others into wedges and make strips of peel for use as garnishes, putting them in separate bowls. Rinse and dry the mint sprigs and place them in another bowl.

Provide plenty of glasses, some long-handled spoons for mixing drinks, and napkins.

SQUEEZING THE JUICE
The best juicer to use is one that both extracts the juice from citrus fruit and separates the juice from the pulp and seeds. Well-made designs that sit stably on a flat surface and can be operated manually are ideal for a juice bar. An orange or grapefruit half is placed in the juicer over a cone. Pulling a lever allows fresh juice to pour into a glass set under the cone. Also provide a citrus reamer for extracting the juice from a lime or lemon half.

Setting Up a Smoothie Station

Cool, frothy smoothies blended from juice and fresh fruit are a delicious way to incorporate fruit into a morning menu. Since smoothies and shakes are best when freshly blended, you can set up a smoothie station so guests can blend their own drinks.

GATHERING THE INGREDIENTS

Using the smoothie recipes on pages 37 and 38 as a foundation, purchase berries—including strawberries, blackberries, and blueberries—bananas, and peaches. You can also offer other fruits, such as mangoes, papayas, and pineapple. As appealing and tempting as it is to combine multiple fruits in one drink, the best smoothies contain only two or three compatible varieties so that the flavor of each stands out in the final drink.

You'll also need fruit juice. Have on hand oranges or other citrus fruits so you can make fresh juice the morning of the party, and purchase one or more varieties of bottled juice, such as apricot, peach, mango, papaya or guava nectar. Chill the bottled juice overnight in the refrigerator.

Have plain and/or vanilla yogurt available for guests to add to their smoothies. You can also put out lemon yogurt, which is particularly good in berry smoothies. Rinse and dry a bunch or two of mint sprigs for guests to use for garnish.

ARRANGING THE STATION

Placement of the station will be determined by access to an electrical outlet for your blender. If your kitchen is spacious enough, set up the station on a counter or at the kitchen table, making sure the blender cord is tucked safely out of the line of traffic. This way, guests will have easy access to the sink for quick, convenient cleanup.

Prepare the various fruits by rinsing, peeling, pitting, coring, or slicing. Put each variety, in its own bowl, near the blender. To prevent the cut fruit from turning brown, sprinkle it with lemon juice and toss gently to coat well. Place bowls of yogurt and mint sprigs near the blender as well. Put a couple of damp cloths in a small basket or other holder close to the blender for wiping up small spills.

Be sure to provide plenty of glasses and a generous supply of napkins. Set out a bucket of ice and tongs for guests who want an extra-cold smoothie. They can add the ice cubes to the glasses or blend them with the drinks.

BLENDING THE DRINKS

You'll want to advise guests to avoid filling the blender more than two-thirds full—and always to put the lid on—to avoid spills when the motor is engaged. Liquids should also be added to the blender first to prevent the fruit from getting stuck on the blade. You can share this advice verbally or write it on an attractive note card and post it with any other tips at the smoothie station.

If you have more than one blender, set them out. The blender container(s) will need to be rinsed between smoothies. If the station cannot be set up near the kitchen sink, have a pitcher of water on hand so guests can clean the container. Set an empty pitcher next to it for the rinse water.

Three-Berry Smoothies

Using frozen berries gives the smoothies a rich, thick texture and allows the drinks to be served without ice, which would dilute the flavor. The night before serving the smoothies, freeze the berries in a plastic container. If fresh fruits are unavailable, use unsweetened frozen berries, available at most markets.

Select 2 tall glasses. In a blender, combine the frozen berries and apricot nectar and process until smooth. Divide among the glasses and garnish each glass with 3 blueberries. Serve at once.

COCONUT-BERRY SMOOTHIES: For a creamier drink, add ¼ cup (2 fl oz/60 ml) coconut milk when processing the berries and only ¾ cup (6 fl oz/180 ml) apricot nectar. The apricot nectar can also be replaced by flavored yogurt, soy milk, or half-and-half (half cream).

CITRUS-BERRY SMOOTHIES: Substitute 1–1¼ cups (8–10 fl oz/250–310 ml) fresh orange juice for the apricot nectar. For a more tropical flavor, use mango or guava nectar in place of the apricot.

TWO-BERRY SMOOTHIES: For a brilliant red smoothie, substitute 6–8 strawberries and 1 cup (4 oz/125 g) raspberries for the strawberries, blackberries, and blueberries. Freeze the berries beforehand and prepare the drink as directed.

6 strawberries, hulled, halved, and frozen

½ cup (2 oz/60g) blackberries, frozen

½ cup (2 oz/60 g) blueberries, frozen, plus 6 berries for garnish

1–1¼ cups (8–10 fl oz/ 250–310 ml) apricot nectar

Banana-Strawberry-Peach Smoothies

1 1/2 **very ripe bananas, peeled and frozen**

4–6 strawberries, hulled and frozen, plus 2 strawberries for garnish

1/2 **peach, pitted, plus 2 thin slices for garnish**

3/4 **cup (6 fl oz/180 ml) peach nectar**

Here, banana is used to give this smoothie a more creamy consistency. Other berries, such as raspberries or blueberries, can be used in place of the strawberries, and other stone fruits, such as nectarines and apricots, can replace the peach.

Select 2 tumblers. In a blender, combine the frozen bananas, strawberries, 1/2 peach, and peach nectar and process until thick and creamy. Divide between the glasses. Garnish each glass with a peach slice and a strawberry and serve at once.

BANANA-STRAWBERRY-MANGO SMOOTHIES: Replace the 1/2 peach with 1/2 mango and the peach nectar with mango nectar.

BANANA-PINEAPPLE SMOOTHIES: Substitute 1 cup (6 oz/185 g) frozen pineapple cubes for the strawberries and peach. Add 1/4 cup (2 oz/60 g) plain yogurt and only 1/4 cup (2 fl oz/60 ml) peach nectar. Other types of nectar such as mango can also be used in place of the peach nectar. Garnish each glass with a pineapple chunk speared on a cocktail pick.

BANANA-KIWIFRUIT SMOOTHIES: Substitute 1 cup (6 oz/185 g) frozen kiwifruit cubes for the strawberries and peach. Substitute 1/4 cup (2 fl oz/60 ml) coconut milk and 1/4 cup (2 fl oz/60 ml) kiwifruit nectar for the peach nectar. Garnish each glass with thin kiwifruit slices.

Balsamic Bloody Mary

Balsamic vinegar adds its characteristic pungent sweetness to this popular brunch cocktail. For the best flavor, choose a good-quality, multifiltered vodka.

Select 4 tall glasses and fill with ice. In a large pitcher, combine the vodka, tomato juice, vinegar, horseradish, Worcestershire sauce, Tabasco sauce, celery salt, and lime juice. Stir well to combine and season to taste with pepper. Pour into the glasses and garnish each glass with a cherry tomato and a chile speared on a cocktail pick. Serve at once.

JALAPEÑO BLOODY MARY: Substitute the vodka with a spicy flavored vodka such as jalapeño vodka or pepper vodka. Omit the balsamic vinegar, cherry tomatoes, and green chiles. Garnish with a jalapeño speared on a cocktail pick.

Ice cubes

1 cup (8 fl oz/250 ml) vodka

2 cups (16 fl oz/500 ml) tomato juice

1 ½ tablespoons balsamic vinegar

1 tablespoon prepared horseradish

1 teaspoon Worcestershire sauce

4 dashes of Tabasco sauce

¼ teaspoon celery salt

Juice of 2 limes

Freshly ground pepper

4 *each* cherry tomatoes and green chiles for garnish

Ramos Gin Fizz

Orange flower water, an essential ingredient for this classic cocktail, is a potent flavoring. The amount called for may look insignificant, but don't be tempted to add more. Look for orange flower water in liquor stores or Mediterranean markets.

Chill 4 tall glasses. In a blender, combine the gin, cream, lemon juice, egg whites, orange flower water, and sugar and process until smooth and frothy. Add enough ice to fill the blender three-fourths full. Cover the blender and shake gently to cool the drink. Strain through a sieve into the chilled glasses, dividing it evenly. Serve at once.

Note: This recipe calls for raw egg whites. While the incidence of bacteria in raw eggs is rare, anyone with a compromised immune system should use caution.

¾ cup (6 fl oz/180 ml) gin

¼ cup (2 fl oz/60 ml) heavy (double) cream

Juice of 4 lemons

4 large egg whites

8 drops of orange flower water

¼ cup (2 oz/60 g) superfine (caster) sugar

Ice cubes

Blackberry Champagne Cocktail

4 blackberries, quartered

¼ cup (2 fl oz/60 ml) triple sec

4 sugar cubes

Angostura bitters

1 bottle (24 fl oz/750 ml) Champagne, Prosecco, or other dry sparkling white wine, chilled

Select 4 Champagne flutes. In a small nonreactive bowl, combine the blackberries and triple sec and let stand for about 15 minutes to let the fruit macerate. Place a sugar cube in each flute and add 1 or 2 dashes of bitters. Spoon 4 pieces of marinated blackberry into each flute. Top with Champagne or other sparkling wine and serve at once.

BLACK RASPBERRY CHAMPAGNE COCKTAIL: Substitute 8 halved black raspberries for the blackberries and Chambord for the triple sec. Garnish with black raspberries.

RED RASPBERRY CHAMPAGNE COCKTAIL: Substitute 8 halved red raspberries for the blackberries, and framboise for the triple sec. Garnish with red raspberries.

BLACKBERRY KIR ROYALE: Substitute 3 tablespoons crème de cassis for the triple sec. Omit the sugar cubes and Angostura bitters.

Brunch is the perfect occasion to serve a Champagne cocktail. Here, the bitterness of triple sec and Angostura bitters pair well with the sweetness of blackberries and sugar cubes. Other berries, such as boysenberries, raspberries, or huckleberries, can be substituted.

Grapefruit Champagne Cocktail

1 cup (8 fl oz/250 ml) grapefruit juice

1 cup (8 fl oz/250 ml) orange juice

2 teaspoons crème de cassis

1 bottle (24 fl oz/750 ml) Champagne, Prosecco, or other dry sparkling white wine, chilled

Select 4 Champagne flutes. Pour equal amounts of the grapefruit juice and the orange juice into each glass and stir to blend. Stir ½ teaspoon of the crème de cassis into each glass. Top each glass with Champagne or other sparkling wine and serve at once.

Grapefruit juice, orange juice, and sparkling wine, all brunch staples, are blended together along with crème de cassis, a black currant liqueur, to make this refreshing cocktail. If time permits, squeeze the juices yourself for the freshest flavor.

Tangerine Mimosa

For a more complex flavor, use a mixture of tangerine varieties such as Pixie, Fairchild, and Dancy, for the juice. You will need 6 to 8 large tangerines to yield the amount needed here.

Select 4 Champagne flutes. Pour the tangerine juice into the flutes, dividing evenly. Top with the Champagne or other sparkling wine. Stir briefly to blend the flavors. Garnish with the tangerine peel strips. Serve at once.

2 cups (16 fl oz/500 ml) fresh tangerine juice, chilled

1 bottle (24 fl oz/750 ml) Champagne, Prosecco, or dry sparkling white wine, chilled

4 tangerine peel strips for garnish

Mango Bellini

This refreshing cocktail is a variation on the traditional Bellini, which is made with peach purée and Prosecco.

Select 4 Champagne flutes. In a blender, combine the mango and mango nectar and process until a smooth purée forms. Taste and add the sugar if needed; the mixture should be sweet but not cloying. Fill each flute about one-third full and top with the Prosecco or other sparkling wine. Serve at once.

1 mango, pitted, peeled, and quartered

½ cup (4 fl oz/125 ml) mango nectar

1 teaspoon superfine (caster) sugar (optional)

1 bottle (24 fl oz/750 ml) Prosecco, Champagne, or other dry sparkling white wine, chilled

Eggs

About Eggs

You have probably cooked eggs so frequently that making scrambled eggs or frying an egg seems second nature. When hosting guests, you may feel distracted by the dual tasks of cooking and socializing. Adding some techniques to your repertoire will help you manage both with ease.

When mixing multiple eggs, most cooks crack the eggs on the edge of a bowl. But eggs will crack more cleanly when gently tapped on the counter or other flat surface.

As you crack open each egg and let the white and yolk fall into the bowl, check for shell fragments. If you spot one, use a spoon to remove and discard it. Avoid scooping up a fragment with an egg-shell half, as the exterior can contaminate the raw egg.

SCRAMBLED AND FRIED EGGS

Eggs cook rapidly on the stove top, and when you are cooking for company, you may be tempted to raise the heat to speed up the process. Cooking eggs over high heat can toughen them, as can overcooking.

Scrambled eggs, such as those in this chapter seasoned with chives (page 54), and omelets (see Setting Up an Omelet Station, page 50) should be cooked over medium heat. Medium-high heat is desirable for fried eggs such as Eggs Over Easy with Peperonata (page 58) and Fried Eggs with Asparagus, Pancetta, and Bread Crumbs (page 57). Maintaining this heat level will give you classic fried eggs with a lacy brown crust around the edges.

When cooking eggs, add butter or olive oil to the pan to prevent sticking, even if you are using a nonstick pan.

PERFECT POACHED EGGS

Many cooks are justifiably intimidated by cooking poached eggs and wonder how they can poach eggs that are done just right and maintain their form. You'll get the best results when you begin with the freshest possible eggs. Eggs that are approaching their sell-by date will not hold their shape as well.

Until you are comfortable with the process, you may want to poach only 4 eggs at a time. Choose a saucepan or frying pan with high sides. You want a pan large enough so the eggs are separated from one another by about 1 inch (2.5 cm). Half fill the pan with water and bring to a simmer over medium heat.

As you'll notice, the recipes in this chapter call for adding fresh lemon juice to the poaching water. Using a small amount of an acidic ingredient such as lemon juice or distilled white vinegar helps the egg whites set more quickly when they come into contact with the hot water.

To control the placement of the eggs in the simmering water, carefully crack each egg into a small bowl. Lower the bowl until it just touches the water, then tilt it slightly and let the egg gently slip into the water. If necessary, adjust the heat under the pan to maintain a simmer. The goal is to cook the eggs in barely simmering water, rather than boil them.

When poached eggs are done—this should take 3 minutes for runny yolks or 5 minutes for set yolks—use a slotted spoon to lift each egg from the water. Let the excess water drip back into the pan, then briefly hold the bottom of the spoon against several layers of paper towels or a clean kitchen towel to absorb any residual moisture and prevent it from getting onto the plate.

Poached eggs are best served soon after cooking, but you can hold them briefly, until you have finished cooking all the eggs in the recipe, by slipping them into a shallow baking dish of warm water (150°–160°F/65°–72°C).

FLAWLESS HARD-BOILED EGGS

Deviled eggs (page 73) can be prepared in advance and set out on a buffet table for guests to help themselves. The recipe is easy to double for a large gathering.

If hard-boiling eggs, choose a spacious saucepan that will hold the eggs in a single layer and allow space around them. Keep in mind that you want the eggs to cook in water that has reached a boil, but you do not want to boil the eggs. Boiling water can cause the eggs to crack against the sides of the pan and the whites to leak out of the crack, giving the cooked eggs an unattractive shape and a tough texture. When so-called hard-boiled eggs are cooked too long at an overly high temperature, the outside of the yolks develop an unappealing greenish cast.

To avoid these pitfalls, place the eggs in a saucepan with cold water to cover, bring the water to a boil over medium-high heat, and immediately remove the pan from the heat. Let the eggs sit in the water for 20 minutes, then remove them from the pan. Pour the hot water out of the pan, refill the pan with cold water, carefully return the eggs to the pan, and let cool for 5 minutes.

Remove the eggs from the water and, if you have time, chill them briefly in the refrigerator to make them easier to peel. One at a time, crack the eggs on a countertop and then hold under a gentle stream of cold water as you remove the shells. To keep the peeled eggs, refrigerate in a bowl of cold water to cover for up to 3 days, changing the water daily.

Setting Up an Omelet Station

Individual omelets cook quickly—in no more than 3 minutes. You can prepare the ingredients in advance and set out the equipment you'll need, creating an omelet station near the stove. Guests choose their own fillings, and no doubt you'll impress them with omelets made to order.

GATHERING THE INGREDIENTS

Using the list on the opposite page as a guide, choose the ingredients you want to offer as fillings for omelets. Fillings customarily include two or three complementary ingredients. One is often cheese, which melts and enriches the filling as the omelet cooks. Depending on the number of guests, provide two or three different types of cheese, along with a choice of vegetables, meat or seafood, and herbs.

A good rule of thumb is to allow 2 eggs per omelet. Remember to have garnishes on hand, such as crème fraîche and salsa.

The night before, you can prepare the ingredients and store them separately in covered bowls in the refrigerator. Dice and sauté vegetables such as onions and bell peppers (capsicums), for instance. Rinse, cook, and chop greens such as spinach; sauté and crumble sausage or bacon; grate or crumble cheeses. You can also rinse, dry, and finely chop fresh herbs.

ARRANGING THE STATION

The best pan for cooking individual omelets has shallow, sloping sides and is about 8 inches (20 cm) in diameter. This shape makes it easier for you to fold and serve the omelet. A frying pan of the same size will work as well. If you are serving vegetarians, use 2 pans, reserving one for omelets with meat fillings. You'll also need a spatula.

On a work surface near the stove or portable burner, set out the bowls of ingredients where they can easily be reached and supply each with a spoon. Have ready unsalted butter. When it's time to cook the omelets, crack the total number of eggs you'll need into a bowl, whisk them together, and season with salt and freshly ground pepper.

Warm plates in a 200°F (95°C) oven. Have paper towels nearby for wiping out the pan(s) in between omelets.

COOKING THE OMELETS

For each omelet, melt 1 tablespoon butter over medium heat until it foams, then tilt the pan to coat. Using a ladle or measuring cup, pour ¼–⅓ cup (2–3 fl oz/60–90 ml) beaten eggs into the pan. Stir gently with the spatula until slightly thickened.

Lift the set portions and let the uncooked parts run underneath. After about 1 minute, the eggs will begin to set, but the top will remain soft and moist. Sprinkle the chosen filling ingredients over one-half of the eggs. Fold the other half over the ingredients and cook until the filling is heated through and the cheese, if using, is melted, about 30 seconds. Slide the finished omelet onto a plate and let guests choose their preferred garnish. If more than 30 minutes will lapse between making omelets, refrigerate the bowl of beaten eggs.

OMELET INGREDIENTS

Dairy: grated firm cheese, such as cheddar, Swiss, or Gruyère; crumbled blue cheese; crumbled fresh goat cheese; crumbled feta cheese; cubed cream cheese; sliced mozzarella cheese

Herbs: fresh flat leaf (Italian) parsley, rosemary, tarragon, basil, chervil, chives

Vegetables: cubed or sliced avocado, cubed seeded tomato, chopped cooked spinach, chopped cooked broccoli, cooked diced onion, minced green (spring) onion, cooked diced red or green bell pepper (capsicum)

Meats: cooked sliced sausage, diced ham, crumbled cooked bacon

Seafood: cooked bay shrimp, flaked cooked crabmeat, diced cooked or smoked salmon

Suggested combinations: broccoli, onions, cheddar cheese; cream cheese, smoked salmon, chives; tomatoes, basil, goat cheese; ham, onions, bell peppers (capsicums), Swiss cheese; shrimp, tarragon, feta cheese; bacon, green (spring) onions, spinach, Gruyère cheese

Finishing options: sour cream or crème fraîche; salsa

Scrambled Eggs with Spinach and White Cheddar

Spinach and cheddar are popular additions to scrambled eggs. Other cheeses, such as Monterey jack, mild yellow cheddar, or even a blue cheese can be used instead. A mixture of minced fresh herbs, including flat-leaf (Italian) parsley, basil, and chives, makes a flavorful substitute for the spinach.

In a bowl, using a fork, beat together the eggs, salt, and pepper until blended.

In a large frying pan over medium heat, melt the butter. When the butter foams, reduce the heat to low. Add the beaten eggs and cook, stirring several times, until curds just begin to form, 1½–2 minutes. Add the spinach and cheese, stir once or twice, and continue to cook just until the curds are soft, 2–3 minutes longer.

Spoon the eggs onto a warmed platter and serve at once.

8 large eggs

½ teaspoon salt

½ teaspoon freshly ground pepper

2 tablespoons unsalted butter

1 cup (1 oz/30 g) baby spinach leaves

2 oz (60 g) white cheddar cheese, coarsely grated

Scrambled Eggs with Chives

18 large eggs

¾ cup (6 fl oz/180 ml) heavy (double) cream

6 tablespoons (½ oz/15 g) snipped fresh chives, plus extra for garnish

1½ teaspoons *each* salt and freshly ground pepper

6 tablespoons (3 oz/90 g) unsalted butter

In each of 2 bowls, whisk together 9 of the eggs, 6 tablespoons (3 fl oz/90 ml) of the cream, 3 tablespoons of the chives, ¾ teaspoon of the salt, and ¾ teaspoon of the pepper until blended.

In a large frying pan over medium heat, melt 3 tablespoons of the butter. When the butter foams, add 1 bowlful of the beaten eggs and cook, without stirring, until warmed through, 2–3 minutes. Continue to cook, stirring the eggs occasionally as they set, until soft curds form, 5–6 minutes longer. Transfer to a warmed platter and keep warm. Repeat with the remaining 3 tablespoons butter and bowlful of beaten eggs. Garnish with the chives and serve at once.

Scrambled eggs are so easy to prepare that they can be made after your guests have arrived. Other herbs, such as rosemary and thyme, can be substituted for the chives.

Soft-Boiled Egg with Rosemary-Chili Salt

1 teaspoon dried rosemary leaves

1 tablespoon salt

½ teaspoon chili powder

4 large eggs

In a spice grinder or a mortar with a pestle, grind the rosemary leaves until they are a fine powder. In a bowl, combine the rosemary, salt, and chili powder and mix well with a fork. Transfer to a small serving bowl. (The rosemary mixture can be prepared in advance and stored in a jar with a tight-fitting lid for up to 4 days.)

Place the eggs in a saucepan and add cold water to cover by 1 inch (2.5 cm). Bring to a boil over medium-high heat. When the water boils, remove the pan from the heat and cover. Let stand for 4–5 minutes for a soft egg, 6–7 minutes for a medium-soft egg, or 8 minutes for a medium egg. Using a slotted spoon, remove the eggs. Pour off the hot water and fill the pan with cold water. Return the eggs to the pan and let cool for 5 minutes.

Place each egg, pointed end down, in an egg cup and serve at once. Diners use a knife to crack the top part of the egg and then lift off the top. Pass the rosemary-chili salt at the table.

Soft-boiled eggs are an English favorite, and it is a rare breakfast or brunch table in the British Isles that doesn't feature them, cooked to the desired stage of doneness: soft, medium-soft, or medium. The seasoning here, rosemary-chili salt, adds spice to this traditional morning fare.

Fried Eggs with Asparagus, Pancetta, and Bread Crumbs

Adding pancetta to classic buttered bread crumbs contributes the taste of bacon without overwhelming the dish. Accompany the eggs and asparagus with toasts drizzled with olive oil to round out the Italian flavors of this simple presentation.

Preheat the oven to 400°F (200°C).

Spread the asparagus in a baking dish large enough to hold them in a single layer. Drizzle with the olive oil and season to taste with salt and pepper. Turn the spears several times to coat them evenly. Roast the asparagus, turning once or twice, until the spears are tender-crisp and the color has darkened slightly, about 15 minutes; the timing will depend on the thickness of the spears. Loosely cover with aluminum foil and set aside.

In a small frying pan over medium-high heat, melt the butter. When the butter begins to foam, add the pancetta and cook, stirring, just until it darkens slightly, about 1 minute. Add the bread crumbs and cook, stirring often, until golden, about 2 minutes. Set aside.

In a large frying pan over medium-high heat, melt the 2 tablespoons butter. When the butter foams, break the eggs into the pan, spacing them about 1 inch (2.5 cm) apart. Reduce the heat to low and season the eggs with salt and pepper. Cover the pan and cook until the whites are set and the yolks begin to firm around the edges, 5–7 minutes. Remove from the heat.

Just before the eggs are ready, divide the asparagus evenly among 4 warmed plates. Using a slotted spatula, transfer the eggs to the plates. Sprinkle the eggs and asparagus with the pancetta-bread crumb mixture and then garnish with a light dusting of Parmesan cheese (if using). Serve at once.

16 asparagus spears, tough ends removed

Olive oil

Salt and freshly ground pepper

2 teaspoons unsalted butter

2 thin slices pancetta, chopped

1 cup (2 oz/60 g) bread crumbs (page 277)

2 tablespoons unsalted butter or canola oil

4 large eggs

Grated Parmesan cheese for garnish (optional)

Eggs Over Easy with Peperonata

1 tablespoon olive oil

2 tablespoons minced shallots

6 large tomatoes, peeled and coarsely chopped, with juices

Salt and freshly ground pepper

1 large red bell pepper (capsicum), seeded and coarsely chopped

2 tablespoons unsalted butter

8 large eggs

In a large frying pan over medium-high heat, warm the olive oil. Add the shallots and cook, stirring, until translucent, about 1 minute. Add the tomatoes, 1/2 teaspoon each salt and pepper and stir to mix. Reduce the heat to medium and cook, stirring occasionally, until the sauce has thickened, about 10 minutes. Add the bell pepper and continue to cook, stirring occasionally, until the pepper is very tender and the sauce is thick, about 15 minutes longer. Cover and set aside.

In another large frying pan over medium-high heat, melt the butter. When the butter foams, break the eggs into the pan, spacing them about 1 inch (2.5 cm) apart. Reduce the heat to low and season the eggs with salt and pepper. Cover the pan and cook until the whites are set and the yolks begin to firm around the edges, 5–7 minutes. Using a slotted spatula, turn the eggs and cook just until the yolks form an opaque film, 30–45 seconds.

Divide the *peperonata* among 4 warmed plates, spreading it to make a bed. Top each serving with 2 eggs. Season to taste with salt and freshly ground pepper. Serve at once.

Peperonata is a favorite Italian preparation of sweet peppers, onions, and tomatoes, cooked down to a chunky sauce. Here, it is served as a base for eggs over easy. When the soft yolk is broken, it enriches the sauce. You can also pair *peperonata* with polenta, grilled meats, or rice. For an extra flourish, garnish each plate with a sprinkle of freshly grated Parmesan cheese.

Ham, Leek, and Gruyère Quiches

The pastry shells for these small, bite-sized quiches can be made up to 2 days in advance and stored in an airtight container, and the filling can be made a day ahead and kept covered in the refrigerator. Spinach, cooked, drained, and minced, can be substituted for the leeks. For a vegetarian version, use sautéed minced mushrooms instead of the minced ham.

To make the pastry, use a pastry blender or fork to cut the butter and vegetable shortening into ³/₄-inch (2-cm) pieces.

BY HAND: In a large bowl, combine the flour, sugar (if using), and salt and stir to mix. Scatter the butter and shortening pieces over the flour mixture. Using a fork, toss to coat with the flour. Using a pastry blender or 2 knives, cut in the butter and shortening until the mixture forms large, coarse crumbs the size of large peas. Drizzle the ice water over the mixture and toss with the fork until the dough is evenly moist and begins to come together in a mass but does not form a ball.

BY FOOD PROCESSOR: Combine the flour, sugar (if using), and salt. Pulse 2 or 3 times to mix. Add the butter and shortening pieces and pulse 8–10 times until the mixture forms large, coarse crumbs the size of large peas. Add the ice water a little at a time and pulse 10–12 times just until the dough begins to come together.

Transfer the dough to a work surface. Divide the dough in half and form each half into a 6-inch (15-cm) disk. Wrap each disk tightly in plastic wrap and refrigerate until well chilled, about 1 hour or for up to overnight.

Position a rack in the middle of the oven, and preheat to 400°F (200°C). Remove 1 disk from the refrigerator. On a lightly floured work surface, roll out into a round about 13 inches (33 cm) in diameter and ¹/₄ inch (6 mm) thick. Using a 2-inch (5-cm) biscuit or cookie cutter, cut out circles of dough. Fit the circles into 24 mini-muffin-pan cups. (If necessary to line all the cups, gather up the scraps, reroll, and cut out more circles.) Place a small ball of crumpled aluminum foil in each cup. Bake for 4 minutes. Remove the foil and reserve, prick the bottom of each pastry with a fork, and continue baking until the pastry is golden, 2–3 minutes longer. Let cool on a wire rack. Set aside. Reduce the oven temperature to 350°F (180°C).

In a frying pan over medium heat, melt the butter. When the butter foams, add the leek and cook, stirring, until it softens, about 5 minutes. Cover, reduce the heat to low, and cook until the leek is translucent and soft, 5–7 minutes. Let cool.

In a bowl, whisk together the eggs, cream, salt, pepper, nutmeg, and ham. Add the leeks and whisk to combine. Spoon the egg mixture into the pastry shells, filling them to the brim.

Bake the quiches until the filling is puffed and lightly golden, 10–12 minutes. Transfer to a wire rack and let cool in the pan. Garnish with the chives and serve warm or at room temperature.

For the pastry

²/₃ cup (5 oz/155 g) cold unsalted butter

6 tablespoons (3 oz/90 g) cold vegetable shortening

2²/₃ cups (13¹/₂ oz/425 g) all-purpose (plain) flour

2 tablespoons sugar (optional)

¹/₂ teaspoon salt

¹/₂ cup (4 fl oz/125 ml) ice water

1¹/₂ tablespoons unsalted butter

1 leek, white part only, minced

2 large eggs

1¹/₃ cups (11 oz/340 ml) heavy (double) cream or half-and-half (half cream)

¹/₄ teaspoon salt

¹/₄ teaspoon white pepper

¹/₈ teaspoon freshly grated nutmeg

¹/₂ cup (3 oz/90 g) minced ham

Finely snipped fresh chives for garnish

Chilaquiles with Poached Eggs and Black Beans

For the tomatillo sauce

12 tomatillos, husks removed

2 cloves garlic, chopped

½ small yellow onion, chopped

2 jalapeño chiles, seeded and coarsely chopped

¼ cup (⅓ oz/10 g) chopped fresh cilantro (fresh coriander)

2 tablespoons canola, sunflower, or grape seed oil

1 cup (8 fl oz/250 ml) chicken broth

½ teaspoon salt

½ teaspoon freshly ground pepper

2 cups (16 fl oz/500 ml) canola oil

18–20 corn tortillas, 6 inches (15 cm) in diameter, torn into strips

½ small yellow onion, chopped

¼ lb (125 g) Monterey jack cheese, shredded

2 tablespoons chopped fresh oregano

1 can (16 oz/500 g) black beans, drained

1 teaspoon fresh lemon juice

4–6 large eggs

¼ lb (125 g) *queso fresco*, crumbled

To make the tomatillo sauce, bring a large pot of water to a boil over high heat. Reduce the heat to medium-high, add the tomatillos, and cook until they soften and become paler in color, 3–4 minutes. Using a slotted spoon, transfer the tomatillos to a cutting board and let cool. Coarsely chop the tomatillos and place in a blender or food processor. Add the garlic, onion, chiles, and cilantro and process until puréed.

In a large saucepan over medium heat, warm the 2 tablespoons oil. Add the tomatillo purée and cook, stirring, until the purée darkens, 4–5 minutes. Gradually add the broth and continue to cook, stirring occasionally, until a medium thick sauce forms, about 10 minutes longer. Stir in the salt and pepper and set aside.

In a heavy frying pan over medium-high heat, warm the oil. Working in batches, add the torn tortillas and fry until golden on one side, about 30 seconds. Turn and fry until golden on the second side, 15–20 seconds. Transfer the strips to paper towels to drain.

Pour off all but 1–2 teaspoons of the oil from the pan and place over medium heat. Add the onion and cook, stirring, until translucent, about 1 minute. Add the tortilla strips and tomatillo sauce and cook stirring gently until the chips are softened, 3–4 minutes. Stir in the cheese and half of the oregano. Continue to cook until the cheese has melted, 4–5 minutes longer. Stir in the remaining oregano.

Meanwhile, in a saucepan over medium heat, warm the beans until they are hot and steaming, about 10 minutes, stirring often to prevent sticking.

Carefully pour water to a depth of 2 inches (5 cm) into a large saucepan and add the lemon juice. Place over medium heat and bring to a gentle simmer. Break the eggs, one at a time, into a small bowl. Hold the bowl so it is just touching the simmering water and slide the egg into the water. Repeat with the remaining eggs, spacing them about 1 inch (2.5 cm) apart. Keep the water at a gentle simmer. Cook until the whites are set and the yolks are glazed over but still soft, 4–5 minutes.

About 1 minute before the eggs are done, spoon some of the *chilaquiles* onto each plate. Using a slotted spoon, lift each egg from the simmering water, letting the excess water drain into the pan. Trim any ragged edges of egg white with kitchen scissors. Top each serving with a poached egg and sprinkle with some of the *queso fresco*. Serve at once, accompanied by the black beans.

This traditional Mexican dish uses leftover tortillas, much as bread puddings were initially a way to use day-old bread. The tortillas, torn into strips as they are here or cut into triangles like chips, are fried, covered with a sauce, and cooked on the stove top or baked in the oven. The sauce for this version is made with fresh tomatillos, a tomato relative with a crisp, clean citrus flavor. The lime green sauce is slightly spiked with chiles. *Chilaquiles* are often served with poached or fried eggs and accompanied by black beans to make a colorful and hearty dish.

Eggs Blackstone with Meyer Lemon Hollandaise

The difference between eggs Blackstone and the better-known eggs Benedict is that the former calls for bacon instead of ham. A ripe, juicy tomato, maybe one of the heirloom varieties such as Brandywine or Marvel Stripe, makes this special brunch dish stellar, but any tomato variety may be used. If Meyer lemons are unavailable, substitute the juice from another variety and add 1/4 teaspoon sugar to replicate the delicate sweetness of the Meyer.

To make the hollandaise sauce, in a saucepan over medium heat, melt the butter. Remove from the heat and keep warm. In a small nonreactive saucepan over low heat, warm the lemon juice. Place the egg yolks in a heatproof bowl or in the top of a double boiler and set over (not touching) barely simmering water in a saucepan. Heat the yolks, whisking constantly, until they begin to thicken, 3–4 minutes. Add 1 tablespoon of the boiling water and whisk until the yolks thicken, about 2 seconds. Add another 1 tablespoon of the boiling water and whisk until the yolks thicken, about 2 seconds. Repeat twice, adding 1 tablespoon boiling water each time. Whisk in the warm lemon juice and remove the bowl from the heat. Whisking constantly, very slowly pour in the melted butter. Whisk in the salt and cayenne and continue to whisk until the sauce triples in volume, 3–4 minutes. To keep the sauce warm until serving, set it over (not touching) hot water in the saucepan and whisk occasionally.

Preheat a broiler (grill). Arrange the bacon slices in a single layer on a baking sheet and place in the broiler about 6 inches (15 cm) from the heat source. Broil (grill) the slices until browned, about 3 minutes. Turn and broil until browned on the second side, about 2 minutes longer. Transfer the bacon to paper towels to drain.

Pour water to a depth of 2 inches (5 cm) into a large frying pan and add the lemon juice. Place over medium heat and bring to a gentle simmer. Break 1 egg into a small bowl or cup. Hold the bowl so it is just touching the simmering water and slide the egg into the water. Quickly repeat with the remaining eggs, one at a time, keeping them about 1 inch (2.5 cm) apart. Adjust the heat to keep the water at a gentle simmer. Cook until the whites are set and the yolks are glazed over but still soft, 4–5 minutes.

About 1 minute before the eggs are done, place 2 muffin halves, cut side up, on each warmed plate. Top each half with 1 tomato slice and 2 bacon slices. Using a slotted spoon, lift each egg from the simmering water, letting the excess water drain into the pan. Trim any ragged edges of egg white with kitchen scissors. Top each muffin half with 1 poached egg and sprinkle with pepper. Spoon 2 tablespoons of the hollandaise sauce over each egg. Serve at once.

For the hollandaise sauce

1/2 cup (4 oz/125 g) unsalted butter

1 1/2 tablespoons fresh Meyer lemon juice

3 large egg yolks

4 tablespoons (2 fl oz/60 ml) boiling water

1/4 teaspoon salt

1/4 teaspoon cayenne pepper

8 slices thick bacon, cut in half lengthwise

1 teaspoon fresh Meyer lemon juice

8 large eggs

4 English muffins, halved and toasted

8 heirloom or regular tomato slices

Freshly ground pepper

Baked Eggs with Tomatoes, Herbs, and Cream

2 teaspoons unsalted butter, plus extra for ramekins

2 or 3 tomatoes, chopped (about 2 cups/12 oz/375 g)

1/2 cup (1 1/2 oz/45 g) chopped fresh basil

1/4 cup (1/3 oz/10 g) chopped fresh flat-leaf (Italian) parsley

1 teaspoon salt

1 teaspoon freshly ground pepper

4 large eggs

4 teaspoons heavy (double) cream

4 teaspoons grated Parmesan cheese (optional)

Position a rack in the middle of the oven, and preheat to 350°F (180°C). Generously butter four 1/2-cup (4–fl oz/125-ml) ramekins.

In a bowl, stir together the tomatoes, basil, parsley, 1/2 teaspoon of the salt, and 1/2 teaspoon of the pepper. Divide evenly among the prepared ramekins. Cut the 2 teaspoons butter into small pieces and divide among the ramekins, sprinkling the pieces evenly over the tomato mixture. Break an egg into each ramekin. Season with the remaining 1/2 teaspoon salt and 1/2 teaspoon pepper, dividing them evenly. Drizzle each egg with 1 teaspoon of the cream. Arrange the ramekins on a rimmed baking sheet.

Bake until the egg whites are opaque and the yolks have firm edges and are soft in the center, about 15 minutes. Remove from the oven and sprinkle each serving with 1 teaspoon of the Parmesan cheese (if using). Serve at once.

Baking eggs in individual ramekins along with a little butter and cream is a classic French dish. Sometimes vegetables, such as the tomatoes here, are a bed for the eggs. Cooked spinach, chard, or kale or sautéed mushrooms or leeks would make delicious substitutions. For another variation, incorporate chopped ham into the vegetables.

Ham and Cheddar Omelet

Omelets are versatile because a wide variety of ingredients can be used for the filling. For example, combine chopped tomato and avocado for a Southwest-style omelet, cooked potatoes and chopped beef for a farmhouse omelet, or curried vegetables for a South Asian–inspired omelet. You can also serve a choice of condiments, such as chutney or salsa.

In a large bowl, whisk together the eggs, salt, and pepper until blended.

In a 14-inch (35-cm) frying pan over medium heat, melt the butter. When the butter foams, tilt the pan to coat evenly. Pour the eggs into the pan and stir slowly with a heatproof rubber spatula until the eggs begin to thicken, about 4 seconds. Reduce the heat to low and cook, without stirring, until the eggs set along the edges, 2–3 minutes. Continue to cook the eggs, gently lifting the set portions with the spatula and tipping the pan to allow the uncooked egg to run underneath, until the eggs are set, about 1 minute for a soft texture. For a firmer texture, cook for about 20 seconds longer.

Sprinkle the ham, cheddar cheese, and herbs on half of the omelet, leaving a 1-inch (2.5-cm) border around the edge. Using the spatula, carefully lift the other half of the omelet and fold it over the filling. Cook until the filling is heated through, 20–40 seconds.

Slide the omelet onto a warmed platter. Using a large knife, cut the omelet crosswise into pieces 2–3 inches (5–7.5 cm) wide. Serve at once.

8 large eggs

½ teaspoon salt

½ teaspoon freshly ground pepper

1½ tablespoons unsalted butter

½ lb (250 g) smoked ham, cut into strips or ½-inch (12-mm) cubes

¼ lb (125 g) white cheese such as Vermont white cheddar, Gruyère, or Swiss, shredded

2 tablespoons fresh herbs such as chervil, flat-leaf (Italian) parsley, or thyme

Frittata with Mixed Herbs, Leeks, and Parmesan Cheese

2 tablespoons unsalted butter

4 cups (12 oz/375 g) thinly sliced leeks, including tender green tops

Salt and freshly ground pepper

6 large eggs

½ cup (¾ oz/20 g) mixed minced fresh flat-leaf (Italian) parsley, basil, and mint

¼ cup (1 oz/30 g) grated Parmesan cheese

The frittata is the Italian version of an omelet. But unlike its French cousin, which carefully folds the egg around the filling, the frittata mixes the filling with the eggs and cooks them together in a large pancake. Here sautéed leeks and herbs are used, but almost any vegetable, from zucchini (courgettes) to peppers (capsicums) to mushrooms can be used.

In an ovenproof 10-inch (25-cm) frying pan over medium heat, melt the butter. When the butter foams, add the leeks, season with salt and pepper, and cook, stirring, until softened, about 15 minutes. Reduce the heat as needed to keep the leeks from browning.

In a bowl, whisk the eggs until blended. Whisk in the herbs and cheese, and season with salt and pepper. Pour the eggs into the pan and stir to distribute the leeks evenly. Reduce the heat to low and cook until the eggs are set around the edges but still a little moist in the center, about 15 minutes. Preheat a broiler (grill).

Place the pan in the broiler about 6 inches (15 cm) from the heat source. Broil (grill) until the top is puffed and golden and the center is firm, about 1 minute. Using a wide spatula, carefully transfer the frittata to a cutting board. Cut into wedges and serve at once.

Deviled Eggs with Lemon Zest, Chives, and Capers

Ever-popular deviled eggs have many variations. Sometimes, as in the French classic *oeufs mimosus,* the yolks are simply mashed with Dijon mustard and seasoned with salt and pepper. Here, a heady mix of shallots, chives, capers, and lemon zest are added to the yolks along with the mustard.

Place the eggs in a large saucepan and add cold water to cover by 1–1 1/2 inches (2.5–4 cm). Bring to a boil over medium-high heat. When the water reaches a boil, remove the pan from the heat and cover. Let stand for 20 minutes. Using a slotted spoon, remove the eggs. Pour off the hot water and fill the pan with cold water. Return the eggs to the pan and let cool for 5 minutes. Remove the eggs and peel them under cold running water.

Cut the eggs in half lengthwise. Carefully remove the yolks and place in a bowl. Set the whites aside. Add the mustard, mayonnaise, salt, pepper, chives, shallots, capers, and lemon zest to the yolks. Using a fork, mash together until the yolk mixture is smooth and fluffy.

Spoon a heaping teaspoonful of the yolk mixture into the cavity of each egg-white half, mounding it slightly. Arrange the deviled eggs on a plate and serve at once. Or, cover and refrigerate for up to 4 hours.

6 large eggs

1 tablespoon Dijon mustard

1 tablespoon mayonnaise

1/2 teaspoon salt

1/2 teaspoon freshly ground pepper

2 tablespoons minced chives

1 teaspoon minced shallots

1 1/2 tablespoons capers, rinsed, drained, patted dry, and coarsely chopped

2 teaspoons grated lemon zest

Grains and Cereals

About Grains and Cereals

Cereals and grains are a classic choice for breakfast and brunch. This chapter's three main ingredients—oatmeal, cornmeal, and grits—can be cooked simply with flavorings such as fruit and honey or they can be dressed up for a more substantial sweet or savory main dish.

Not only are grains hearty and satisfying, but they are easy to cook whether you are serving them on their own or as the foundation for another recipe. For cooking the oatmeal, grits, and cornmeal in the recipes here, your most practical piece of equipment is a heavy saucepan or one with a heavy bottom.

Although grains are cooked in at least twice as much liquid—either milk or water—they thicken quickly while simmering on the stove. Stirring the hot mixture frequently helps prevent it from sticking to the pan. A heavy saucepan, along with a vigilant eye, provides an extra measure of insurance.

POLENTA STEP BY STEP

Cornmeal, in particular, absorbs a substantial amount of liquid. The ratio of liquid to cornmeal—4 cups (32 fl oz/1 l) liquid for 1 cup (5 oz/155 g) cornmeal—is much greater than for oatmeal and other grains.

Traditional polenta recipes call for adding dry cornmeal to boiling water in a slow, steady stream while stirring continuously to prevent lumps from forming. In the polenta recipes in this chapter, the cornmeal is first mixed with milk before adding it to the water—another way to help avoid lumps. Even with this method, you should add the milk-polenta mixture slowly to the boiling water as you stir steadily with a whisk.

To make sure the polenta remains smooth and all the grains cook evenly, you will need to stir it frequently as it cooks, preferably switching from the whisk to a wooden spoon.

At this stage, you want to follow a couple of precautions. As the polenta thickens, it will start to bubble and may even spatter above the rim of the pan. To protect your hand and arm from scalding polenta, wear oven mitts and use a long-handled spoon.

You know that the polenta is almost done when it starts to pull away from the sides of the pan. If the polenta is not quite ready but looks like it is losing moisture, you can add water by tablespoons, stirring each addition into the polenta before adding more.

WORKING WITH BEATEN EGGS

Grits, which like polenta are made from corn, cook into a similarly thick, silken cereal that can be lightened with eggs, enriched with cheese, and baked into a savory pudding. The recipe here, Cheddar Cheese Grits (page 83), can be prepared a day ahead and warmed the next morning before serving.

Using grits in a soufflé is another classic recipe. A grits soufflé, like the one made with dark greens and sweet onions on page 85, will not rise as high or be as delicate as other, lighter sweet or savory soufflés. Nevertheless, to help guarantee buoyant results, you must adhere to three steps: carefully separating the egg whites from the yolks; beating the whites until they form stiff peaks; and adding the whites to the soufflé base in two stages.

Start by removing the eggs from the refrigerator immediately before you separate them. Crack each egg on a flat surface and hold it in a clean, cupped hand, letting

the white run through your fingers into a bowl. Separate each egg individually and collect the whites in a small bowl. The whites will not beat properly if they contain even a small speck of the yolk. If you accidentally break the yolk into the white, reserve the entire egg for another use.

Make sure your mixing bowl and electric beaters are spotlessly clean. You can also use a clean whisk. To determine when the eggs have reached the right stage, lift the beaters or whisk. The beaten egg whites should stand up in stiff peaks and not fall to one side.

Finally, stir only one-fourth of the beaten egg whites into the soufflé base, which will lighten the mixture. Then, using a rubber spatula, fold in the remaining whites, carefully sweeping the spatula through, under, and over both mixtures, and giving the bowl a quarter turn with each fold. Do not overmix. It's fine if a few streaks of egg whites remain.

FINISHING TOUCHES

For hot oatmeal and polenta, you can offer guests accompaniments in addition to the ones in each recipe. Maple syrup and toasted nuts are as delicious with oatmeal as they are in the polenta recipe on page 79.

You can vary the compote made for the oatmeal on page 90 to suit the season by using stone fruits in summer and apples and pears in autumn and winter. Or, serve with one of the basic recipes at the back of the book.

If you want a lighter accompaniment than cream, set out a bowl of Greek-style yogurt, the variety used to make the granola parfait on page 89. If you are unable to find this thick yogurt, make your own by spooning regular yogurt into a fine-mesh sieve lined with cheesecloth (muslin), set the sieve over a bowl, and refrigerate overnight to drain.

Polenta with Mascarpone, Maple Syrup, and Toasted Pecans

Polenta, a specialty of northern Italy, is made from cornmeal. It is cooked with water, milk, broth, or a mixture of liquids to a soft consistency. Mascarpone, another Italian specialty, is an exceptionally creamy fresh cow's milk cheese that makes an ideal garnish. Warm maple syrup and crunchy toasted pecans top off this hearty contemporary breakfast dish.

In a small saucepan over low heat, warm the maple syrup. Keep warm while preparing the polenta.

To prepare the polenta, in a large, heavy saucepan over medium-high heat, bring 3 cups (24 fl oz/750 ml) water and the salt to a boil. In a small bowl, stir together the cornmeal and milk. Gradually stir the cornmeal mixture into the boiling water. Stirring constantly, bring the mixture to a boil, about 2 minutes. Reduce the heat to medium-low and cook, stirring frequently, until the polenta is thick and creamy, about 25 minutes. Add up to 1/2 cup (4 fl oz/125 ml) water by tablespoons if the polenta begins to stick. (Be careful, as the hot polenta can bubble and spatter.)

Divide the polenta among 4 shallow serving bowls. Drizzle about 2 tablespoons of the warm maple syrup over the polenta in each bowl. Stir the mascarpone (this thins it slightly) and spoon about 2 tablespoons on top of each bowl of polenta. Sprinkle with the toasted pecans and serve at once.

1/2 cup (5 1/2 fl oz/170 ml) maple syrup

1 1/2 teaspoons salt

1 cup (5 oz/155 g) coarse-ground polenta

1 cup (8 fl oz/250 ml) whole milk

1/2 cup (4 oz/125 g) mascarpone cheese

1/2 cup (2 oz/60 g) toasted pecan halves (page 277), coarsely chopped

Grilled Polenta with Sausages and Bell Peppers

For the polenta

1½ teaspoons salt

1 cup (5 oz/155 g) coarse-ground polenta

1 cup (8 fl oz/250 ml) whole milk

Unsalted butter for pan

For the sausages

1 tablespoon olive oil

1 lb (500 g) sweet Italian sausages, cut into slices ½ inch (12 mm) thick

1 yellow onion, coarsely chopped

1 green bell pepper (capsicum), seeded and coarsely chopped

1 red bell pepper (capsicum), seeded and coarsely chopped

¼ cup (2 fl oz/60 ml) chicken broth

Salt and freshly ground pepper

1 tablespoon olive oil

1 tablespoon finely chopped flat-leaf (Italian) parsley

To prepare the polenta, in a large, heavy saucepan over medium-high heat, bring 3 cups (24 fl oz/750 ml) water and the salt to a boil. In a small bowl, stir together the cornmeal and milk. Gradually stir the cornmeal mixture into the boiling water. Stirring constantly, bring the mixture to a boil, about 2 minutes. Reduce the heat to medium-low and cook, stirring frequently, until the polenta is thick and creamy, about 25 minutes. Add up to ½ cup (4 fl oz/125 ml) water by tablespoons if the polenta begins to stick. (Be careful, as the hot polenta can bubble and spatter.)

Butter a rimmed baking sheet. Using a rubber spatula, spread the hot polenta on the prepared pan to form a 10-inch (25-cm) square about ½ inch (12 mm) thick. Cover the polenta with waxed paper and refrigerate until cold, about 2 hours.

To prepare the sausages, in a frying pan over medium heat, warm the olive oil. Add the sausage slices and cook, stirring frequently, until browned on all sides, about 8 minutes. Spoon off any excess fat. Add the onion and cook until softened, about 3 minutes. Add the bell peppers and cook, stirring frequently, until the vegetables are tender, about 5 minutes. Add the broth and bring to a simmer, stirring to scrape up any browned bits from the pan bottom. Season with salt and pepper. Remove from the heat and keep warm.

Preheat the broiler (grill). Cut the polenta into 12 rectangles or squares, and brush the tops with half of the olive oil. Using a wide spatula, transfer the polenta pieces to a rimmed baking sheet, arranging them bottom side up. Brush with the remaining oil. Place in the broiler about 6 inches (15 cm) from the heat source. Broil, turning once, until both sides are golden, about 5 minutes per side.

Arrange 2 pieces of polenta on each plate and surround with the sausage mixture, dividing it evenly. Sprinkle with the chopped parsley and serve at once.

You can get a head start on this dish. Cook the polenta, spread it on the baking sheet, and then refrigerate it for up to 3 days. Then, just before serving, cut it into pieces and broil it. Italian sausages, cooked with red and green bell peppers, make a colorful accompaniment.

GRAINS AND CEREALS   81

Polenta with Prosciutto, Poached Eggs, and Pecorino Cheese

2 teaspoons olive oil

8 thin slices prosciutto

1½ teaspoons salt

1 cup (5 oz/155 g) coarse-ground polenta

1 cup (8 fl oz/250 ml) whole milk

1 teaspoon fresh lemon juice

4 large eggs

½ cup (2 oz/60 g) grated pecorino cheese

Freshly ground pepper

In a large frying pan over medium heat, warm the olive oil. Add the prosciutto slices in a single layer and cook, turning once with tongs, until the slices are hot and begin to crisp at the edges, about 5 minutes total. Remove from the heat and keep warm.

To prepare the polenta, in a large, heavy saucepan over medium-high heat, bring 3 cups (24 fl oz/750 ml) water and the salt to a boil. In a small bowl, stir together the polenta and milk. Gradually stir the polenta mixture into the boiling water. Stirring constantly, bring the mixture to a boil, about 2 minutes. Reduce the heat to medium-low and cook, stirring frequently, until the polenta is thick and creamy, about 25 minutes. Add up to ½ cup (4 fl oz/125 ml) water by tablespoons if the polenta begins to stick. (Be careful, as the hot polenta can bubble and spatter.)

Pour water to a depth of 2 inches (5 cm) into a large saucepan and add the lemon juice. Place over medium heat and bring to a gentle simmer. Break 1 egg into a small bowl or cup. Hold the bowl so it is just touching the simmering water and slide the egg into the water. Quickly repeat with the remaining eggs, one at a time, spacing them about 1 inch (2.5 cm) apart. Adjust the heat to keep the water at a gentle simmer. Cook until the whites are set and the yolks are glazed over but still soft, 4–5 minutes.

About 1 minute before the eggs are done, divide the polenta among 4 individual plates or shallow bowls. Lay 2 prosciutto slices over each serving. Using a slotted spoon, lift each egg from the simmering water, letting the excess water drain into the pan. Trim any ragged edges of egg white with kitchen scissors. Place the egg on the prosciutto and sprinkle with about 2 tablespoons of the pecorino cheese. Season lightly with salt and pepper and serve at once.

This is breakfast Italian style—polenta for the cereal, prosciutto for the ham, and a poached egg topped with aged sheep's milk cheese. When poaching the eggs, be sure to keep the water at a gentle simmer so they do not break apart before the whites have set.

Cheddar Cheese Grits

Grits, also called hominy grits, are the ground white or yellow meal made from dried, hulled corn kernels. Look for organic grits, produced from hominy that has not been treated with lye. When grits are combined with cheddar cheese and lightened with eggs and milk, they bake into a pudding that is ideal for brunch. You can make the dish a day ahead. Let the grits cool in the baking dish, then cover and refrigerate overnight. To serve the grits, heat in a 325°F (165°C) oven until hot, about 20 minutes.

Position a rack in the middle of the oven, and preheat to 325°F (165°C). Butter a 2-qt (2-l) baking dish.

In a bowl, whisk together the eggs and milk until blended. Set aside.

In a heavy saucepan over medium-high heat, bring 2 cups (16 fl oz/500 ml) water and the salt to a boil. Slowly stir in the grits. Reduce the heat to low, cover, and cook, stirring frequently, until the grits are soft and the water is absorbed, about 20 minutes. Adjust the heat as needed to keep the grits cooking gently. Remove from the heat and let stand, covered, for 5 minutes. The grits will be thick.

Spoon the hot grits into a bowl. Add the egg mixture and whisk until blended, about 2 minutes. A few small lumps will remain. Whisk in 1 1/2 cups (6 oz/185 g) of the grated cheese and season with pepper. Using a rubber spatula, scrape the grits into the prepared baking dish. Sprinkle with the remaining grated cheese. Bake until the edges are brown and the center is set when the dish is jiggled slightly, about 55 minutes. Remove from the oven and serve at once.

Unsalted butter for pan

3 large eggs

1 cup (8 fl oz/250 ml) whole milk

1 teaspoon salt

3/4 cup (4 1/2 oz/140 g) grits

2 cups (8 oz/250 g) grated sharp cheddar cheese

Freshly ground pepper

Grits Soufflé with Greens and Sweet Onion

Grits, served with milk and butter, is a breakfast staple in much of the American south, and greens are on nearly every southern table. Here, they are paired in a homey soufflé flavored with two kinds of onions and two kinds of cheese. It will not rise as tall as its French namesake, but it will puff up and lighten in texture.

Position a rack in the middle of the oven, and preheat to 350°F (180°C). Lightly butter a 9-by-13-inch (23-by-33-cm) baking dish.

Stack 5 or 6 leaves of the greens on top of one another and roll up tightly. Cut on a diagonal into thin strips. Repeat with the remaining greens. In a large frying pan over medium-high heat, melt the 4 tablespoons butter. Add the greens, sweet onion, and garlic and cook, stirring occasionally, until the greens are wilted, about 10 minutes. Add the broth, reduce the heat to medium, cover partially, and cook until the greens are tender, about 20 minutes longer. Remove from the heat and let cool. Pour the greens into a sieve and drain well, pressing out any excess liquid. Transfer to a large bowl.

In a heavy saucepan over medium heat, bring the milk and cream to a simmer. Slowly stir in the grits, green onions, and thyme, and season with salt and pepper. Reduce the heat to low, cover, and cook, stirring frequently, until the grits are soft and the liquid is absorbed, about 20 minutes. Adjust the heat as needed to keep the grits cooking gently. Remove from the heat and stir in the cheddar cheese. Spoon the hot grits into the bowl with the greens and stir well to combine.

In a small bowl, lightly beat the egg yolks with a fork and quickly stir into the grits mixture. In a large bowl, using an electric mixer on high speed, beat the egg whites until stiff peaks form. Stir one-fourth of the beaten whites into the grits mixture. Using a rubber spatula, gently fold the lightened grits mixture into the remaining egg whites. Pour into the prepared dish. Sprinkle with the Parmesan cheese.

Bake until puffed and golden, about 40 minutes. Serve at once.

4 tablespoons (2 oz/60 g) unsalted butter, plus extra for pan

1/2 lb (250 g) mixed greens such as turnip, collard, mustard, or Swiss chard, tough stems removed

1/2 Vidalia or other sweet onion, chopped

1 clove garlic, chopped

1/4 cup (2 fl oz/60 ml) chicken broth

1 3/4 cups (14 fl oz/430 ml) whole milk

1/2 cup (4 fl oz/125 ml) heavy (double) cream

3/4 cup (4 1/2 oz/140 g) grits

3 green (spring) onions, white and pale green parts only, chopped

1 1/2 teaspoons fresh thyme leaves

Salt and freshly ground pepper

1/2 cup (2 oz/60 g) shredded cheddar cheese

3 large eggs, separated

1/2 cup (2 oz/60 g) grated Parmesan cheese

Granola with Greek Yogurt, Blueberries, and Rosemary Honey

For the granola

3 cups (9 oz/280 g) rolled oats

¼ cup (1 oz/30 g) *each* walnuts and almonds, coarsely chopped

¼ cup (1½ oz/45 g) cashew halves

2 tablespoons shredded coconut

¼ cup (2½ fl oz/75 ml) maple syrup

1 teaspoon vanilla extract

¼ cup (2 fl oz/60 ml) sesame oil

½ cup (3 oz/90 g) dried apricots, cut into pieces

½ cup (3 oz/90 g) dried cranberries

2 cups (16 oz/500 g) Greek-style yogurt

2 cups (8 oz/250 g) blueberries

½ cup (6 fl oz/185 ml) rosemary or other flavored honey

Position a rack in the middle of the oven, and preheat to 325°F (165°C).

To make the granola, in a large bowl, using a large spoon, mix together the oats, walnuts, almonds, cashews, and coconut. In a small bowl, stir together the maple syrup, vanilla, and sesame oil. Drizzle the maple syrup mixture over the oat mixture and stir to moisten evenly. Transfer the oat mixture to a rimmed baking sheet and spread in an even layer.

Bake, stirring about every 7 minutes, until the oats just begin to turn golden, about 30 minutes total. The granola should feel dry, rather than moist; it becomes crisp as it cools. Stir in the apricots and cranberries. Let cool on the baking sheet. Store in an airtight container at room temperature for up to 1 week.

Divide the yogurt among 4 shallow bowls. Top each serving with about one-fourth of the granola. Sprinkle with one-fourth of the blueberries and drizzle with 2 tablespoons honey. Serve at once.

Rolled oats combined with sesame oil and maple syrup bake into a crisp, crunchy granola. Feel free to use any combination of nuts and dried fruits that suit your taste or that of your guests. Make a double batch of the granola and use the extra to make Granola and Ricotta Cream Parfait (page 89), serve with milk, spoon over vanilla ice cream, or enjoy as a satisfying snack. Greek yogurt is thicker and less tart than other commercial yogurts, but regular yogurt can also be used. Rosemary honey adds a subtle herbal taste and aroma but any flavored honey can be used.

Oatmeal with Blueberries and Cream

4 cups (32 fl oz/1 l) whole milk

¼ teaspoon salt

2 cups (6 oz/185 g) rolled oats

½ cup (4 fl oz/125 ml) heavy (double) cream

2 cups (8 oz/250 g) blueberries

In a heavy saucepan over medium-high heat, bring the milk and salt to a gentle boil, about 3 minutes. Slowly stir in the oats. Reduce the heat to medium and cook uncovered at a gentle boil, stirring frequently, until the oatmeal is soft and the milk is absorbed, about 5 minutes. Adjust the heat as needed to keep the oatmeal boiling gently. Remove from the heat, cover, and let stand for 3 minutes. After the oatmeal has rested, stir in the cream just until blended.

Using a large spoon, gently stir the blueberries into the hot oatmeal. Divide among individual bowls and serve at once.

Oatmeal with raisins is a classic combination, but adding fresh fruit to the morning bowl is even better. Strawberries or blackberries, chopped peaches or nectarines, or a combination of fruits makes a delicious alternative.

Old-fashioned Oatmeal with Raspberry Compote

4 cups (32 fl oz/1 l) whole milk

¼ teaspoon salt

2 cups (6 oz/185 g) rolled oats

Raspberry Compote (page 275)

In a heavy saucepan over medium-high heat, bring the milk and salt to a gentle boil, about 3 minutes. Slowly stir in the oats. Reduce the heat to medium and cook uncovered at a gentle boil, stirring frequently, until the oatmeal is soft and the milk is absorbed, about 5 minutes. Adjust the heat as needed to keep the oatmeal boiling gently. Remove from the heat, cover, and let stand for 3 minutes.

Spoon the hot oatmeal into individual bowls, top each one evenly with the compote and serve at once.

Nothing is more warming on a cold morning than a bowl of steaming oatmeal. Here, it is topped with fresh raspberries in almond syrup, a delicious combination. Cooking the oats in milk, even nonfat milk, rather than water produces a hot cereal with a rich, creamy texture. Be sure to use rolled oats, rather than quick-cooking oats, for their nutty flavor.

Brûléed Oatmeal with Baked Apples

Brown sugar glazes the top of this oatmeal, which is served topped with slices of warm baked apples. Be sure to sprinkle the brown sugar evenly over the oatmeal so that it will melt into a uniform topping. And don't leave it in under the broiler too long. It is ready when it bubbles and turns golden brown.

To make the baked apples, position a rack in the middle of the oven, and preheat to 375°F (190°C). Line a rimmed baking sheet with parchment (baking) paper.

In a bowl, combine the apples, lemon juice, melted butter, and brown sugar and stir to evenly coat the apples. Spread the apples on the prepared sheet and bake until the liquid is bubbling and the apples are tender and glazed with the brown sugar mixture, about 20 minutes. Remove from the oven and keep warm. Preheat the broiler (grill).

Meanwhile, in a heavy saucepan over medium-high heat, bring the milk and salt to a gentle boil, about 3 minutes. Stir in the oats. Reduce the heat to medium and cook uncovered at a gentle boil, stirring frequently, until the oatmeal is soft and the milk is absorbed, about 5 minutes. Adjust the heat as needed to keep the oatmeal boiling gently. Remove from the heat.

Divide the hot oatmeal among 4 shallow baking dishes about 6 inches (15 cm) in diameter, spreading it evenly in the dishes. Evenly sprinkle 2 tablespoons of the brown sugar over each serving. Using a spoon or your fingers, gently press the brown sugar into a uniform layer.

Arrange the baking dishes on a baking sheet and place in the broiler about 6 inches (15 cm) from the heat source. Broil (grill) until the topping melts and bubbles vigorously, about 3 minutes. Rotate the baking sheet halfway through baking to ensure uniform browning, and watch carefully to prevent the topping from burning. Place each baking dish on a serving plate. Top with the warm apple slices and serve at once.

For the baked apples

2 apples such as Granny Smith or Baldwin, peeled, cored, and cut into wedges ¼ inch (6 mm) thick

2 teaspoons fresh lemon juice

1 tablespoon unsalted butter, melted

2 tablespoons firmly packed light brown sugar

4 cups (32 fl oz/1 l) whole milk

¼ teaspoon salt

2 cups (6 oz/185 g) rolled oats

½ cup (3½ oz/105 g) firmly packed light brown sugar

Breads and Pastries

About Breads and Pastries

Homemade baked goods can elevate even the simplest morning meal into a special occasion. Some recipes, like those for muffins, can be assembled in minutes and baked ahead of time. Brioche and other yeast breads take more time but are worth the effort.

Many important factors go into producing moist, tender baked goods. Leaveners create gas bubbles in dough or batter that expand in the oven and give the baked item a light texture. Fats—the most common are butter and oil—contribute flavor and moisture. Eggs add leavening, richness, and structure. The proportions of ingredients and the way they are combined also determine the outcome.

MIXING QUICK BREADS AND CAKES

In this chapter, there are three basic techniques for combining wet and dry ingredients. Each one adheres to a particular progression of tasks, though you will notice slight variations in some of the recipes.

Quick mixing is the method used most often for muffins and for quick breads in loaf form. First, the dry ingredients are stirred together in a bowl. In a separate bowl, the wet ingredients are blended together. Then the dry ingredients are added to the wet ingredients and stirred by hand or beaten with an electric mixer just until the dry ingredients are moistened. At this point, raisins, chopped nuts, and/or other additions are folded into the batter.

For scones (page 104) and the Irish Soda Bread (page 111), small pieces of cold butter are added to the dry ingredients and then are quickly worked into even smaller pieces with a pastry blender or 2 knives. Lastly, the wet ingredients are blended into the butter mixture. This technique is also used for making the pastry for Rustic Apple Galettes (page 127).

Cake batters, like the one for Almond Breakfast Cake (page 123), are often mixed using the creaming method. After the dry ingredients are stirred together in a bowl, room-temperature butter and sugar—as well as almond paste in the case of the breakfast cake—are beaten together to incorporate air and lighten the mixture. The eggs are blended in next, followed by the dry ingredients. For the breakfast cake, the dry ingredients are incorporated in batches alternately with milk.

It is essential to follow the instructions specific to each recipe. Of particular importance is to avoid overmixing. You want to stop just as the dry and wet ingredients are blended. Overworking the batter causes it to toughen and become dense when baked.

WORKING WITH YEAST DOUGH

If you are new to baking, you'll probably feel more comfortable making quick breads. But at some point, you'll want to make yeast breads for the sheer satisfaction of making your own focaccia, sticky buns, brioche, or beignets.

The recipes in this chapter call for two types of yeast. In recipes using active dry yeast, the yeast is dissolved in warm liquid before the dough is mixed, while quick-rise yeast can be mixed with other dry ingredients before the liquid is introduced.

Doughs made with quick-rise yeast rise in half the time of those leavened with active dry yeast. The doughs for sticky buns (page 112) and focaccia (page 128), both leavened with quick-rise yeast, double in bulk in less

than 1 hour, while the dough for brioche (page 119), which uses active dry yeast, must stand for nearly 5 hours. You'll want to keep this in mind when planning your menu.

You can mix yeast doughs by hand or, for ultimate convenience, with a stand mixer. After the dough is mixed, it is kneaded—a critical step for combining the ingredients and developing the gluten that gives the final baked item its essential structure and texture.

When you are kneading the dough, pay attention to the look and feel of the dough as well as the timing in the recipe. Whether kneaded by hand or by machine, the dough should appear smooth and feel elastic to the touch. You can also use a technique that bakers call the "windowpane test" to check the structure of the dough: Pull off a piece of dough and, holding it in both hands, gently stretch it until it forms a sheet. If the dough tears, it is not ready. If it holds together and is thin enough that you can see light through it, the dough is ready.

BAKING QUICK BREADS

You can bake recipes for standard muffins in different-sized pans by adjusting the baking time. Spoon the batter into jumbo muffin pans and increase the time by 8 to 12 minutes, or into miniature muffin pans and reduce the time by 5 to 7 minutes.

Standard quick breads, usually baked in pans measuring 9 by 5 inches (23 by 13 cm), can also be made in small loaf pans. Divide the batter between two 6-by-3½ inch (15-by-9 cm) pans and reduce the oven temperature by one-third.

If you prefer to use glass baking pans or pans with nonstick finishes, reduce the oven temperature by 25°F (15°C) so the baked item does not overbrown.

Setting Up a Bagel Bar

Guests will feel they're being treated to an opulent spread when you offer a buffet of bagels and fixings. Much of the preparation can be done in advance, and as guests choose their bagels and toppings, you can be cooking a dish that requires your attention in the kitchen.

GATHERING THE INGREDIENTS

Bagels tend to go stale quickly, so place your order at your local bagel shop in advance to be picked up the afternoon before, or the morning of, the event. If keeping them overnight, store in an airtight container at room temperature.

Select traditional bagel flavors, such as plain, poppy seed, sesame seed, salt, onion, and garlic. For guests who might like sweet bagels, include flavors like cinnamon raisin and blueberry. You can also find miniature bagels, which are about one-third the size of an ordinary bagel.

Cream cheese is essential. Either offer a block, or look for whipped cream cheese, which is easier to spread. You can also put out a selection of flavored cream-cheese spreads, such as sun-dried tomato, chive, smoked salmon, and vegetable.

Thinly sliced lox is the other classic topping. Allow about $^1/_2$ lb (250 g) for 4 servings. You can use smoked sable or whitefish in place of, or in addition to, the lox.

Have on hand garnishes for the bagels. Review the list at right and select any other ingredients for the bar.

ARRANGING THE BAR

The day before the event, decide on the best location—a counter if your kitchen is large enough and the bar won't interfere with your cooking, or a suitable table in your dining or living room. Some guests will want to toast their own bagels, so select a spot with access to an electrical outlet and set up a toaster.

Cut the bagels in half horizontally and arrange them on a platter or in a napkin-lined basket, keeping the sweet and savory bagels

separate. Place the bagels near the toaster along with plates, utensils, and napkins.

Mound the cream cheese and any other spreads in small serving dishes, and put a stick of butter in a butter dish. Provide a generous number of butter knives.

Choose a platter for the lox or other fish and lay out the slices in an attractive overlapping pattern. As you set the slices in place, separate them so they can easily be picked up with a serving fork—but be sure to handle them gently to avoid tearing.

Cut tomatoes into thin slices and thinly slice and/or chop the onions. Arrange them on a plate or cutting board.

Rinse capers, drain them well, and put them in a dish with a small serving spoon. Cut the lemons into wedges and put them on a plate. Set out a pepper mill.

ASSEMBLING THE BAGELS

As guests arrive, have them start garnishing their bagels. They can garnish the bagels with a sprinkle of capers, a squeeze of lemon, and a grinding of pepper.

BAGEL BAR TOPPINGS

Avocado

Baby spinach or mâche

Butter

Bacon or pancetta

Capers

Cream cheese

Cucumber

Fresh herbs

Freshly ground pepper

Gruyère cheese

Ham

Honey

Jam or other preserves

Lemons

Lox, smoked sable,
and/or smoked whitefish

Pastrami

Red onions

Roasted bell peppers (capsicums)

Smoked Gouda cheese

Swiss cheese

Tomatoes

Vermont white cheddar cheese

Raspberry-Lemon Muffins

The sweetness of raspberries pairs well with the tartness of lemons in these tender, colorful muffins. If fresh berries are out of season, frozen berries will still yield a delicious result. It is important to not overmix the batter, which causes the gluten in the flour to develop, producing long tunnels in the finished muffins.

Position a rack in the middle of the oven, and preheat to 375°F (190°C). Butter 12 standard muffin-pan cups or line with paper liners.

In a bowl, stir together the flour, baking powder, cinnamon, and salt. Set aside.

BY HAND: In a large bowl, whisk together the eggs and milk until blended. Add the oil, brown sugar, lemon zest, lemon juice, vanilla, and almond extract and whisk just until blended. Add the dry ingredients and stir with a rubber spatula just until moistened. Do not overmix. Fold in the berries.

BY MIXER: In a large bowl, combine the eggs and milk and beat on low speed just until blended. Add the oil, brown sugar, lemon zest, lemon juice, vanilla, and almond extract and beat just until blended. Add the dry ingredients and mix on low speed just until moistened. Do not overmix. Fold in the raspberries with a rubber spatula.

Spoon the batter into the prepared muffin cups, filling each to within 1/4 inch (6 mm) of the rim. Bake until a toothpick inserted into the center of a muffin comes out clean, about 25 minutes if using fresh raspberries or 25–30 minutes if using frozen raspberries. Transfer to a wire rack and let cool in the pan for 15 minutes, then turn out onto the rack. Serve warm or at room temperature with Honey Butter (if using). Store in an airtight container at room temperature for up to 3 days.

Unsalted butter for pan

2 cups (10 oz/315 g) all-purpose (plain) flour

1 1/2 teaspoons baking powder

1/2 teaspoon ground cinnamon

1/2 teaspoon salt

2 large eggs

1 cup (8 fl oz/250 ml) whole milk

2/3 cup (5 fl oz/160 ml) canola or corn oil

1 1/3 cups (9 1/2 oz/295 g) firmly packed light brown sugar

2 teaspoons grated lemon zest

2 tablespoons fresh lemon juice

1 teaspoon vanilla extract

1/4 teaspoon almond extract

1 cup (4 oz/125 g) fresh or frozen raspberries

Honey Butter (page 274), optional

Blueberry-Cornmeal Muffins

6 tablespoons (3 oz/90 g) unsalted butter, melted, plus extra for pan

1$\frac{1}{2}$ cups (7$\frac{1}{2}$ oz/235 g) all-purpose (plain) flour

$\frac{1}{2}$ cup (2$\frac{1}{2}$ oz/75 g) fine-ground cornmeal

2 teaspoons baking powder

$\frac{1}{2}$ teaspoon baking soda (bicarbonate of soda)

$\frac{1}{4}$ teaspoon salt

$\frac{1}{4}$ teaspoon freshly grated nutmeg

$\frac{2}{3}$ cup (5 oz/155 g) firmly packed light brown sugar

2 large eggs

1 cup (8 fl oz/250 ml) whole milk

1 cup (4 oz/125 g) fresh or frozen blueberries

2 tablespoons granulated sugar mixed with 1 teaspoon ground cinnamon

Orange Butter (page 274) for serving (optional)

Position a rack in the middle of the oven, and preheat to 400°F (200°C). Butter 12 standard muffin-pan cups or line with paper liners.

In a bowl, stir together the flour, cornmeal, baking powder, baking soda, salt, nutmeg, and brown sugar. Set aside.

BY HAND: In a large bowl, whisk the eggs until blended. Whisk in the milk and butter. Add the dry ingredients and stir with a rubber spatula just until moistened. Do not overmix. Fold in the berries.

BY MIXER: In a large bowl, combine the eggs, milk, and butter and beat on low speed just until blended. Add the dry ingredients and mix on low speed just until moistened. Do not overmix. Fold in the berries with a rubber spatula.

Spoon the batter into the prepared muffin cups, filling each about three-fourths full. Sprinkle the cinnamon sugar evenly over the tops. Bake until a toothpick inserted into the center of a muffin comes out clean, 15–18 minutes. Transfer to a wire rack and let cool in the pan for 2 minutes, then turn out onto the rack. Serve warm or at room temperature with Orange Butter (if using). Store in an airtight container at room temperature for up to 2 days.

These cornmeal muffins have a coarser, heartier texture than wheat flour-based muffins. To keep the berries from sinking to the bottom of the muffins, toss them in a sieve with 1 tablespoon flour before adding them to the batter.

Banana Bread with Walnuts and Orange Zest

Using bananas that are very ripe and have some brown spots will give this bread extra sweetness. For an elegant finishing touch, place walnut halves in a line down the center of the loaf before baking. You can also dust the top lightly with Demerara sugar, which, when baked, will form a caramelized topping. Toasted pecans can be substituted for the walnuts.

Position a rack in the middle of the oven and preheat to 350°F (180°C). Butter and flour a 9-by-5-inch (23-by-13-cm) loaf pan.

In a small bowl, using a fork, mash the bananas. You should have 1⅓ cups (10 oz/315 g). In a separate bowl, stir together the 1½ cups (7½ oz/235 g) all-purpose flour, whole-wheat flour, baking powder, baking soda, salt, nutmeg, orange zest, and nuts. Set aside.

BY HAND: In a large bowl, whisk the eggs until blended. Stir in the brown sugar, 6 tablespoons butter, and milk. Add the dry ingredients in 3 batches alternately with the bananas in 2 batches, beginning and ending with the dry ingredients, and stir with a rubber spatula just until the batter is moistened. Do not overmix.

BY MIXER: In a large bowl, combine the eggs, brown sugar, 6 tablespoons butter, and milk. Beat on medium-low speed just until blended. Add the dry ingredients in 3 batches alternately with the bananas in 2 batches, beginning and ending with the dry ingredients, and mix on low speed just until mixed. Do not overmix.

Pour the batter into the prepared pan and smooth the top with the rubber spatula. Bake until a toothpick inserted into the center comes out clean, 55–60 minutes. If the surface starts to brown too much, cover with a sheet of aluminum foil the last 15 minutes of baking.

Transfer to a wire rack and let cool in the pan for 5 minutes, then turn out onto the rack and let cool completely. If desired, serve with Maple Butter or store in an airtight container at room temperature for up to 3 days.

6 tablespoons (3 oz/90 g) unsalted butter, melted, plus extra for pan

1½ cups (7½ oz/235 g) all-purpose (plain) flour, plus extra for pan

2 large bananas, peeled

½ cup (2½ oz/75 g) whole-wheat (wholemeal) flour

2 teaspoons baking powder

½ teaspoon baking soda (bicarbonate of soda)

½ teaspoon salt

¼ teaspoon freshly ground nutmeg

1 tablespoon grated orange zest

½ cup (2 oz/60 g) toasted (page 277) and chopped walnuts

2 large eggs

¾ cup (6 oz/185 g) firmly packed light brown sugar

½ cup (4 fl oz/125 ml) whole milk

Maple Butter (page 274) for serving (optional)

Scones with Currants and Lemon Zest

For the dough

2 cups (10 oz/315 g) all-purpose (plain) flour

¼ cup (2 oz/60 g) granulated sugar

1 tablespoon baking powder

½ teaspoon salt

2 teaspoons grated lemon zest

6 tablespoons (3 oz/90 g) cold unsalted butter, cut into ½-inch (12-mm) pieces

½ cup (3 oz/90 g) dried currants

¾ cup (6 fl oz/180 ml) heavy (double) cream OR whole milk

For the topping

1 tablespoon granulated, Demerara, or turbinado sugar

1 teaspoon ground cinnamon

2 teaspoons whole milk or heavy (double) cream

Position a rack in the middle of the oven, and preheat to 425°F (220°C). Line a rimless baking sheet with parchment (baking) paper.

BY HAND: In a bowl, stir together the flour, granulated sugar, baking powder, salt, and lemon zest. Using a pastry blender or 2 knives, cut in the butter until the mixture forms large, coarse crumbs the size of peas. Stir in the currants. Pour the cream over the dry ingredients and mix with a fork or rubber spatula just until the dry ingredients are moistened.

BY FOOD PROCESSOR: Combine the flour, granulated sugar, baking powder, salt, and lemon zest and pulse 2 or 3 times to mix. Add the butter and pulse 7 or 8 times just until the mixture forms large, coarse crumbs the size of peas. Scatter the currants over the dough. Pour in the cream and pulse just until moistened.

Turn the dough out onto a lightly floured work surface and press gently until the dough clings together in a ball. Pat out into a round about ½ inch (12 mm) thick and 6½ inches (16.5 cm) in diameter. Cut the round into 6 wedges, or use a 3-inch (7.5-cm) biscuit cutter to cut out rounds. Place 1 inch (2.5 cm) apart on the prepared pan.

To make the topping, in a small bowl, stir together the sugar and cinnamon. Brush the dough with the milk and sprinkle evenly with the cinnamon sugar.

Bake until golden brown, 13–17 minutes. Transfer to a wire rack and let cool slightly. Serve warm or at room temperature. Store in an airtight container at room temperature for up to 2 days.

Working quickly with a light touch and baking the dough as soon as it is formed will help ensure tender scones. So, too, does baking the scones in a hot oven, which gets the baking powder working right away. Serve the scones warm, split open, and topped with fresh clotted cream, Berry Jam (page 275) or Lemon Curd (page 276).

Blueberry Tea Cake

Here, aromatic cardamom, which has a slight citrusy flavor, and a little dark rum give this easy-to-make moist cake an intriguing flavor. Once the batter is mixed, put the cake in the oven right away, so none of the leavening power of the baking powder and baking soda is lost. Other berries, such as blackberries or raspberries, can be substituted for the blueberries.

Position a rack in the middle of the oven, and preheat to 350°F (180°C). Butter and flour an 8-inch (20-cm) square baking dish.

In a bowl, stir together the 2 cups (10 oz/315 g) flour, baking powder, baking soda, salt, and cardamom. Set aside.

BY HAND: In a large bowl, whisk together the eggs and brown sugar until thick and fluffy. Using a wooden spoon, stir in the 1/2 cup melted butter, rum, and lemon zest. Add the dry ingredients in 3 batches alternately with the yogurt in 2 batches, beginning and ending with the dry ingredients, and mix just until smooth. Fold in the blueberries with a rubber spatula.

BY MIXER: In a large bowl, combine the eggs and brown sugar. Beat on low speed until thick and fluffy. Add the 1/2 cup (4 oz/125 g) melted butter, rum, and lemon zest and beat just until blended. Add the dry ingredients in 3 batches alternately with the yogurt in 2 batches, beginning and ending with the dry ingredients, and mix on low speed just until smooth. Fold in the blueberries with a rubber spatula.

Pour the batter into the prepared baking dish and smooth the top with the rubber spatula. Bake until a toothpick inserted into the center comes out clean, 50–60 minutes. Transfer to a wire rack and let cool completely. If desired, using a fine-mesh sieve, dust the cake with confectioners' sugar. Store in an airtight container at room temperature for up to 2 days.

1/2 cup (4 oz/125 g) unsalted butter, melted and cooled, plus extra for pan

2 cups (10 oz/315 g) all-purpose (plain) flour, plus extra for pan

1 teaspoon baking powder

1/2 teaspoon baking soda (bicarbonate of soda)

1/4 teaspoon salt

1/4 teaspoon ground cardamom

2 large eggs

1 1/2 cups (10 1/2 oz/330 g) firmly packed light brown sugar

2 tablespoons dark rum

1/2 teaspoon grated lemon zest

1 cup (8 oz/250 g) plain yogurt

2 cups (8 oz/250 g) fresh or frozen blueberries

Confectioners' (icing) sugar for dusting (optional)

Poppy Seed Bread
with Lemon Curd

Unsalted butter for pan

2 large eggs

¾ cup (6 fl oz/180 ml) whole milk

½ cup (4 fl oz/125 ml) canola or corn oil

¾ cup (6 oz/185 g) granulated sugar

1 teaspoon grated lemon zest

1 teaspoon vanilla extract

1¾ cups (9 oz/280 g) all-purpose (plain) flour

¾ teaspoons baking powder

½ teaspoon salt

2 tablespoons poppy seeds

½ cup (4 fl oz/125 ml) Lemon Curd (page 276)

Confectioners' (icing) sugar for dusting (optional)

Position a rack in the middle of the oven, and preheat to 350°F (180°C). Butter a 9-by-5-inch (23-by-13-cm) loaf pan. Line the bottom with parchment (baking) paper and butter the paper.

In a large bowl, whisk together the eggs and milk until blended. Add the oil, granulated sugar, lemon zest, and vanilla and whisk to blend. In another bowl, using a large wooden spoon, stir together the flour, baking powder, and salt. Stir in the poppy seeds. Pour the wet ingredients into the dry ingredients and stir just until blended.

Using a rubber spatula, spread about three-fourths of the batter in the prepared pan. Using a teaspoon, drizzle half of the lemon curd over the batter. Spread the remaining batter over the curd. The batter will not cover the curd completely. Spoon the remaining lemon curd over the batter. Insert a small knife about halfway into the batter and gently swirl it through the curd once or twice.

Bake until lightly browned and a toothpick inserted into the center comes out clean, about 50 minutes. Transfer to a wire rack and let cool in the pan for 10 minutes, then turn out onto the rack and peel off the parchment paper. Turn the loaf top side up and let cool completely on the rack. If desired, using a fine-mesh sieve, dust the top lightly with confectioners' sugar. Store in an airtight container at room temperature for up to 3 days.

Poppy seeds add a crunchy texture and slightly nutty taste to this sunny yellow quick bread. Because the batter is particularly thick, the citrus curd can be spread on top of it and will remain there, rather than sink to the bottom of the pan. The addition of lemon zest to the batter intensifies the bread's citrus flavor.

Irish Soda Bread

Popular throughout Ireland, soda bread is commonly made from flour, buttermilk (or sour milk in the past), and salt and leavened with baking soda, rather than yeast. Here, yogurt has been used in place of the buttermilk and rolled oats have been added for a bit more texture. Cut into slices and serve with a flavored butter such as Brandy Butter (page 274) and Berry Jam (page 275) or Orange Marmalade (page 275).

Position a rack in the middle of the oven, and preheat to 425°F (220°C). Place a baking sheet in the oven to preheat.

In a large bowl, stir together the flour, oats, bran, baking soda, and salt. Using a pastry blender or 2 knives, cut in the butter until the mixture resembles coarse meal. Add the yogurt and stir to blend, forming a rough ball. The dough will start rising as soon as the baking soda comes in contact with the yogurt, so work quickly to form the dough.

Turn the dough out onto a lightly floured work surface and knead gently for about 30 seconds. The dough should feel soft to the touch. Dust a clean work surface with flour and set the ball of dough on it. Flatten slightly into a 7-inch (18-cm) dome and sprinkle with flour, spreading the flour lightly over the surface. Using a sharp knife, cut a shallow X in the loaf from one side to the other. Transfer the loaf to the preheated baking sheet.

Bake until the loaf sounds hollow when tapped on the bottom, 30–35 minutes. Transfer to a wire rack to cool slightly. Serve warm. Any leftover bread can be stored in an airtight container for up to 2 days.

2¼ cups (11½ oz/360 g) bread flour

½ cup (1½ oz/45 g) rolled oats

¼ cup (½ oz/15 g) wheat bran

1½ teaspoons baking soda (bicarbonate of soda)

1 teaspoon salt

4 tablespoons (2 oz/60 g) cold unsalted butter, cut into ½-inch (12-mm) pieces

1½ cups (12 oz/375 g) plain yogurt

Sticky Buns

½ cup (4 fl oz/125 ml) whole milk

¾ cup (6 oz/185 g) unsalted butter, at room temperature, plus extra for pans

4½–5 cups (22½–25 oz/ 700–780 g) bread flour

½ cup (4 oz/125 g) granulated sugar

1 teaspoon salt

1 package (2¼ teaspoons) quick-rise yeast

2 large eggs

1 cup (7 oz/220 g) firmly packed light brown sugar

1 teaspoon ground cinnamon

⅔ cup (4 oz/125 g) raisins

⅔ cup (2½ oz/75 g) coarsely chopped pecans

In a saucepan over low heat, combine the milk, ¼ cup (2 oz/60 g) of the butter, and ½ cup (4 fl oz/125 ml) water and heat to warm (105°–115°F/40°–46°C).

BY HAND: In a large bowl, combine 1½ cups (7½ oz/235 g) of the flour, the granulated sugar, salt, and yeast. Using a wooden spoon, slowly beat the warm milk mixture into the dry ingredients. Beat in the eggs. Gradually stir in 2½ cups (12½ oz/390 g) more flour to make a soft dough that holds its shape. Turn the dough out onto a lightly floured work surface and knead, adding more flour as needed, until smooth and elastic, about 10 minutes.

BY STAND MIXER: In the 5-qt (5-l) bowl of a stand mixer, combine 1½ cups (7½ oz/235 g) of the flour, the granulated sugar, salt, and yeast. Place the bowl on the mixer, attach the dough hook, and gradually beat the warm milk mixture into the dry ingredients on low speed. Beat in the eggs. Gradually beat in 2½ cups (12½ oz/390 g) more flour to make a soft dough that holds its shape. Knead with the dough hook, adding more flour as needed, until the dough is smooth and elastic and comes away from the sides of the bowl, 6–7 minutes.

Form the dough into a ball, transfer to a lightly oiled bowl, turn to coat with the oil, and cover with plastic wrap. Let the dough rise in a warm spot until it doubles in bulk, 1¼ –1¾ hours. Punch down the dough and turn out onto a floured work surface. Cut it in half. Roll out each half into an 8-by-15-inch (20-by-37.5-cm) rectangle. Spread each rectangle with 2 tablespoons of the butter. In a bowl, stir together ½ cup (3½ oz/110 g) of the brown sugar, the cinnamon, and the raisins. Sprinkle half of the mixture evenly over the 2 dough rectangles.

Starting at the long side of each rectangle farthest from you, roll up the rectangle into a log. Pinch the seams to seal. Cut each log crosswise into 10 equal slices. Butter two 9-inch (23-cm) round cake pans. Add the remaining ½ cup brown sugar and remaining ¼ cup butter to the remaining brown sugar mixture, and stir to blend. Stir in the pecans. Spread the pecan mixture evenly in the pans. Arrange 10 slices, cut side up, in each pan. Cover loosely with a kitchen towel and let them rise in a warm, draft-free spot until doubled in size, 60–75 minutes.

Position a rack in the middle of the oven, and preheat to 350°F (180°C). Bake the buns until a toothpick inserted into the center of a bun comes out clean, 30–35 minutes. Transfer to a wire rack and let cool in the pans for 5 minutes. Invert each pan onto a plate. When the buns are cool to the touch, pull them apart. Store the buns in an airtight container at room temperature for up to 2 days.

Also known as cinnamon buns, these popular morning treats are ideal for entertaining because you can make them a day ahead and they are still delicious the next morning. Here, they are baked in round cake pans, but they can also be baked in two 8-inch (20-cm) square pans. Instead of cutting each log into 10 slices, cut each log into 9 slices.

Beignets

In the United States, the same term is sometimes used for filled deep-fried pastries. It is more typically linked to the plain deep-fried pastry dough dusted with confectioners' sugar and served in New Orleans accompanied by café au lait made from the local chicory-flavored coffee.

In a small bowl, sprinkle the yeast over the warm water and let stand until creamy, about 5 minutes. In a small saucepan over medium heat, combine the milk and butter and heat gently until the milk is warm but not steaming and the butter melts. Remove from the heat.

BY HAND: In a large bowl, stir together 3 cups (15 oz/470 g) of the flour, the granulated sugar, and the salt. Gradually add the milk mixture to the dry ingredients and, using a wooden spoon, stir until blended. Add the egg, the yeast mixture, and the remaining 1 1/2 cups (7 1/2 oz/235 g) flour and stir just until a soft dough forms.

BY FOOD PROCESSOR: Combine 3 cups (15 oz/470 g) of the flour, the granulated sugar, and the salt and pulse 2 or 3 times to mix. With the processor running, pour the milk mixture through the feed tube and process until well blended. Add the egg, the yeast mixture, and the remaining 1 1/2 cups (7 1/2 oz/235 g) flour and process just until a soft dough forms.

Position a rack in the middle of the oven, and preheat to 200°F (95°C). Line an ovenproof platter with paper towels. Pour the oil to a depth of 3 inches (7.5 cm) into a deep, heavy saucepan and heat to 360°F (182°C) on a deep-frying thermometer. Turn the dough out onto a lightly floured work surface and divide in half. Knead 1 piece of the dough briefly until soft but not sticky. Roll into a rectangle about 1/4 inch (6 mm) thick. Cut into 6 equal rectangles.

When the oil is hot, place 2 or 3 rectangles into the oil and fry, turning once, until puffed and brown, about 2 minutes per side. Using a slotted spoon, transfer to the paper towels to drain and keep warm in the oven. Repeat with the remaining rectangles and then with the remaining dough. Arrange on a serving plate. Using a fine-mesh sieve, dust with confectioners' sugar and serve immediately.

1 package (2 1/2 teaspoons) active dry yeast

1/4 cup (2 fl oz/60 ml) warm water (105°–115°F/40–46°C)

1 cup (8 fl oz/250 ml) whole milk

4 tablespoons (2 oz/60 g) unsalted butter

4 1/2 cups (22 1/2 oz/705 g) all-purpose (plain) flour

3 tablespoons granulated sugar

3/4 teaspoon salt

1 large egg

Peanut or canola oil for deep-frying

Confectioners' (icing) sugar for dusting

Buttermilk Doughnuts

2¼ cups (11½ oz/360 g) all-purpose (plain) flour

¾ teaspoon freshly ground nutmeg

½ teaspoon ground cinnamon

½ teaspoon baking powder

½ teaspoon baking soda (bicarbonate of soda)

½ teaspoon salt

1 large egg

½ cup (4 oz/125 g) granulated sugar

1 tablespoon unsalted butter, melted

½ cup (4 fl oz/125 ml) buttermilk

Peanut or canola oil for deep-frying

Confectioners' (icing) sugar for dusting

In a bowl, sift together the flour, nutmeg, cinnamon, baking powder, baking soda, and salt. Set aside.

BY HAND: In a large bowl, whisk the egg and granulated sugar until creamy and pale. Add the melted butter and buttermilk and whisk until blended. Add the flour mixture and mix with a wooden spoon until the dough holds together.

BY MIXER: In a large bowl, mix the egg and granulated sugar on low speed until creamy and pale. Add the melted butter and buttermilk and beat until blended. Add the flour mixture and mix on low speed until the dough holds together.

Line a platter with paper towels. Pour the oil to a depth of 2 inches (5 cm) into a deep, heavy saucepan and heat to 365°F (185°C) on a deep-frying thermometer. Turn the dough out onto a lightly floured work surface. Roll out to a 9-inch (23-cm) circle about ½ inch (12 mm) thick. Use a 2¾-inch (7-cm) biscuit cutter to cut out circles, then use a ½-inch (12-mm) cutter to cut a circle from the center of each.

When the oil is hot, place 2 doughnuts and 2 doughnut holes into the oil and fry until deep golden brown, about 2 minutes. Using a slotted spoon, turn and fry on the second side, about 1½ minutes. Using the slotted spoon, transfer to the paper towels to drain. Repeat with the remaining doughnuts and doughnut holes.

Arrange the doughnuts and holes on a serving plate. Using a fine-mesh sieve, dust with confectioners' sugar and serve at once.

These old-fashioned cake doughnuts, aromatic with cinnamon and nutmeg, are easy to prepare. You will need a deep-frying thermometer, as you must keep the oil at a steady 365°F (185°C) for the doughnuts to turn out golden brown and crisp and not the least bit oily. While they are immersed in the oil, they will almost triple in thickness, so be sure to fry them in two batches to avoid crowding.

Cinnamon-Raisin Brioche Pudding with Caramel Glaze

Sunny yellow brioche, rich in eggs and butter, is an ideal choice for a bread pudding. Have all of the dough ingredients at room temperature for the best results. Also, you'll find the soft, sticky dough is easier to shape If you refrigerate it overnight. Serve the pudding with a pitcher of warmed cream, if desired. Reserve the leftover brioche for making toast the following morning.

To make the brioche, in the 5-qt (5-l) bowl of a stand mixer, combine the warm water, yeast, and sugar. Place the bowl on the mixer, attach the paddle attachment, and mix on low speed to dissolve the yeast. Let stand until foamy, about 5 minutes. Beat in 4 of the eggs until blended. Add the flour and salt and mix until incorporated. Add the butter pieces to the flour, and mix until incorporated. Continue mixing on low speed until the dough is smooth, 8–10 minutes. Periodically stop the mixer and scrape down the sides of the bowl. Transfer to a buttered bowl, cover the bowl with plastic wrap, and refrigerate for at least 5 hours or up to overnight.

Butter a 9-by-5-inch (23-by-13-cm) loaf pan. Remove the dough from the refrigerator. Punch the dough down and turn out onto a lightly floured work surface. Cut into 4 equal pieces. With floured hands, roll each piece into an oval about 4 inches (10 cm) long and 2 inches (5 cm) thick. Place the ovals side by side in the prepared pan. Cover the dough loosely with a kitchen towel and let rise in a warm, draft-free spot until almost doubled in size, about 1 1/2 hours.

Position a rack in the middle of the oven, and preheat to 375°F (190°C). Beat the remaining egg and use it to brush the top of the loaf. Bake until a toothpick inserted into the center comes out clean, about 45 minutes. Let cool in the pan on a rack for 5 minutes, then turn out onto the rack and cool completely.

To make the pudding, position a rack in the middle of the oven, and preheat to 325°F (165°C). Butter a 3-qt (3-l) baking dish. Cut 4 slices from the brioche loaf, each about 3/4 inch (2 cm) thick, then cut the slices into cubes. Place the cubes in the prepared dish, sprinkle with the raisins, and toss to combine. Set aside.

In a large bowl, whisk the eggs. Whisk in the melted butter, sugar, milk, vanilla, and cinnamon. Pour the milk mixture over the brioche mixture, stirring if necessary to moisten the brioche evenly.

Bake for 20 minutes. Evenly drizzle the Caramel Glaze over the top and continue to bake until the top is lightly browned, the liquid has been absorbed, and the edges are bubbling, about 25 minutes longer. Let the pudding stand for 10 minutes. Serve warm.

For the brioche

1/4 cup (2 fl oz/60 ml) warm water (105°–115°F/40°–46°C)

1 package (2 1/2 teaspoons) active dry yeast

1 teaspoon sugar

5 large eggs, at room temperature

2 1/4 cups (11 1/2 oz/360 g) all-purpose (plain) flour

1/2 teaspoon salt

3/4 cup (6 oz/185 g) unsalted butter, cut into 1/2-inch (12-mm) pieces, plus extra for pan

For the pudding

3/4 cup (4 1/2 oz/140 g) raisins

2 large eggs

2 tablespoons unsalted butter, melted, plus extra for pan

1/4 cup (2 oz/60 g) sugar

2 cups (16 fl oz/500 ml) whole milk

1 teaspoon vanilla extract

1 teaspoon ground cinnamon

Caramel Glaze (page 276)

Swedish Cardamom Twist

½ cup (4 fl oz/125 ml) whole milk

4 tablespoons (2 oz/60 g) unsalted butter, at room temperature

Seeds from 10 cardamom pods, crushed

2½–3 cups (12½–15 oz/ 390–465 g) bread flour

¼ teaspoon salt

¼ cup (2 oz/60 g) sugar

1 package (2¼ teaspoons) quick-rise yeast

Canola oil for bowl

For the filling

4 tablespoons (2 oz/60 g) unsalted butter, at room temperature, cut into ½-inch (12-mm) pieces

¼ cup (2 oz/60 g) sugar

1 teaspoon ground cinnamon

1 egg yolk beaten with 1 teaspoon water

In a saucepan over low heat, combine the milk, butter, ½ cup (4 fl oz/125 ml) water, and the cardamom pods. Heat to warm (105°–115°F/40°–46°C).

BY HAND: In a bowl, combine 1 cup (5 oz/155 g) of the flour, salt, sugar, and yeast. Using a spoon, beat in the warm milk mixture until smooth. Gradually beat in 1½ cups (7½ oz/235 g) more flour to make a soft dough that holds its shape. Turn the dough out onto a lightly floured work surface and knead, adding the remaining flour as needed, until smooth and elastic, about 10 minutes.

BY STAND MIXER: In the 5-qt (5-l) bowl of a stand mixer, combine 1 cup (5 oz/ 155 g) of the flour, salt, sugar, and the yeast. Place the bowl on the mixer, attach the dough hook, and gradually beat in the warm milk mixture on low speed. Gradually beat in 1½ cups (7½ oz/235 g) more flour to make a soft dough that holds its shape. Knead with the dough hook, adding the remaining flour as needed, until the dough is smooth and comes away from the sides of the bowl, 6–7 minutes.

Form the dough into a ball, transfer to a lightly oiled bowl, turn to coat with the oil, and cover the bowl with plastic wrap. Let the dough rise in a warm, draft-free spot until it doubles in bulk, 1½–2 hours.

Meanwhile, make the filling: In a small bowl, cream together the butter, sugar, and cinnamon.

Dust a rimmed baking sheet with flour. Punch down the dough and turn out onto a lightly floured surface. Form into a ball and knead until smooth, about 1 minute. Let rest for 10 minutes. Roll out the dough into a 9-by-12-inch (23-by-30-cm) rectangle. Spread the filling evenly over the dough, leaving a 1-inch (2.5-cm) plain border on all sides. Starting at the long side farthest from you, roll up the rectangle toward you into a log. Place the roll, seam side down, on the baking sheet.

Using scissors and cutting at an angle, snip the roll at ½-inch (12-mm) intervals, cutting almost halfway through. Pull and push the snipped sections of dough alternately to the left and right, twisting each section slightly to expose the spiral inside. Cover loosely with a kitchen towel and let rise in a warm, draft-free spot until doubled in size, about 1 hour.

Position a rack in the middle of the oven, and preheat to 375°F (190°C). Brush the loaf with the yolk mixture. Bake until golden brown, 25–30 minutes. Let cool on a wire rack. Store in an airtight container at room temperature for up to 2 days.

Because this recipe uses quick-rise yeast, early birds can put together this fragrant bread before their guests arrive, pop it into the oven just as the doorbell starts to ring, and then serve it warm. It is delicious served alone or with butter and jam, and because it is so handsome when it comes out of the oven, serve it whole and let guests cut the slices themselves.

Almond Breakfast Cake

Almond paste, almond extract, and sliced almonds deliver a triple dose of almond flavor to this single-layer cake. Make sure to use almond paste rather than marzipan, which contains sugar. Fresh almond paste is soft and blends easily with the butter. To keep it fresh, always store it tightly wrapped so that it doesn't take on moisture.

Position a rack in the middle of the oven, and preheat to 350°F (180°C). Butter a 9-inch (23-cm) round cake pan.

To make the crumb topping, in a bowl, stir together the flour, brown sugar, and cinnamon until blended. Add the melted butter and stir together until the mixture is evenly moistened and crumbly. Gently stir in the almonds just until evenly distributed. Set the bowl aside.

To make the cake, in a bowl, sift together the flour, baking powder, and salt. Set the bowl aside.

BY HAND: In a large bowl, combine the butter and almond paste. Using a wooden spoon, beat until smooth. Add the sugar and beat until blended. Add the eggs, vanilla, and almond extract and stir until blended, about 1 minute. The mixture may look slightly curdled. Add the dry ingredients in 2 batches alternately with the milk in 1 batch, beginning and ending with the dry ingredients, and mix just until blended.

BY MIXER: In a large bowl, combine the butter and almond paste. Beat on medium speed until smooth. Add the sugar and beat until blended. Add the eggs, vanilla, and almond extract and beat until blended, about 1 minute. The mixture may look slightly curdled. Add the dry ingredients in 2 batches alternately with the milk in 1 batch, beginning and ending with the dry ingredients, and mix on low speed just until blended.

Pour the batter into the prepared pan and smooth the top with a rubber spatula. Sprinkle the crumb topping evenly over the surface. Bake until a toothpick inserted into the center comes out clean, about 55 minutes. Transfer to a wire rack and let cool completely in the pan. Serve at once or cover the cake with plastic wrap and store at room temperature for up to 3 days.

Unsalted butter for pan

For the crumb topping

6 tablespoons (2¼ oz/70 g) all-purpose (plain) flour

⅓ cup (2½ oz/75 g) firmly packed light brown sugar

¼ teaspoon ground cinnamon

2 tablespoons unsalted butter, melted

1 cup (4 oz/125 g) sliced (flaked) almonds

For the cake

2 cups (10 oz/315 g) all-purpose (plain) flour

1½ teaspoons baking powder

¼ teaspoon salt

½ cup (4 oz/125 g) unsalted butter, at room temperature

¼ lb (125 g) almond paste, at room temperature

1 cup (8 oz/250 g) granulated sugar

2 large eggs

1 teaspoon vanilla extract

½ teaspoon almond extract

¾ cup (6 fl oz/180 ml) whole milk

Cinnamon-Walnut Coffee Cake

Canola or corn oil for pan

For the filling and topping

1 cup (5 oz/155 g) finely chopped walnuts

¹⁄₃ cup (3 oz/90 g) granulated sugar

2 teaspoons ground cinnamon

For the cake

2³⁄₄ cups (11 oz/345 g) cake (soft-wheat) flour

1 teaspoon baking powder

¹⁄₂ teaspoon baking soda (bicarbonate of soda)

¹⁄₂ teaspoon salt

3 large eggs

2 cups (1 lb/500 g) granulated sugar

1 cup (8 fl oz/250 ml) canola or corn oil

2 teaspoons vanilla extract

1 cup (8 oz/250 g) sour cream

Confectioners' (icing) sugar for dusting (optional)

Caramel Glaze (page 276) for serving (optional)

Position a rack in the middle of the oven, and preheat to 350°F (180°C). Oil a 9¹⁄₂- or 10-inch (24- or 25-cm) tube pan with sides at least 3³⁄₄ inches (9.5 cm) high. Line the bottom with parchment (baking) paper and oil the paper.

To make the filling and topping, in a bowl, stir together the walnuts, sugar, and cinnamon. Set aside.

To make the cake, in a bowl, sift together the flour, baking powder, baking soda, and salt. Set aside.

BY HAND: In a large bowl, whisk together the eggs and granulated sugar until the mixture is light in color and fluffy, about 2 minutes. Slowly whisk in the oil and vanilla. Add the dry ingredients and mix with a rubber spatula just until incorporated. Mix in the sour cream just until no white streaks remain.

BY MIXER: In a large bowl, combine the eggs and granulated sugar. Beat on medium speed until the mixture is light in color and fluffy, about 2 minutes. Slowly add the oil and vanilla and beat on low speed. Add the dry ingredients and beat on low speed just until incorporated. Mix in the sour cream just until no white streaks remain.

Pour about two-thirds of the batter into the prepared pan and smooth the top with the rubber spatula. Set aside ¹⁄₄ cup (2 oz/60 g) of the walnut-cinnamon mixture to use as a topping. Sprinkle the remaining mixture evenly over the batter. Insert a small knife about halfway into the batter and gently swirl it through the walnut-cinnamon filling to create a swirled effect. Pour the remaining batter evenly over the filling and smooth the top with the spatula. The batter will not cover the filling completely. Sprinkle evenly with the reserved topping.

Bake until a toothpick inserted into the center of the cake comes out clean, about 55 minutes. Transfer to a wire rack and let cool for 15 minutes. Run a thin knife around the sides and center tube of the pan to loosen the cake sides. Invert a wire rack on top of the pan and invert both the rack and the pan. Lift off the pan. Remove and discard the parchment. Turn the cake top side up and let cool completely on the rack. Using a fine-mesh sieve, dust with confectioners' sugar or drizzle each slice with Caramel Glaze (if using). Cover the cake with plastic wrap and store at room temperature for up to 3 days.

The same cinnamon-walnut mixture that is swirled through this tender, fine-grained cake also serves as a crunchy topping. The cake's light structure develops during a thorough beating of the eggs and sugar. It is hard to overmix the batter at this stage, so don't skimp on the beating time.

Rustic Apple Galettes

Galettes can take many shapes. This square version has an especially crisp crust. Apples with a firm texture, such as Cortland, Granny Smith, Rome Beauty, and Baldwin, will hold their shape during baking. The secret to the tender crust is to use milk for the liquid.

BY HAND: In a large bowl, combine the all-purpose and cake flours, sugar, and salt and stir to mix. Scatter the butter and shortening pieces over the flour mixture. Using a fork, toss to coat with the flour. Using a pastry blender or 2 knives, cut in the butter and shortening until the mixture forms large, coarse crumbs the size of large peas. Drizzle 3 tablespoons of the milk over the mixture and toss with the fork until the dough is evenly moist and begins to come together in a mass but does not form a ball. Slowly drizzle in the remaining milk by teaspoons, if the mixture still seems dry.

BY FOOD PROCESSOR: Combine the all-purpose and cake flours, sugar, and salt and pulse 2 or 3 times to mix. Add the butter and shortening pieces and pulse 8–10 times until the mixture forms large, coarse crumbs the size of large peas. Add 3 tablespoons of the milk a little at a time and pulse 10–12 times just until the dough begins to come together in a mass but does not form a ball. Slowly drizzle in the remaining milk by teaspoons, if necessary.

Transfer the dough to a work surface and shape into a 6-inch (15-cm) disk. Wrap the disk tightly in plastic wrap and refrigerate until well chilled, about 1 hour or for up to overnight.

Position a rack in the lower third of the oven, and preheat to 375°F (190°C). Line a large rimmed baking sheet pan with parchment (baking) paper.

Remove the dough from the refrigerator. If it is cold and hard to roll, let it stand at room temperature for 10–20 minutes. On a lightly floured work surface, roll out the dough into a 9-by-14-inch (23-by-35-cm) rectangle about 1/8 inch (3 mm) thick. Trim the edges even. Carefully roll the dough around the pin, transfer it to the prepared pan, and unroll it.

To make the filling, in a large bowl, gently toss together the apples, apricot jam, sugar, flour, lemon juice, and cinnamon until evenly distributed. Spread the filling evenly over the dough, leaving a 1 1/2-inch (4-cm) plain border on all sides. Fold the border up and over the filling, forming loose pleats around the corners and leaving the center open. Drizzle the melted butter over the filling. Brush the dough border with the egg mixture, then sprinkle it with the sugar. You will not need all of the egg mixture.

Bake until the crust is golden brown and the apples are tender when pierced with a toothpick, about 40 minutes. Transfer to a wire rack and let cool on the pan. Serve warm or at room temperature topped with whipped cream, if desired.

For the dough

1 cup (5 oz/155 g) all-purpose (plain) flour

1/3 cup (1 1/2 oz/ 45 g) cake (soft-wheat) flour

1 tablespoon sugar

1/2 teaspoon salt

6 tablespoons (3 oz/90 g) cold unsalted butter, cut into 1/2-inch (12-mm) pieces

2 tablespoons cold vegetable shortening, cut into 1/2-inch (12-mm) pieces

3–4 tablespoons cold whole milk

For the filling

4 apples, peeled, cored, and cut into 3/4-inch (2-cm) pieces

2 tablespoons apricot jam

2 tablespoons sugar

2 tablespoons all-purpose (plain) flour

1 tablespoon fresh lemon juice

1/4 teaspoon ground cinnamon

1 tablespoon unsalted butter, melted

1 large egg beaten with 2 tablespoons heavy (double) cream

1 tablespoon sugar

Whipped cream (page 276) for serving (optional)

Herb and Olive Focaccia

1 package (2¼ teaspoons) quick-rise yeast

1¼ cups (10 fl oz/310 ml) lukewarm water (110°F/43°C)

3½ tablespoons olive oil, plus extra for pan

3 tablespoons chopped fresh oregano, rosemary, or sage

1 teaspoon salt

Freshly ground pepper

3½–4 cups (17½–20 oz/ 545–625 g) bread flour

1 small yellow onion, quartered and sliced

24 oil-cured black olives, pitted and chopped

This savory Italian bread is a versatile addition to your repertoire of brunch recipes. You can serve it alongside soups, salads, or frittatas or as an accompaniment to a cheese platter. Or, you can top it with slices of tomato and fresh mozzarella cheese for an easy open-faced sandwich.

BY HAND: In a large bowl, dissolve the yeast in the lukewarm water. Add 2 tablespoons of the olive oil, 1 tablespoon of the oregano, the salt, and a generous grinding of pepper. Using a wooden spoon, gradually stir in 3 cups (15 oz/470 g) of the flour to make a soft dough that holds its shape. Turn the dough out onto a lightly floured work surface and knead, adding the remaining flour as needed, until smooth and elastic, about 10 minutes.

BY STAND MIXER: In the 5-qt (5-l) bowl of a stand mixer, dissolve the yeast in the lukewarm water. Add 2 tablespoons of the olive oil, 1 tablespoon of the oregano, the salt, and a generous grinding of pepper. Place the bowl on the mixer, attach the dough hook, and gradually beat in 3 cups (15 oz/470 g) of the flour to make a soft dough that holds its shape. Knead with the dough hook, adding the remaining flour as needed, until the dough is smooth and elastic and comes away from the sides of the bowl, 6–7 minutes.

Form the dough into a ball, transfer to a lightly oiled bowl, turn to coat with the oil, and cover the bowl with plastic wrap. Let the dough rise in a warm, draft-free spot until it doubles in bulk, 45–60 minutes.

Meanwhile, in a bowl, combine the onion, the remaining 2 tablespoons oregano, the olives, and 1 tablespoon of the remaining olive oil and mix well. Set aside.

Oil a rimmed baking sheet. Punch down the dough and turn out onto a lightly floured work surface. Form the dough into a ball, transfer to the prepared baking sheet, and let rest for 5 minutes. Using your fingers, stretch the dough so it evenly covers the bottom of the baking sheet. Cover the dough loosely with a clean kitchen towel and let rise in a warm, draft-free place until puffy, 30–40 minutes.

Position a rack in the middle of the oven, and preheat to 425°F (220°C). Using your fingertips, make a pattern of dimples at 2-inch (5-cm) intervals over the entire surface of the dough. Brush with the remaining oil. Sprinkle evenly with the olive mixture. Bake until golden brown, 18–20 minutes. Serve warm.

Tomato Tarts with Basil and Fresh Goat Cheese

For the best flavor, prepare this tart at the height of summer when all of the colorful heirloom tomatoes are at the farmers' market. Select a goat cheese with a rich, creamy consistency and a full, tangy, though not overly assertive flavor.

Position a rack in the middle of the oven, and preheat to 400°F (200°C).

In a small bowl, combine two-thirds of the basil strips, garlic, and cherry tomatoes. Add the 1/4 cup olive oil, season with salt, and toss gently to combine. Set aside.

Place the puff pastry sheet on a lightly floured work surface. Cut into 6 rectangles, each about 4 by 5 inches (10 by 13 cm). Place the rectangles on a baking sheet and prick them all over with a fork to prevent the pastry from rising. Bake until light golden brown, 10–12 minutes. Remove from the oven and let stand on the baking sheet. Leave the oven on.

Meanwhile, in a small bowl, using a fork, mash the goat cheese. Slowly pour in the milk, stirring until the cheese mixture has a smooth consistency but is not runny. You may not need all of the milk. Cut the large tomatoes into slices 1/2 inch (12 mm) thick and season with salt. Gently spread 1 heaping tablespoon of the goat cheese mixture onto each pastry rectangle. Using only the large, center slices of the large tomatoes (reserve the remainder for another use), place a slice on each tart. Bake the tarts until warmed through, about 5 minutes.

Place the tarts on individual plates. Season the tomato quarters with salt and scatter around the tarts, dividing them evenly. Top each tart with a mound of the cherry tomato and basil mixture, again dividing evenly. Drizzle olive oil over the tomatoes. Garnish the tarts with the remaining basil strips and serve at once.

20–25 fresh basil leaves, cut into thin strips

2 cloves garlic, finely minced

2 cups (12 oz/375 g) cherry tomatoes, halved

1/4 cup (2 fl oz/60 ml) extra-virgin olive oil, plus extra for drizzling

Salt

1 sheet frozen puff pastry, about 10 by 12 inches (25 by 30 cm), partially thawed

5 oz (155 g) fresh goat cheese

About 1/2 cup (4 fl oz/125 ml) whole milk

1 large red tomato

1 large yellow tomato

6 medium tomatoes, quartered

Parmesan-Romano Cheese Twists

1 cup (5 oz/155 g) plus
2 tablespoons all-purpose
(plain) flour

1/2 teaspoon freshly ground
pepper

1/2 teaspoon baking soda
(bicarbonate of soda)

1/2 teaspoon salt

1/2 cup (4 oz/125 g) cold
unsalted butter, cut into
16 pieces

1/4 cup (2 oz/60 g) cold
sour cream

1 large egg beaten
with 2 tablespoons heavy
(double) cream

1/2 cup (2 oz/60 g) grated
Parmesan cheese

1/2 cup (2 oz/60 g) grated
Romano cheese

In a large bowl, sift together the flour, pepper, baking soda, and 1/4 teaspoon of the salt.

BY HAND: Using a pastry blender or 2 knives, cut in the butter until the largest pieces are the size of small beans. The butter pieces will be different sizes, and there will still be some loose flour. Add the sour cream and mix with a wooden spoon until clumps of smooth dough form, about 2 minutes.

BY MIXER: Add the butter pieces to the dry ingredients and mix on low speed until the largest pieces are the size of small beans, about 1 minute. The butter pieces will be different sizes, and there will still be some loose flour. Add the sour cream and mix on low speed until large clumps of smooth dough pull away from the sides of the bowl, about 30 seconds.

Transfer the dough to a work surface and form into a smooth ball. Divide in half and shape each piece into a disk. Wrap each disk tightly in plastic wrap and refrigerate for 30–60 minutes or for up to overnight.

Remove the dough from the refrigerator. If it is cold and too hard to roll, let it stand at room temperature for 10–20 minutes. Position a rack in the middle of the oven, and preheat to 375°F (190°C). Line a rimmed baking sheet with parchment (baking) paper.

On a lightly floured work surface, roll out each disk into a 6-by-12-inch (15-by-30-cm) rectangle. Using a large sharp knife, cut the rectangle lengthwise into 6 strips, each 1 inch (2.5 cm) wide. Then cut the strips in half crosswise. You will have 12 strips each, 6 inches (5 cm) long and 1 inch (2.5 cm) wide. Lightly brush the strips with the egg mixture. Sprinkle evenly with half of the Parmesan cheese and half of the Romano cheese, pressing the cheese lightly so it adheres to the dough. Pick up each strip by the ends and twist the strip in opposite directions 4 or 5 times to make a tight spiral. Place the strips on the prepared pan, spacing them 1 inch (2.5 cm) apart. Sprinkle the strips with 1/8 teaspoon of the salt. Repeat with the second disk of dough and the remaining cheese and salt.

Bake until lightly browned, about 14 minutes. Transfer to a wire rack and let cool in the pan for 10 minutes, then place on the rack and cool completely. Store in an airtight container at room temperature for up to 3 days.

These twists are a welcome change from the traditional crackers and breads that accompany soups and salads. They are flavored with two types of aged cheese—Parmesan, made from cow's milk, and Romano, made from sheep's milk—which together give the twists a pleasant salty, sharp taste.

Cheddar-Jalapeño Corn Bread

Cornmeal is sold in fine, medium, and coarse grind, and any of these grinds can be used for this recipe. A medium grind will yield a lightly textured bread that still retains some bite. If you choose the more nutritious stone-ground cornmeal, which retains some of the hull and germ, your bread will be heavier and denser than if you use steel-ground cornmeal, which is mostly endosperm.

Position a rack in the middle of the oven, and preheat to 375°F (190°C). Butter a 9-inch (23-cm) square baking pan.

In a bowl, sift together the flour, cornmeal, sugar, baking powder, baking soda, and salt. Set aside.

BY HAND: In a large bowl, whisk together the buttermilk, egg, and melted butter until blended. Add the dry ingredients and stir with a large spoon just until evenly moistened. The batter will have some small lumps. Stir in half of the grated cheese and the chile.

BY MIXER: In a large bowl, beat the buttermilk, egg, and melted butter on medium speed until blended. Add the dry ingredients and mix on low speed just until evenly moistened. The batter will have some small lumps. Stir in half of the grated cheese and the chile.

Pour the batter into the prepared pan and evenly smooth the top with a rubber spatula. Sprinkle with the remaining cheese. Bake until the top is lightly browned and a toothpick inserted into the center comes out clean, about 16 minutes. Transfer to a wire rack and let cool in the pan for 5 minutes. Serve warm with Honey Butter, if desired. Store in an airtight container at room temperature for up to 3 days. To rewarm the corn bread, wrap tightly in aluminum foil and heat in a 300°F (150°C) oven for about 10 minutes.

Unsalted butter for pan

1 cup (5 oz/155 g) all-purpose (plain) flour

1¼ cups (6 oz/185 g) yellow cornmeal

2 tablespoons sugar

2 teaspoons baking powder

1 teaspoon baking soda (bicarbonate of soda)

½ teaspoon salt

1¼ cups (10 fl oz/310 ml) buttermilk

1 large egg

4 tablespoons (2 oz/60 g) unsalted butter, melted

6 oz (185 g) sharp cheddar cheese, grated

1 jalapeño chile, seeded and finely chopped

Honey Butter (page 274) for serving (optional)

Pancakes, Waffles, and French Toast

About Pancakes, Waffles, and French Toast

All of these classic morning dishes are hearty enough to be the centerpiece of breakfast or brunch. They are made from a wide variety of distinctive ingredients, and each is a delicious foundation for condiments, from fresh fruits to flavored syrups to chutneys.

In many ways, pancakes and waffles are quick breads made on the stove top, in the case of the former, or in a special appliance, in the case of the latter. Batters for both are prepared following the quick-mixing method used for muffins and other quick breads: dry ingredients are stirred together in one bowl, the wet ingredients blended in another, and the two then combined. As when mixing batters for other quick breads, you need to blend the dry and wet ingredients quickly, just until the dry ingredients are moistened. You will see some lumps in the batter, but don't be tempted to continue stirring in order to eliminate them.

COOKING PERFECT PANCAKES

One of the best pans for cooking pancakes is a griddle. This flat pan, either round, square, or rectangular, sits over one or two burners on the stove top. You can also use a large frying pan with low, sloping sides. This shape allows you to turn the pancakes easily with a spatula.

To ensure your pancakes are golden brown on the outside and light and tender on the inside, you must preheat the pan to just the right temperature. If you will be cooking several batches of pancakes, put a small bowl of water next to the stove. Dip a finger or two into the water and flick a few drops onto the surface. If the water sizzles and immediately evaporates, the pan is the right temperature.

Pancakes should be cooked in a minimal amount of fat. Rather than melt the butter in the pan, you want to coat the surface with a thin film. Have on hand a small amount of melted butter and a pastry brush. After the pan is preheated, brush butter onto the surface, covering it evenly.

For uniform pancakes, use a measuring cup or ladle for scooping up the batter and hold it steady in one spot as you pour the batter into the hot pan. The batter will spread, so be sure to allow enough space between pancakes.

You know that it's time to turn a pancake when small bubbles appear on the surface. You can also gently lift the edge of a pancake with a spatula and look underneath to see if the first side is golden brown.

Crepes and blintzes have less body than pancakes and serve as delicate wrappers for sweet or savory fillings. The technique for cooking them is the same as for pancakes, but they are made individually in a frying pan 9 or 10 inches (23 or 25 cm) in diameter. You can purchase a crepe pan or use a general-purpose frying pan of the right size.

USING A WAFFLE MAKER

In this chapter, you'll find recipes for two types of waffles: classic and Belgian. Both have a grid of pockets for holding syrup and other embellishments; the pockets of Belgian waffles are especially deep. Each type needs to be cooked in a waffle maker with plates designed to create the characteristic pockets.

Waffle makers, also called waffle irons, are convenient appliances that turn out uniform waffles with a delightfully crisp and golden brown exterior in 5 minutes or less. They have a number of handy features, depending on the model: timers that signal doneness, plates with nonstick surfaces, even reversible plates that allow you to cook either classic or Belgian waffles using the same appliance.

You'll want to adhere to the instructions accompanying the waffle maker while following some general guidelines. All waffle makers should be preheated, and the plates (even if they are nonstick) should be lightly brushed with oil. To create uniform waffles and to prevent the batter from overflowing, measure it before pouring it onto the center of the bottom plate, following the manufacturer's directions for how much to use (usually about 1 cup/8 fl oz/250 ml batter for a 4-inch/10-cm waffle). Then use a small spatula to spread the batter evenly almost to the edge.

Avoid opening the waffle maker until the waffle is done. The best indications are when steam is no longer being released from the sides and the lid is slightly raised. Many waffle makers also chime when the waffles are ready. Ever so slightly lift the handle. If you sense resistance, the waffle is not yet ready. If the waffle maker opens easily, the waffle is done.

COOKING AND HOLDING

Pancakes and waffles are cooked in batches, and you'll want to keep them warm so you can serve all of your guests at once. Place them uncovered on a heatproof serving platter and put the platter on the middle rack of the oven, preheated to 250°F (120°C). Otherwise, the waffles or pancakes will become soggy. You can also hold French toast briefly in a warm oven.

Crepes and the wrappers for blintzes can be held even longer. Layer them between pieces of waxed paper, put them in an airtight container, and store them in the refrigerator for up to 2 days.

Gingerbread Pancakes

Traditional gingerbread spices—cinnamon, ginger, and cloves—flavor these tender, cakelike pancakes. Molasses gives them an appealing light brown color. Don't worry if these pancakes appear a bit thicker than the typical pancake. They are still light and tender.

Position a rack in the middle of the oven, and preheat to 250°F (120°C).

In a large bowl, whisk together the flour, baking powder, baking soda, salt, cinnamon, ginger, and cloves. In another bowl, whisk together the brown sugar, eggs, molasses, 2 tablespoons melted butter, and $3/4$ cup (6 fl oz/180 ml) water. Add the egg mixture to the flour mixture and stir just until blended. There will be some small lumps.

Place a large griddle or frying pan with low sloping sides over medium heat until hot enough for a drop of water to sizzle and then immediately evaporate. Brush with about $1/2$ teaspoon of the melted butter. For each pancake, ladle about $1/4$ cup (2 fl oz/60 ml) batter onto the hot surface. Reduce the heat to medium-low and cook until small bubbles appear and the edges start to look dry, about 4 minutes. After 3 minutes, lift a pancake to check if the underside is done; do not let the pancakes darken too much. Carefully turn the pancakes and cook until lightly browned on the second sides, about 1 minute longer. Transfer to an ovenproof platter and place in the oven to keep warm; do not cover the pancakes, or they will get soggy. Repeat with the remaining batter and butter to make about 8 pancakes, each about 4 inches (10 cm) in diameter.

Serve the pancakes at once, accompanied by the syrup.

$1\frac{1}{4}$ cups ($6\frac{1}{2}$ oz/200 g) all-purpose (plain) flour

1 teaspoon baking powder

$1/2$ teaspoon baking soda (bicarbonate of soda)

$1/2$ teaspoon salt

1 teaspoon ground cinnamon

$3/4$ teaspoon ground ginger

$1/8$ teaspoon ground cloves

$1/4$ cup (2 oz/60 g) firmly packed dark brown sugar

2 large eggs

2 tablespoons light molasses

4 tablespoons unsalted butter, melted

Orange Blossom Maple Syrup (page 274) or regular maple syrup

Lemon-Ricotta Pancakes

1½ cups (7½ oz/235 g) all-purpose (plain) flour

1 teaspoon baking soda (bicarbonate of soda)

½ teaspoon salt

1½ cups (12 fl oz/375 ml) buttermilk

2 large eggs, separated

¼ cup (2 oz/60 g) sugar

¾ cup (6 oz/185 ml) whole-milk or part-skim ricotta cheese

1 tablespoon grated lemon zest

2 teaspoons unsalted butter, melted

12 strawberries, hulled, sliced, and tossed with 1 tablespoon sugar (optional)

Position a rack in the middle of the oven, and preheat to 250°F (120°C).

In a large bowl, whisk together the flour, baking soda, and salt. In another bowl, whisk together the buttermilk, egg yolks, sugar, ricotta, and lemon zest. Add the buttermilk mixture to the flour mixture and stir just until blended. There will be some small lumps.

In a separate bowl, using a mixer on medium speed or a whisk, beat the whites until soft peaks form. Using a rubber spatula, carefully fold the beaten whites into the ricotta mixture just until blended.

Place a large griddle or frying pan with low sloping sides over medium heat until hot enough for a drop of water to sizzle and then immediately evaporate. Brush with about ½ teaspoon of the melted butter. For each pancake, ladle about ¼ cup (2 fl oz/60 ml) batter onto the hot surface. Reduce the heat to medium-low and cook until small bubbles appear, the edges start to look dry, and the bottoms are golden brown, about 4 minutes. Carefully turn the pancakes and cook until lightly browned on the second sides, about 1½ minutes longer. Transfer to an ovenproof platter and place in the oven to keep warm; do not cover the pancakes or they will get soggy. Repeat with the remaining batter and butter to make about 16 pancakes, each about 4 inches (10 cm) in diameter.

Serve the pancakes at once, accompanied by the strawberries.

Ricotta and beaten egg whites give these pancakes a light, fluffy texture. A pan heated just hot enough to quickly evaporate a drop of water guarantees that the pancakes will brown properly and release easily. The butter used to coat the pan should be bubbling, but not browned, when the batter is ladled into the pan. Pass the butter at the table for anyone who wants a little extra richness.

Apple Oven Pancake

Preheating the baking dish before adding the fruit and batter gives the pancake a head start, so that once it is in the oven it billows like a popover. Anjou or Red Bartlett (Williams') pears can be substituted for the apples. Serve plain or with a syrup such as Orange Blossom Maple Syrup (page 274).

Position a rack in the lower third of the oven, and preheat to 425°F (220°C).

In a large frying pan over medium-high heat, melt 2 tablespoons of the butter. Add the apples and cook, turning as needed, just until tender, 5–7 minutes. Sprinkle evenly with the brown sugar, lemon juice, and cinnamon and stir to combine. Remove from the heat.

Place a large baking dish 12 inches (30 cm) in diameter or 9 by 13 inches (23 by 33 cm) in the oven to heat for 5 minutes. Remove the dish from the oven, add the remaining 2 tablespoons butter, and tilt the dish to coat the bottom and sides with the butter. Spoon the apples over the bottom of the dish in an even layer.

In a bowl, whisk together the eggs, milk, flour, vanilla, and salt until blended. Carefully pour the batter over the hot fruit.

Bake until puffed and golden brown, 20–25 minutes. Remove from the oven. Using a fine-mesh sieve, dust the top with confectioners' sugar. Serve at once.

4 tablespoons (2 oz/60 g) unsalted butter

4 cups (1 lb/500 g) diced peeled tart apples such as Granny Smith

2 tablespoons firmly packed light brown sugar

Juice of $\frac{1}{2}$ lemon

$\frac{1}{2}$ teaspoon ground cinnamon

4 large eggs, lightly beaten

1 cup (8 fl oz/250 ml) whole milk

1 cup (5 oz/155 g) all-purpose (plain) flour

1 teaspoon vanilla extract

$\frac{1}{8}$ teaspoon salt

Confectioners' (icing) sugar for dusting

Cornmeal Pancakes with Ham

1½ cups (7½ oz/235 g)
fine-grind white or yellow
cornmeal

1 teaspoon salt

1 teaspoon sugar

1½ cups (12 fl oz/375 ml)
boiling water

1 small yellow onion, grated

¼–½ cup (2–4 fl oz/60–125
ml) whole milk

½ cup (3 oz/90 g) finely
chopped cooked ham

Freshly ground pepper

2–3 tablespoons unsalted
butter, melted

Sour cream for garnish

Chopped red onions and
chives for garnish

The cornmeal gives these savory pancakes an appealing crunch. They are delicious served plain, or with a dollop of sour cream and a scattering of chopped red onion and snipped fresh chives, or with a drizzle of warm maple syrup.

Position a rack in the middle of the oven, and preheat to 250°F (120°C).

In a large bowl, whisk together the cornmeal, salt, and sugar. Slowly and carefully stir in the boiling water, whisking until smooth and quite stiff. Let the batter stand for 5 minutes. Stir in the onion. Stir in enough of the milk to make a batter with the consistency of porridge. Stir in the ham and season with pepper.

Place a large griddle or frying pan with low sloping sides over medium heat until hot enough for a drop of water to sizzle and then immediately evaporate. Brush with about 1½ teaspoons of the melted butter. For each pancake, ladle about ¼ cup (2 fl oz/60 ml) batter onto the hot surface. Flatten the cakes with a spatula so they cook evenly. Cook until browned and crisp, 5–7 minutes. Using a spatula, carefully turn the pancakes and cook until browned and crisp on the second sides, 5–7 minutes. Do not let the pancakes cook too quickly; the insides should remain a bit moist. Transfer to an ovenproof platter and place in the oven to keep warm; do not cover the pancakes, or they will get soggy. Repeat with the remaining butter and batter.

Serve the pancakes accompanied by a dollop of sour cream, and a sprinkling of red onions and chives.

Potato Pancakes with Sour Cream and Applesauce

Potato pancakes are traditionally served to celebrate the Jewish holiday of Hanukkah, but they can be enjoyed year-round. For the best result, use starchy russet potatoes and be sure to shred them on the biggest holes of a box grater or with the medium or coarse shredding blade of the food processor to ensure large shreds that will cook up into crisp pancakes.

Position a rack in the middle of the oven, and preheat to 250°F (120°C).

Peel the potatoes and shred them on the coarsest holes of a box grater. Enclose half of the grated potatoes in a clean dish towel and twist the towel to press out as much liquid as possible. Repeat with the remaining grated potatoes. Place the potatoes in a large bowl and add the onion, eggs, sour cream, salt, and pepper. Using a wooden spoon, stir to blend.

Line an ovenproof platter with paper towels. Pour the oil to a depth of 1/4 inch (6 mm) into a heavy frying pan and heat over medium heat to 365°F (185°C) on a deep-frying thermometer. For each pancake, ladle 1/4 cup (2 fl oz/60 ml) of the potato mixture onto the hot surface. Cook the pancakes until brown and crisp, about 2 minutes. Using a slotted spoon, carefully turn the pancakes and cook until brown and crisp on the second sides, about 2 minutes. Using the slotted spoon, transfer to the paper towel–lined platter and place in the oven to keep warm; do not cover the pancakes, or they will get soggy. Repeat with the remaining potato mixture to make about 18 pancakes. The pancakes can be kept warm in the oven for 20 minutes.

Serve at once, accompanied by the sour cream and applesauce.

2 lb (1 kg) russet potatoes

1/2 yellow onion, finely grated

2 large eggs, lightly beaten

2 tablespoons sour cream

3/4 teaspoon salt

1/4 teaspoon freshly ground pepper

Canola or corn oil for frying

1 cup (8 oz/250 g) sour cream

2 cups (18 oz/560 g) applesauce (page 277)

Raised Waffles with Strawberry-Rhubarb Compote

1 package (2¹⁄₂ teaspoons) active dry yeast

1 teaspoon granulated sugar

¹⁄₄ cup (2 fl oz/60 ml) warm water (105°–115°F/40°–46°C)

1 cup (8 fl oz/250 ml) whole milk

2 tablespoons unsalted butter

1 cup (5 oz/155 g) all-purpose (plain) flour

2 tablespoons firmly packed light brown sugar

¹⁄₄ teaspoon salt

1 teaspoon canola or corn oil

1 large egg

¹⁄₄ teaspoon baking soda (bicarbonate of soda)

Strawberry-Rhubarb Compote (page 275)

If your morning will be busy, this is the ideal recipe. The batter for these especially crisp, yeast-leavened waffles can be quickly mixed the night before serving, so it is ready to be poured into the waffle iron in the morning, while the compote can be prepared up to 2 days in advance and refrigerated until the waffles are ready.

In a large bowl, dissolve the yeast and granulated sugar in the warm water and let stand until foamy, about 5 minutes. In a saucepan over low heat, combine the milk and butter and heat to lukewarm (about 115°F/46°C).

In a small bowl, whisk together the flour, brown sugar, and salt. Stir the warm milk mixture into the dissolved yeast. Add the flour mixture and stir until blended. Cover the bowl and refrigerate overnight. The batter will thicken slightly.

To cook the waffles, preheat a regular waffle iron for 5 minutes, then brush with some of the oil. Stir the egg and baking soda into the chilled batter until blended. Following the manufacturer's directions, ladle enough batter for 1 waffle into the center of the waffle iron (usually about ¹⁄₂ cup/4 fl oz/125 ml), and spread with a small spatula to fill the holes. Close the waffle iron and cook until the steam stops escaping from the sides and the top opens easily, or according to the manufacturer's directions, 4–5 minutes. The timing will depend on the specific waffle iron used. The waffle should be browned and crisp. Repeat with the remaining oil and batter. Transfer the waffle to a warmed platter and repeat with the remaining oil and batter.

Serve the waffles at once, accompanied by the compote.

Buttermilk Belgian Waffles with Orange Blossom Maple Syrup

1 cup (5 oz/155 g)
all-purpose (plain) flour

2 tablespoons sugar

1¼ teaspoons baking powder

½ teaspoon baking soda
(bicarbonate of soda)

½ teaspoon salt

1½ cups (12 fl oz/375 ml)
buttermilk

4 tablespoons (2 oz/60 g)
unsalted butter, melted

2 large eggs

1 teaspoon vanilla extract

1 teaspoon canola or corn oil

Orange Blossom Maple Syrup
(page 274) or regular maple
syrup

1 cup (4 oz/125 g) fresh
blueberries (optional)

In a large bowl, whisk together the flour, sugar, baking powder, baking soda, and salt. In another bowl, whisk together the buttermilk, melted butter, eggs, and vanilla until blended. Add the buttermilk mixture to the flour mixture and whisk just until blended. There will be some small lumps.

To cook the waffles, preheat a Belgian waffle iron for 5 minutes, then brush with some of the oil. Following the manufacturer's directions, ladle enough batter for 1 waffle into the center of the waffle iron (usually about ½ cup/4 fl oz/125 ml), and spread with a small spatula to fill the holes. Close the waffle iron and cook until the steam stops escaping from the sides and the top opens easily, or according to the manufacturer's directions, 4–5 minutes. The timing will depend on the specific waffle iron used. The waffle should be browned and crisp. Transfer the waffle to a warmed platter and repeat with the remaining oil and batter.

Serve the waffles at once with the syrup and with the blueberries, if desired.

The grid on the waffle iron traditionally used for Belgian waffles is deeper than the grid on a conventional waffle iron. The result is more generous pockets for capturing more thick, sweet syrup. But these light, crisp Belgian waffles cook up nicely on any iron.

Sweet Crepes with Banana Cream

Both the pastry cream that fills these crepes and the sauce that covers them are flavored with fresh banana slices. All of the elements of this dish—the crepes, the pastry cream, and the sauce—can be made up to 2 days in advance, cooled, covered tightly, and refrigerated. Reheat the sauce over low heat before serving.

BY HAND: To make the crepe batter, in a bowl, combine the flour, sugar, and salt. Add the eggs, milk, and ³/₄ cup (6 fl oz/180 ml) water and whisk until smooth and blended. Add the melted butter and whisk until smooth. Cover tightly and refrigerate for 1 hour.

BY FOOD PROCESSOR: To make the crepe batter, combine the flour, sugar, and salt. Add the eggs, milk, and ³/₄ cup (6 fl oz/180 ml) water and process until smooth and blended, about 10 seconds. Add the melted butter and process until smooth, about 4 seconds. Pour into a bowl, cover, and refrigerate for 1 hour.

To cook the crepes, place a 9-inch (23-cm) frying pan with low, sloping sides over medium heat and heat until hot enough for a drop of water to sizzle and then immediately evaporate. Brush with about ¹/₂ teaspoon of the soft butter. For each crepe, ladle about ¹/₄ cup (2 fl oz/60 ml) batter into the center of the pan, and tilt the pan so that the batter forms a thin layer on the bottom. Cook until the edges just begin to brown and the top of the crepe is set, 1¹/₂–2 minutes. Using a wide spatula, carefully turn the crepe and cook for about 1 minute longer. Turn out onto a plate and repeat with the remaining soft butter and batter. Stack the crepes on the plate, putting a piece of waxed paper between the crepes. You will have at least 12 crepes. The crepes can be covered and refrigerated for up to 2 days.

To make the sauce, in a heavy saucepan over medium heat, heat the cream and brown sugar, stirring constantly, until the brown sugar dissolves. Adjust the heat so the sauce simmers gently and continue to cook, uncovered, until the sauce reduces slightly, about 20 minutes. Remove from the heat and stir in the banana slices. The sauce can be cooled, covered, and refrigerated for up to 2 days. To serve, warm over low heat.

To serve the crepes, stir the sliced banana into the chilled pastry cream. Spread about 2 tablespoons of banana pastry cream in the center of each crepe and fold in half. Place 2 filled crepes on each individual plate. Spoon the warm sauce over the crepes and serve at once.

For the crepes

1 cup (5 oz/155 g) all-purpose (plain) flour

2 tablespoons sugar

¹/₂ teaspoon salt

3 large eggs

³/₄ cup (6 fl oz/180 ml) whole milk

3 tablespoons unsalted butter, melted

2 tablespoons unsalted butter, softened

For the sauce

1 cup (8 fl oz/250 ml) heavy (double) cream

1¹/₄ cups (9 oz/280 g) firmly packed dark brown sugar

1 banana, sliced

1 banana, sliced, for serving

1 batch Pastry Cream (page 276)

Buckwheat Crepes with Smoked Salmon and Crème Fraîche

Buckwheat gives these crepes a nutty flavor that pairs well with savory fillings. Since buckwheat flour has no gluten, it is often mixed with wheat flour to ensure a tender texture, as it is here. A buckwheat batter is also thicker than an all-wheat batter, so you must be careful to work quickly to spread the batter once it is in the pan.

BY HAND: To make the crepe batter, in a large bowl, combine the all-purpose and buckwheat flours and salt. Add the eggs, milk, and ³/₄ cup (6 fl oz/180 ml) water and whisk until well blended. Cover and refrigerate for about 20 minutes.

BY FOOD PROCESSOR: To make the crepe batter, combine the all-purpose and buckwheat flours and the salt and pulse 2 or 3 times to mix. Add the eggs, the milk, and ³/₄ cup (6 fl oz/180 ml) water and process until well blended, about 10 seconds. Pour into a bowl, cover, and refrigerate for about 20 minutes.

To cook the crepes, place a 9- or 10-inch (23- or 25-cm) frying pan with low, sloping sides over medium heat and heat until hot enough for a drop of water to sizzle and then immediately evaporate. Brush lightly with some of the oil. For each crepe, ladle about 6 tablespoons (3 fl oz/90 ml) batter into the center of the pan, tilting the pan so that the batter forms a thin layer on the bottom. Cook until the top of the crepe is set, about 2 minutes. Using a wide spatula, carefully turn the crepe and cook for about 1 minute longer. Turn out onto a plate and repeat with the remaining oil and batter. Stack the crepes on the plate, putting a piece of wax paper between the crepes. You will have 8 crepes.

Divide the salmon evenly among the crepes, fold into quarters, and arrange on a platter. Spoon the crème fraîche on top and sprinkle with pepper and chives.

½ cup (2½ oz/75 g) all-purpose (plain) flour

½ cup (2½ oz/75 g) buckwheat flour

½ teaspoon salt

2 large eggs

¾ cup (6 fl oz/180 ml) whole milk

1 tablespoon canola or corn oil

½ lb (250 g) thinly sliced smoked salmon

1 cup (8 oz/250 g) crème fraîche (page 276)

Freshly ground pepper

Snipped fresh chives for garnish

Cheese Blintzes with Berry Jam

For the blintzes

1 cup (5 oz/155 g) all-purpose (plain) flour

½ teaspoon salt

3 large eggs

¾ cup (6 fl oz/180 ml) whole milk

3 tablespoons unsalted butter, melted

About 2 tablespoons unsalted butter, softened

For the filling

1 cup (7½ oz/235 g) farmer cheese

1 cup (8 oz/250 g) whole-milk or part-skim ricotta cheese

2 tablespoons sugar

¼ teaspoon grated lemon zest

½ teaspoon vanilla extract

4 teaspoons unsalted butter

Berry Jam (page 275)

Blueberries and raspberries for garnish

BY HAND: To make the blintz batter, in a bowl, combine the flour and the salt. Add the eggs, the milk, and ¾ cup (6 fl oz/180 ml) water and whisk until smooth and blended. Add the melted butter and whisk until smooth. Cover and refrigerate for 1 hour.

BY FOOD PROCESSOR: To make the blintz batter, combine the flour and the salt. Add the eggs, the milk, and ¾ cup (6 fl oz/180 ml) water and process until smooth and blended, about 10 seconds. Add the melted butter and process until smooth, about 4 seconds. Pour into a bowl, cover, and refrigerate for about 20 minutes.

To cook the blintzes, place a 9-inch (23-cm) frying pan with low, sloping sides over medium heat and heat until hot enough for a drop of water to sizzle and then immediately evaporate. Brush with about ½ teaspoon of the softened butter. For each blintz, ladle about ¼ cup (2 fl oz/60 ml) batter into the center of the pan, tilting the pan so that the batter forms a thin layer on the bottom. Cook until the edges begin to brown and the top of the blintz is set, 1½–2 minutes. Using a wide spatula, carefully turn the blintz and cook for about 1 minute longer. Turn out onto a plate and repeat with the remaining butter and batter. Stack the blintzes on a plate, putting a piece of wax paper between each. You will have at least 12 blintzes. The blintzes can be covered and refrigerated for up to 2 days.

To make the filling, in a large bowl, combine the farmer and ricotta cheeses, sugar, lemon zest, and vanilla and stir until blended.

Spread about 2 tablespoons of the cheese filling in the center of each blintz. Fold the sides over the filling. Fold in the ends to enclose the filling completely and form a rectangle.

In a large frying pan over medium heat, melt 2 teaspoons of the butter. When the butter just begins to sizzle, add half of the blintzes, seam side down, and fry until browned, about 2 minutes. Repeat with the remaining butter and blintzes. Serve hot with the jam and berries on top.

Blintzes can be filled with a sweet or savory filling. Here, farmer and ricotta cheeses are mixed with a little sugar and lemon zest to create a smooth, creamy filling with just a hint of sweetness. If you decide to create your own filling, make sure that it does not contain too much liquid, which will make the blintzes soggy.

Challah French Toast with Cranberry-Apple Compote

Always choose a firm-textured, flavorful bread for the best French toast. Slices of gold, egg-rich challah are a good choice because they soak up the batter, yet retain their shape during cooking. The addition of maple syrup to the batter both flavors it and encourages browning.

In a bowl, whisk together the eggs, milk, maple syrup, cinnamon, and salt. Pour the batter into a baking dish.

In a large frying pan over medium heat, melt half of the butter and continue to heat until it foams but does not brown.

Place 4 of the bread slices in the egg mixture and let stand for 5 seconds. Turn and let stand for 5 seconds longer. Using tongs, lift the slices from the batter, letting any excess drip back into the baking dish, and transfer to the hot pan. Cook until browned, about 3 minutes. Turn and cook until browned on the second side, about 2 minutes longer. Using the clean tongs, transfer to a warmed platter. Repeat with the remaining butter, batter, and bread slices.

Serve at once, accompanied by the compote.

3 large eggs

¾ cup (6 fl oz/180 ml) whole milk

2 tablespoons maple syrup

1 teaspoon ground cinnamon

⅛ teaspoon salt

1 tablespoon unsalted butter for pan

8 slices day-old challah, each ¾ inch (2 cm) thick, with crusts

Cranberry-Apple Compote (page 275)

Mascarpone-Stuffed French Toast with Blackberries

¼ lb (125 g) mascarpone cheese

1 tablespoon sugar

1 teaspoon fresh lemon juice

½ teaspoon vanilla extract

8 slices firm-textured bread such as brioche (page 119) or challah, each ½ inch (12 mm) thick, with crusts

For the batter

2 large eggs

½ cup (4 fl oz/125 ml) whole milk

½ teaspoon vanilla extract

⅛ teaspoon salt

1 tablespoon unsalted butter for pan

2 cups (8 oz/250 g) blackberries

Orange Blossom Maple Syrup (page 274) or regular maple syrup

In a bowl, whisk together the mascarpone, sugar, lemon juice, and vanilla. Spread 2 tablespoons of the mascarpone mixture on 4 of the bread slices, leaving a ¼-inch (6-mm) plain border on all sides. Top with the remaining bread slices.

To make the batter, in a bowl, whisk together the eggs, milk, vanilla, and salt. Pour the batter into a baking dish.

In a large frying pan over medium heat, melt half of the butter and continue to heat until it foams but does not brown.

Place each of the sandwiches in the batter and let stand for 5 seconds. Turn and let stand for 5 seconds longer. Using a wide spatula, carefully lift the sandwiches from the batter, letting any excess drip back into the baking dish, and transfer to the hot pan. Cook until browned, about 3 minutes. Add the remaining butter to the pan, turn the sandwiches, and cook until browned on the second sides, about 2 minutes. Using a clean, wide spatula, transfer the sandwiches to a cutting board.

Cut each in half on the diagonal. Divide among individual plates, top with the blackberries, dividing them evenly, and serve at once with the maple syrup.

These sandwiches, filled with a lightly sweetened mascarpone cheese filling, elevate French toast to the centerpiece of a brunch party. Other fresh berries or fruits, such as blackberries, olallieberries, peaches, nectarines or plums, can be added to, or substituted for, the blackberries. If you are expecting a crowd, this recipe can be easily doubled.

Brioche French Toast
with Fresh Figs

Sweet, dark purple Mission figs are a favorite for this dish, but golden Calimyrnas, yellow-green Kadotas, and green Adriatics are also good choices, or use a mix of varieties. Choose figs that are soft to the touch but not bruised and use them promptly, as they spoil quickly. If you have brioche left over from making the bread pudding on page 119, this is a great way to use it.

To make the batter, in a bowl, whisk together the eggs, milk, orange juice, sugar, orange zest, vanilla, and salt. Pour the batter into a baking dish.

In a large frying pan over medium heat, melt 1 teaspoon butter and continue to heat until it foams but does not brown.

Place 4 of the bread slices in the batter and let stand for 5 seconds. Turn and let stand for 5 seconds longer. Using tongs, lift the slices from the batter, letting any excess drip back into the baking dish, and transfer to the hot pan. Cook until browned, about 3 minutes. Turn and cook until browned on the second sides, about 2 minutes longer. Using clean tongs, transfer to a warmed platter. Repeat with the remaining butter, batter, and bread slices.

Divide the French toast among individual plates and arrange the figs on top and alongside. Serve at once. Pass the syrup at the table.

For the batter

2 large eggs

¾ cup (6 fl oz/180 ml) whole milk

¼ cup (2 fl oz/60 ml) fresh orange juice

1 tablespoon sugar

2 teaspoons grated orange zest

½ teaspoon vanilla extract

⅛ teaspoon salt

2 teaspoons unsalted butter for pan

8 slices day-old brioche (page 119), ¾ inch (2 cm) thick, with crusts

8 fresh figs such as Mission, quartered

Orange Blossom Maple Syrup (page 274) or regular maple syrup

Main Dishes

About Main Dishes

Brunch, combining two meals, calls for substantial fare, making main dishes, from pasta and tacos to savory bread pudding, excellent choices for serving guests. The recipes here are appropriate for breakfast as well, especially the breakfast pizzas and tarts, both of which include eggs.

Whether you are hosting breakfast or brunch, many main dishes are ideal for a buffet. A number can be served at room temperature, and several can be made ahead or left to cook so you can attend to other tasks. Following the tips below will help you be more efficient in the kitchen as well as ensure the best results for your guests.

WORKING WITH PASTRY

The recipe on page 188, Fennel Sausage and Egg Tartlets, calls for prebaking the pastry in the pans. This process, called blind baking, prevents the bottom crust from becoming soggy when the filling is largely liquid.

To help the pastry hold its shape, line each pastry-lined pan with aluminum foil or parchment (baking) paper. Fill the bottom with pastry weights, small metal or ceramic balls made especially for this purpose. If you don't have pastry weights, use dried beans or uncooked rice which will work just as well. When the prebaked pastry comes out of the oven, be sure to put the pans on a wire rack. This helps keep the crust dry and crisp.

The Chicken Potpies on page 177 call for already prepared frozen puff pastry, an option that saves considerable time over making your own. You can purchase the puff pastry well ahead as long as you store it in the freezer in its original package. The pastry must be thawed before rolling. You'll find instructions on the package, but as a general rule, you can move the package to the refrigerator and leave it there to thaw overnight.

When handling puff pastry, you do not want the layers of dough and butter to dry out. Work with only one sheet at a time and store the remaining sheet(s), well wrapped, in the refrigerator, rather than leave it exposed at room temperature.

PREPARING SEAFOOD AND MEAT

When cooking with seafood, you want to make sure that fish and shellfish are free of bones and shell fragments.

Fillets like the salmon used on page 170 may still have small bones, called pin bones, embedded in the flesh. To locate them, move your fingers over the surface, pressing down slightly. When you feel a bone, pull it out with sturdy tweezers or small needle-nosed pliers. You may need to coax the tip of the bone from the flesh so you can grab onto it.

When you purchase already cooked crabmeat for the crab cakes on page 173, it sometimes contains small pieces of shell. Spread the crabmeat on a plate and pick through it with your fingers or a fork. Remove any shell fragments and discard.

Shrimp (prawns) need to be peeled and deveined before using in the tacos on page 174. Begin by pulling off the legs of each shrimp. Starting at the head, pry the shell away from the body and work toward the tail, removing that as well. Use a small, sharp knife to make a shallow cut along the back to expose the dark intestinal vein. You can then lift it out easily with the tip of the knife. Finally, rinse all of the shrimp under cold

running water, then pat dry with paper towels. Sausage casings are sometimes tough and chewy, so you need to remove them from the sausages used in the *strata* on page 187 and in the gravy on page 179. To accomplish this, slit each sausage from end to end with a sharp knife or kitchen scissors, then peel away the casing. When cooking the meat, be sure to break up any clumps with a wooden spoon so the meat cooks evenly and can be mixed with other ingredients.

The flank steak for the hash on page 191 needs to be cut into a neat $1/2$-inch (12-mm) dice so that all of the ingredients are about the same size. For ease of handling, freeze the meat briefly, which makes it easier to cut.

COOKING PASTA AND RISOTTO

Pasta and noodles are welcome at just about any meal—unless they are underdone and too chewy, or overcooked and too soft. For any type of pasta, look for high-quality brands made with semolina. You will want to cook it in a generous amount of boiling water in a large pot to ensure even cooking.

After the water comes to a boil, add the pasta and about 2 tablespoons salt. Stir to circulate the pasta in the water, then stir occasionally until it is done. Cooking times are stated on the packaging, but you want to test the pasta a bit sooner than the time given. You can cook it longer if it is not yet al dente—tender but firm to the bite—but you cannot turn back the clock if it is overdone so be sure to watch it carefully.

Risotto, which needs to cook slowly to release the starch in the rice kernels, should be prepared in a large pan to prevent scorching or cooking too rapidly. If you are making the risotto cakes on page 169, remove the rice from the heat when the kernels are still firm.

Risotto Cakes with Cherry Tomatoes

These stick-to-your-ribs rice cakes are crispy on the outside and pleasantly soft on the inside. The accompanying tomatoes add a slight acidic counterpoint along with a splash of vibrant color. For a subtle variation, use a mixture of yellow and red cherry tomatoes. Accompany the cakes with a salad of fresh seasonal greens or a colorful fruit salad.

To make the risotto, line an 8-inch (20-cm) square baking pan with aluminum foil. In a saucepan over medium heat, warm the broth until bubbles appear around the edge of the pan. Adjust the heat to maintain a gentle simmer.

In a frying pan over medium-high heat, warm 2 tablespoons of the olive oil. Add the onion and cook, stirring occasionally, until translucent, 3–5 minutes. Stir in the rice and add the remaining 2 tablespoons olive oil. Reduce the heat to medium and cook, stirring, until the grains turn translucent at the edges, about 1 minute. Pour in the wine and stir until it is absorbed, about 3 minutes.

Add 1/2 cup (4 fl oz/125 ml) of the hot broth and cook, stirring constantly, until most of the liquid is absorbed, 3–5 minutes. Continue adding broth, 1/2 cup (4 fl oz/125 ml) at a time, and cook, stirring constantly, until all of the broth is used, and the risotto is creamy, 20–25 minutes. Remove from the heat. Stir in the Parmesan and herbs, and season with salt and pepper. Pour into the prepared pan and spread evenly. Let cool, cover, and chill in the refrigerator until firm, for at least 2 hours.

To prepare the tomatoes, position a rack in the middle of the oven, and preheat to 250°F (120°C). Line a rimmed baking sheet with parchment (baking) paper. Place the tomatoes in a bowl. Drizzle with the olive oil, season with salt and pepper, and toss to coat. Arrange the tomatoes, cut sides up, on the prepared pan. Roast until curly around the edges, slightly darkened, and partially dried, about 1 1/2 hours.

Turn the solidified rice out onto a work surface and remove the foil. Cut in half on the diagonal. Cut each half into 3 wedges, and then cut each wedge in half.

Place the flour, eggs, and *panko* in 3 separate bowls. Next to the bowls, set a large wire rack over a sheet of waxed paper. Season the wedges on all sides with salt and pepper. Working with 1 wedge at a time, roll it first in the flour to coat. Using tongs, dip it in the bowl of beaten egg several times. Lift the wedge, transfer to the bowl of *panko* and turn with tongs to coat completely. Place on the rack and repeat with the remaining wedges. The wedges can be coated up to 1 hour in advance and kept covered at room temperature until ready to fry.

In a large frying pan over medium-high heat, melt 1 tablespoon each of the butter and oil. When the mixture stops foaming, add 6 of the wedges and cook, turning once, until well browned on both sides, about 10 minutes total. Transfer to a plate. Repeat with the remaining butter, oil, and 6 wedges.

Place 2 risotto cakes on each plate. Garnish with the roasted tomatoes and serve.

For the risotto

4 cups (32 fl oz/1 l) chicken broth

4 tablespoons (2 fl oz/60 ml) olive oil

1 yellow onion, chopped

1 1/2 cups (10 1/2 oz/330 g) Arborio rice

1/2 cup (4 fl oz/125 ml) dry white wine such as Sauvignon Blanc

1/4 cup (1 oz/30 g) grated Parmesan cheese

1/2 cup (3/4 oz/20 g) chopped mixed fresh herbs such as basil, thyme, oregano, chervil, and flat-leaf (Italian) parsley

Salt and freshly ground pepper

For the tomatoes

3 cups (18 oz/560 g) small cherry tomatoes, halved

1 tablespoon olive oil

Salt and freshly ground pepper

1 cup (5 oz/155 g) all-purpose (plain) flour

2 large eggs, lightly beaten

2 cups (8 oz/250 g) *panko*

Salt and freshly ground pepper

2 tablespoons unsalted butter

2 tablespoons canola oil

Gravlax with Mustard-Dill Sauce

For the gravlax

2 same-sized salmon fillets, 1½ lb (12 oz/375 g) each, with skin

6 lemons

½ cup (4 oz/125 g) granulated sugar

½ cup (4 oz/125 g) coarse salt

3 tablespoons cracked peppercorns

3 tablespoons coriander seeds, lightly crushed

3 tablespoons vodka or aquavit

For the sauce

⅓ cup (2½ oz/75 g) Dijon mustard

3 tablespoons firmly packed light brown sugar

2 tablespoons cider vinegar

⅓ cup (3 fl oz/80 ml) sunflower oil

3 tablespoons finely chopped fresh dill

To make the gravlax, trim any fat from the salmon. Run your fingers gently over the fish to check for small bones, and remove any with sturdy tweezers or small needle-nosed pliers. Finely grate the zest from the 6 lemons, then cut the lemons into thin slices and discard any seeds. In a bowl, stir together the lemon zest, granulated sugar, salt, peppercorns, and coriander seeds. Rub the vodka over the flesh side of the salmon fillets. Coat the flesh sides of both fillets with the peppercorn mixture.

Place 1 fillet, flesh side up, in a nonreactive dish just large enough to hold it. Cover the fillet with a layer of lemon slices, then top with the remaining fillet, flesh side down. Cover the dish with plastic wrap and top with a piece of cardboard cut slightly smaller than the dish. Weight the salmon evenly with heavy cans of food. Refrigerate for 48 hours, turning the fillets 4–6 times and draining away any accumulated liquid. The heavy weight and the salt will force the liquid out of the fish, leaving it firm and easy to slice.

To make the sauce, in a small bowl, whisk together the mustard, brown sugar, and vinegar until smooth. Add the sunflower oil in a slow, steady stream, whisking constantly until the sauce is emulsified. Stir in the dill. The sauce can be prepared up to 3 days ahead, covered tightly, and stored in the refrigerator. Before serving, whisk the sauce well and transfer to a small serving bowl.

Uncover the salmon and scrape off the lemon slices and most of the peppercorn mixture. Using a thin, sharp knife, cut the salmon on the diagonal into very thin slices. Lift the slices from the skin and arrange on a serving platter. The salmon may be sliced up to 6 hours ahead and refrigerated, tightly covered, until serving. Garnish with the lemon slices. Serve at once with the sauce.

Salmon cured with spices and vodka or aquavit, a Scandinavian caraway-flavored spirit, makes an elegant brunch dish. Serve with thin slices of toasted rye bread or good-quality crackers.

Dungeness Crab Cakes with Cabbage Slaw

The Dungeness crab, which lives along the western shores of the United States, is prized for the particularly delicate, sweet flavor of its meat. If Dungeness crabmeat is unavailable, look for the meat of king crab or blue crab. If possible, always buy freshly cooked crabmeat for its superior taste.

To make the crab cakes, in a bowl, stir together the mayonnaise, mustard, salt, and cayenne pepper. Stir in the celery and green onions. Gently fold in the crabmeat and half of the bread crumbs. Spread the remaining bread crumbs on a sheet of waxed paper. Shape the crab mixture into 8 patties, each 1 inch (2.5 cm) thick. They will only reluctantly hold together; do not overwork them. Place each cake in the bread crumbs and turn to coat evenly. Arrange the cakes on a baking sheet, cover with plastic wrap, and refrigerate for 1 hour.

Meanwhile, to make the slaw, in a small bowl, whisk together the buttermilk, mayonnaise, dill, and garlic. In a large bowl, toss together the cabbage, carrots, and green onions. Add the dressing and toss well. Season with salt and black pepper and toss again. Taste and add as much lemon juice as desired.

To cook the crab cakes, heat 2 large frying pans over medium heat. In each pan, melt 2 teaspoons of the butter with 2 teaspoons of the oil. Place 4 crab cakes in each pan and cook until golden brown, about 3 minutes. Turn and cook until the cakes are well browned on the second sides and hot throughout, 3–4 minutes longer. Transfer to individual plates and serve at once with the lemon wedges and the slaw.

For the crab cakes

½ cup (4 fl oz/125 ml) mayonnaise

2 teaspoons dry mustard

Pinch of salt

Pinch of cayenne pepper

1 celery stalk, finely minced

2 green (spring) onions, white and pale green parts, finely minced

1 lb (500 g) cooked Dungeness crabmeat, picked over for shell fragments

2 cups (4 oz/125 g) fresh bread crumbs

For the cabbage slaw

¼ cup *each* (2 fl oz/60 ml) buttermilk and mayonnaise

2 tablespoons minced fresh dill

1 clove garlic, minced

4 cups (12 oz/375 g) thinly sliced Napa cabbage

3 carrots, grated

2 green (spring) onions, white and pale green parts, minced

Salt and freshly ground black pepper

Fresh lemon juice to taste

4 teaspoons unsalted butter

4 teaspoons olive oil

4 lemon wedges

Shrimp Tacos with Melon-Pineapple Salsa

For the salsa

½ small cantaloupe, about 1¼ lb (625 g), peeled, seeded, and cut into ½-inch (12-mm) dice

½ small pineapple, about 1 lb (500 g), peeled, cored, and cut into ½-inch (12-mm) dice

½ red onion, finely chopped

½ bell pepper (capsicum), seeded and finely chopped

1 small cucumber, about 6 oz (185 g), peeled, seeded, and cut into ½-inch (12-mm) dice

½ jalapeño chile, seeded and finely chopped

½ cup (¾ oz/20 g) chopped fresh cilantro (fresh coriander)

2 tablespoons *each* fresh lime juice and olive oil

Salt and freshly ground pepper

For the tacos

24 medium shrimp (prawns), about 1 lb (500 g) total weight, peeled and deveined

4 tablespoons (2 oz/60 g) unsalted butter

½ teaspoon chipotle chile powder

1 small clove garlic, minced

4 corn tortillas, each 6 inches (15 cm) in diameter

Serve this colorful dish in the summertime, when the cantaloupe is at the height of its season. If you can't find cantaloupe in the market, Persian, Sharlyn, or Crenshaw melon is a good substitute. Any color bell pepper—red, green, gold, orange—will work in the salsa.

To make the salsa, in a large bowl, combine the cantaloupe, pineapple, onion, bell pepper, cucumber, jalapeño, and cilantro. Add the lime juice and olive oil, and season with salt and pepper. Stir well to combine. Cover and refrigerate until ready to serve.

To make the tacos, prepare a charcoal or gas grill for direct grilling over medium-high heat, or preheat a broiler (grill). Oil the rack. Thread the shrimp on long metal skewers. In a small saucepan over medium-high heat, melt the butter. Remove from the heat, let cool slightly, and stir in the chile powder and garlic. Brush the shrimp with the butter mixture.

BY GRILL: Using tongs, place the shrimp over the hottest part of the fire or directly over the heat elements and grill until bright pink, about 2 minutes. Turn and grill until bright pink on the second side, about 2 minutes longer. The shrimp should be firm to the touch at the thickest part. Transfer to a plate. Lightly brush the tortillas with the remaining butter mixture and place over the hottest part of the grill. Grill until they start to puff up, about 1 minute. Using tongs, turn and grill until puffed on the second sides, about 1 minute longer.

BY BROILER: Arrange the shrimp in a single layer on a baking sheet and place in the broiler at least 6 inches (15 cm) from the heat source. Broil (grill) until they are bright pink, about 2 minutes. Using tongs, turn the shrimp and broil until bright pink on the second side, about 2 minutes longer. The shrimp should be firm to the touch at the thickest part. Transfer to a plate. Lightly brush the tortillas with the remaining butter mixture. Arrange in a single layer on the baking sheet and broil until they start to puff up, about 1 minute. Using tongs, turn and broil until puffed on the second sides, about 1 minute longer.

Place 1 tortilla on each plate. Arrange 6 shrimp in the center and top with a spoonful of the salsa. Serve at once, passing the remaining salsa at the table.

Chicken Potpies

Underneath the golden, buttery pastry of these hearty potpies, your guests will find chunks of chicken and vegetables suspended in a velvety sauce. For the best flavor, check the label and buy only puff pastry made with all butter. Also, make sure the pastry is cooked through before you remove the pies from the oven.

Remove the giblets from the chicken and save for another use or discard. Place the chicken in a large pot. Slice 2 of the carrots and add to the pot. Add the celery, onion, peppercorns, and bay leaf. Pour in cold water to cover the chicken by 1 inch (2.5 cm). As the water comes to a boil, use a large spoon to skim off any scum and foam that rise to the surface. Reduce the heat to medium and simmer, partially covered until the chicken is tender and falling off the bone, 1 1/2–2 hours. Lift out the chicken, transfer to a platter, and let cool. Cover with plastic wrap and refrigerate. Pour the broth through a fine-mesh sieve into a large bowl. Discard the solids. Let cool, then cover and refrigerate for 6–8 hours or for up to overnight.

Using a spoon, lift off the layer of fat on top of the chilled broth. Pour the broth into a large saucepan and bring to a boil over high heat. Reduce the heat to medium-high and simmer, uncovered, until reduced by half, 30–40 minutes. Set aside 4 cups (32 fl oz/1 l) broth (save any remaining broth for another use).

In a large saucepan over medium-high heat, melt the butter. Add the flour and whisk until blended. Continue to cook, whisking constantly, for about 2 minutes. Pour in the broth, raise the heat to high, bring to a boil, and whisk until thickened and smooth. Season with salt and pepper. Partially cover the sauce and set aside.

Remove the chicken from the bones, discarding the skin and gristle. Cut into 1/2-inch (12-mm) pieces. Place the potatoes in a saucepan and add water to cover. Season with salt, bring to a boil, and cook until almost tender, about 5 minutes. Drain, rinse under cold running water, and add to the sauce. Cut the remaining 2 carrots into 1/2-inch dice and cook, drain, and rinse as you did the potatoes. Add the carrots, chicken, peas, corn, and parsley to the sauce and season with salt and pepper. Divide the mixture among four 2-cup (16–fl oz/500-ml) ramekins.

Position a rack in the middle of the oven, and preheat to 400°F (200°C). Cover a rimmed baking sheet with aluminum foil. Place the puff pastry on a lightly floured work surface and roll out 1/8 inch (3 mm) thick. Cut out 4 circles each 1/2 inch (12 mm) larger than the diameter of the ramekins. Lightly brush 1 side of each circle with the beaten egg. Place brushed side down on a ramekin and press the pastry firmly against the outside of the ramekin to seal. Cut a small X in the center to allow steam to escape. Brush the tops with the remaining beaten egg. Place the ramekins on the prepared sheet. Bake until the pastry is golden brown and the filling is bubbly, about 45 minutes.

Place each ramekin on a serving plate and serve immediately.

1 chicken, 3–4 lb (1.5–2 kg)

4 carrots

2 celery stalks, sliced

1 yellow onion, quartered

1 teaspoon peppercorns

1 bay leaf

1/3 cup (3 oz/90 g) unsalted butter

1/3 cup (2 oz/60 g) all-purpose (plain) flour

Salt and freshly ground pepper

3 small Yukon gold potatoes, peeled and cut into 1/2-inch (12-mm) dice

1 cup (5 oz/155 g) small fresh or frozen green peas

1 cup (6 oz/185 g) fresh or frozen corn kernels

1/4 cup (1/3 oz/10 g) finely chopped fresh flat-leaf (Italian) parsley

1 package (14-oz /440-g) frozen puff pastry, thawed according to package directions

1 egg lightly beaten with 1 teaspoon water

Chicken Hash with Artichokes and Red Peppers

½ lemon

6 artichokes, 10–12 oz (315–375 g) each

2 tablespoons olive oil

1 red bell pepper (capsicum), seeded and thinly sliced

1 yellow onion, sliced

4 Yukon gold potatoes, about 1¼ lb (625 g) total weight, peeled and cut into ½-inch (12-mm) dice

2 skinless, boneless chicken breasts, each split into halves, 6 oz (185 g) total weight, cut into ½-inch (12-mm) dice

Salt and freshly ground pepper

½ cup (4 fl oz/125 ml) heavy (double) cream

Fill a bowl three-fourths full with cold water. Squeeze in the juice of the lemon half. Working with 1 artichoke at a time, cut off the top ¾ inch (2 cm) of the leaves with a serrated knife to remove the prickly tips. Trim the stem even with the bottom. Pull off the tough, dark green outer leaves until you reach the tenderest, pale green inner leaves. Cut off the stem and trim the base, and then cut the artichoke in half lengthwise. Using a small spoon, scrape out the prickly fibers, or choke, from the center, and then drop the halves into the lemon water to prevent the cut portions from turning brown.

In a large frying pan over medium-high heat, warm the olive oil. Add the bell pepper and onion and cook, stirring, until slightly softened, 3–5 minutes. Add the potatoes and cook, stirring, until almost tender, 5–7 minutes. Season the chicken with salt and pepper, add to the pan, and cook, stirring, until opaque and firm to the touch, about 5 minutes.

Drain the artichoke hearts, cut lengthwise into thin slices, add to the pan, and mix well. Stir in the cream, reduce the heat to medium, and simmer gently, stirring from time to time, until the artichokes and potatoes are soft, 8–10 minutes.

Spoon into warmed serving bowls and serve at once.

Hash is a hearty mixture of chopped meat (usually corned beef), potatoes, and onions. Here, the use of chicken, artichokes, and red bell pepper adds a contemporary twist to an old-fashioned favorite.

Baking Powder Biscuits and Sausage Gravy

Biscuits and gravy is an iconic breakfast dish, especially in the southern United States. Both the fluffy baking powder biscuits and the milk gravy are easy to assemble, making this recipe a good choice when a casual get-together—either sit-down or buffet—is on your calendar.

Position a rack in the middle of the oven, and preheat to 450°F (230°C).

BY HAND: In a large bowl, combine the flour, baking powder, salt, and baking soda and stir to mix. Using a pastry blender or 2 knives, cut in the shortening and butter until the mixture forms large, coarse crumbs the size of small peas. Pour in the buttermilk and mix quickly with a fork or rubber spatula just until the dry ingredients are moistened. Do not overmix the dough.

BY FOOD PROCESSOR: Combine the flour, baking powder, salt, and baking soda and pulse 2 or 3 times to mix. Add the shortening and butter and pulse 3 or 4 times or just until the mixture forms large, coarse crumbs the size of small peas. Pour in the buttermilk and pulse for a few seconds or just until the dry ingredients are moistened. Do not overmix the dough.

Turn the dough out onto a lightly floured work surface and knead into a ball. Roll out into a round about ½ inch (12 mm) thick. Use a 3-inch (7.5-cm) biscuit cutter to cut out 4 biscuits. Gently gather the scraps, knead into a ball, and roll out again. Cut out 2 more biscuits.

Arrange the biscuits on a rimmed baking sheet. Bake until golden brown, about 15 minutes. Remove the biscuits and transfer to a wire rack and let cool.

To make the sausage gravy, in a frying pan over medium-high heat, warm the oil. Cook the sausage meat, breaking it up with a wooden spoon, until no trace of pink remains, 12–15 minutes. Using a slotted spoon, transfer to paper towels to drain. Pour off all but 2 tablespoons of the fat in the pan and place over medium-high heat. Stir in the flour and cook, stirring, for 2 minutes. Slowly stir in the milk to prevent lumps from forming, raise the heat to high, and bring to a boil, stirring to scrape up any browned bits from the pan bottom. Reduce the heat to low and cook, stirring, until lightly thickened, about 2 minutes. Return the sausage to the pan, and season with salt and pepper.

Split the biscuits in half. Place the bottom halves, cut sides up, on individual plates. Ladle about ½ cup (4 fl oz/250 ml) of the sausage gravy over each biscuit bottom. Cover with the top halves and serve at once.

For the biscuits

2 cups (10 oz/315 g) all-purpose (plain) flour

2 teaspoons baking powder

1 teaspoon salt

¼ teaspoon baking soda (bicarbonate of soda)

4 tablespoons (2 oz/60 g) cold vegetable shortening, cut into ½-inch (12-mm) pieces

2 tablespoons cold unsalted butter, cut into ½-inch (12-mm) pieces

1 cup (8 fl oz/250 ml) cold buttermilk

For the sausage gravy

2 tablespoons canola oil

¾ lb (375 g) sweet or hot pork sausage, casings removed and meat crumbled

3 tablespoons all-purpose (plain) flour

2 cups (8 fl oz/500 ml) whole milk

Salt and freshly ground pepper

Pizzas with Eggs and Bacon

1 recipe Pizza Dough (page 277)

8 thick slices bacon, about ½ lb (250 g) total weight, cut into 1½-inch (4-cm) pieces

½ cup (2 oz/60 g) grated Parmesan cheese

4 large eggs

Salt and freshly ground pepper

Snipped fresh chives for garnish

Position a rack in the middle of the oven, and preheat to 400°F (200°C). Oil a large rimless baking sheet.

Punch down the pizza dough and turn out onto a lightly floured work surface. Cut the dough into 4 equal pieces. Roll out each piece, stretching the dough if necessary, into a 6- to 8-inch (15- to 20-cm) round. Carefully transfer the rounds to the prepared pan. The dough is elastic and will tend to lose shape; use oiled fingertips to reform the rounds on the pan, stretching and pulling the dough as needed. Brush with olive oil. Bake until puffed and lightly browned, about 20 minutes. Remove from the oven.

Meanwhile, in a small frying pan over medium heat, cook the bacon, stirring, until crisp, 5–7 minutes. Using a slotted spoon, transfer to paper towels to drain.

Evenly sprinkle one-fourth each of the bacon and Parmesan cheese over the top of each pizza. To prevent the egg yolks from breaking, crack each egg into a shallow bowl or saucer, then slide it onto the center of a pizza. Season lightly with salt and pepper. Continue baking until the egg whites are set and the yolks are glazed over but still soft, about 10 minutes. Slide each pizza onto an individual plate, garnish with chives, and serve at once.

A breakfast pizza is a delicious way to dress up bacon and eggs. To save time in the morning, make the dough the day before and let it rise slowly in the refrigerator. Serve the pizzas right out of the oven with a simple green salad or a platter of sliced tomatoes drizzled with fruity olive oil.

Sausage Strata with Cheddar Cheese and Sun-Dried Tomatoes

A *strata,* which is a layered casserole made primarily of bread, eggs, and cheese, can often be assembled the day before serving and refrigerated until it goes into the oven. This recipe makes an excellent focal point for a breakfast buffet, accompanied with a Caesar salad or a fruit salad. If the *strata* is fully baked but the top isn't brown enough, slip the dish (make sure it is flameproof) under the broiler (grill) for 2–3 minutes.

In a frying pan over medium-high heat, cook the sausage meat, breaking it up with a wooden spoon, until no trace of pink remains, 10–12 minutes. Using a slotted spoon, transfer to paper towels to drain.

Pour off all but 1 tablespoon of the fat from the pan, return to medium-high heat, and add the onion. Cook, stirring frequently, until softened, 3–5 minutes. Stir in the tomatoes and remove from the heat. In a large bowl, whisk the eggs. Whisk in the milk, salt, and pepper until blended.

Butter a 9-by-13-inch (23-by-33-cm) baking dish. Arrange 6 of the bread slices in a single layer on the bottom of the prepared dish. Top evenly with half of the sausage, half of the tomato mixture, and half of the grated cheddar cheese. Repeat with the remaining bread slices, sausage, tomato mixture, and cheddar cheese.

Slowly pour the milk mixture evenly over the layers. Wrap securely in plastic wrap and weight with large cans to submerge the layers. Refrigerate for at least 2 hours or for up to overnight.

Position a rack in the middle of the oven, and preheat to 350°F (180°C). Bake until puffed and golden brown, 30–40 minutes. Remove to a wire rack and let cool for 5 minutes. Cut into pieces and serve.

½ lb (250 g) sweet or hot pork sausages, casings removed and meat crumbled

1 yellow onion, finely chopped

1 cup (3 oz/90 g) slivered dry-packed sun-dried tomatoes

8 large eggs

2 cups (16 fl oz/500 ml) whole milk

½ teaspoon salt

¼ teaspoon freshly ground pepper

Unsalted butter for the pan

12 slices soft white bread, each ½ inch (12 mm) thick, crusts removed

¼ lb (125 g) cheddar cheese, grated

Fennel Sausage and Egg Tartlets

For the pastry

1 cup (5 oz/155 g) all-purpose (plain) flour

½ teaspoon salt

½ cup (4 oz/125 g) cold unsalted butter, cut into ½-inch (12-mm) pieces

1 large egg, lightly beaten

For the filling

½ lb (250 g) fennel sausages, casing removed and meat crumbled

4 large eggs

Salt and freshly ground pepper

2 tablespoons grated Parmesan cheese

1 tablespoon chopped fresh flat-leaf (Italian) parsley

BY HAND: To make the pastry, in a large bowl, combine the flour and salt. Scatter the butter pieces over the flour mixture. Using a fork, toss to coat with the flour. Using a pastry blender or 2 knives, cut in the butter until the mixture resembles coarse sand. Drizzle with the egg and toss with the fork until the dough is evenly moist and begins to come together in a smooth mass.

BY FOOD PROCESSOR: To make the pastry, combine the flour and salt, and pulse 2 or 3 times to mix. Add the butter pieces and process until the mixture resembles coarse sand, about 10 seconds. Add the egg and process just until the dough gathers into a ball around the blades, about 15 seconds.

Turn the dough out onto a lightly floured work surface and form into a disk. Wrap tightly in plastic wrap and refrigerate until well chilled, about 2 hours or for up to overnight.

Cut the dough into 4 equal pieces. On a lightly floured work surface, roll each piece into a 5-inch (13-cm) round. Line four 4½-inch (11.5-cm) tartlet pans with the dough. Refrigerate until chilled, about 30 minutes or for up to overnight.

Position a rack in the middle of the oven, and preheat to 375°F (190°C). Line each chilled tartlet with aluminum foil and fill with dried beans, uncooked rice, or ceramic or metal pie weights. Bake until the pastry begins to turn light brown, about 20 minutes. Remove the weights and foil. Return the tartlets to the oven and bake until the pastry is dried out and lightly browned, 5–7 minutes. Transfer to a wire rack.

Meanwhile, make the filling: In a large frying pan over medium-high heat, cook the sausage meat, breaking it up with a wooden spoon, until no trace of pink remains, 10–12 minutes. Transfer to paper towels to drain.

Scatter one-fourth of the sausage over the bottom of each tartlet, then top each with 1 egg. To prevent the egg yolks from breaking, crack each egg into a saucer, then slide it onto the sausage in each tartlet. Season with salt and pepper. Bake until the pastry is golden brown and the eggs are set, 15–20 minutes. Remove from the oven and sprinkle with the Parmesan cheese and parsley, dividing evenly. Serve at once.

Delicate pastry shells filled with sausage and eggs make an elegant first course for a formal brunch. The pastry can be prepared in stages over three days: make the dough one day, roll it out and line the pans the next day, and bake the third day. Other favorite sausages can be substituted for the fennel sausages.

Flank Steak Hash with Bell Peppers

The word "hash" is used for a multitude of preparations that combine chopped meat and potatoes—some are crispy and others are soft, some are thinly sauced and others are creamy. This colorful version calls for flank steak, a relatively lean beef cut; a mix of bell peppers; and a toasty bread crumb topping that gives the finished dish an appealing crunchy texture.

Position a rack in the middle of the oven, and preheat to 375°F (190°C). Butter a 2-qt (2-l) baking dish.

In a frying pan over medium-high heat, warm the oil. Add the onion, bell peppers, and cumin and cook, stirring frequently, until the vegetables are softened, 5–7 minutes. Add the potatoes, reduce the heat to medium, cover, and cook, stirring often, until they are almost tender but still hold their shape, about 15 minutes. When you stir, be sure to scrape the bottom of the pan to ensure the potatoes don't stick. Add 1 tablespoon of water if the pan becomes too dry.

Stir in the steak and tomatoes, raise the heat to medium-high, and cook, stirring frequently, until the meat shows no traces of pink, 3–5 minutes. Stir in the cream and season with salt and pepper. Transfer to the prepared baking dish. (At this point, the hash can be covered tightly and refrigerated for up to 1 day before baking.)

Position a rack in the middle of the oven, and preheat to 375°F (190°C). Sprinkle the *panko* evenly over the hash and drizzle with the melted butter. Bake until the top is golden brown and the hash is heated through, about 15 minutes (or a little longer if the dish has been refrigerated). Serve at once.

Unsalted butter

2 tablespoons olive oil

1 yellow onion, chopped

1 red bell pepper (capsicum), seeded and chopped

1 yellow bell pepper (capsicum), seeded and chopped

1 green bell pepper (capsicum), seeded and chopped

1 teaspoon ground cumin

3 Yukon gold potatoes, about 1 lb (500 g) total weight, cut into ½-inch (12-mm) dice

1 lb (500 g) flank steak, cut into ½-inch (12-mm) dice

2 tomatoes, peeled, seeded, and chopped

2 tablespoons heavy (double) cream

Salt and freshly ground pepper

1½ cups (6 oz/185 g) *panko* or Herbed Bread Crumbs (page 277)

½ cup (4 oz/125 g) unsalted butter, melted

Noodles with Ginger-Garlic Sauce

2 tablespoons peanut oil

1 teaspoon red pepper flakes

2 large cloves garlic, minced

2 tablespoons minced fresh ginger

3 tablespoons Asian sesame oil

2 tablespoons soy sauce

1½ tablespoons balsamic vinegar

1½ tablespoons sugar

2 tablespoons salt

1 lb (500 g) fresh thin Chinese egg noodles

12 green (spring) onions, white and pale green parts, thinly sliced

2 tablespoons sesame seeds

⅓ cup (½ oz/15 g) coarsely chopped fresh cilantro (fresh coriander)

In a small frying pan over medium heat, warm the peanut oil. Add the red pepper flakes and cook, stirring, until the oil turns slightly red and the pepper flakes are fragrant. Add the garlic and ginger and cook, stirring, until fragrant and slightly soft, about 1 minute. Remove from the heat. In a small bowl, whisk together the sesame oil, soy sauce, balsamic vinegar, and sugar. Whisk in the ginger mixture. Season the sauce with salt.

Bring a large pot three-fourths full of water to a boil. Add the salt and the noodles, stir well, and cook until al dente, 2–3 minutes. Drain and rinse under cold running water until cold. Drain thoroughly, then transfer to a large bowl.

Add the sauce and toss to coat the noodles. Add the green onions, reserving about 2 tablespoons for garnish. Toss to mix. Cover and let stand at room temperature, 1–2 hours, tossing occasionally so the noodles absorb the seasonings evenly.

Just before serving, in a small, dry frying pan over medium heat, toast the sesame seeds, stirring frequently, until fragrant and lightly colored, about 5 minutes. Pour onto a plate to cool. Add the sesame seeds and cilantro to the noodles, reserving 2 tablespoons of the cilantro for garnish. Transfer to a large platter. Garnish with the reserved green onions and cilantro and serve at once.

This Asian-inspired cold noodle dish is refreshing on a warm day. It goes together quickly and then must sit for a while, leaving you plenty of time to assemble the other elements of your menu. Sliced cucumbers dressed with rice vinegar, a light green salad, or cubed papaya tossed with fresh lime juice would make a good side dish. Look for the Chinese egg noodles in the cold case of an Asian grocery or a well-stocked supermarket.

Pasta with Arugula, Cherry Tomatoes, and Goat Cheese

Here, pleasantly peppery arugula is nicely balanced by sweet cherry tomatoes. Almost any short tubular or curled pasta shape, such as penne, *garganelli,* or *mostaccioli,* can be used. Accompany the pasta with room-temperature asparagus or green beans dressed with a vinaigrette and coarse country bread.

Bring a large pot three-fourths full of water to a boil. Add 2 tablespoons salt and the pasta and cook according to package directions until al dente. Drain the pasta, reserving about ¼ cup (2 fl oz/60 ml) of the cooking water, and place the pasta in a warmed serving bowl. Mix in the arugula and keep warm.

Just before the pasta is ready, in a large frying pan over medium-high heat, warm the olive oil. Add the tomatoes and, holding the pan handle, roll the tomatoes around by jerking the pan toward you, then pushing it away. Sprinkle with the garlic and keep the tomatoes moving until their skins crack, 1–3 minutes. Remove from the heat and season lightly with salt. Spoon the tomatoes over the pasta.

Dollop the goat cheese, 1 tablespoon at a time, on top of the tomatoes. Using a large fork and spoon, toss to combine, adding 1 or 2 tablespoons, or more, of the cooking water if the pasta seems dry. Season with pepper and serve at once.

Salt

¾ lb (375 g) fusilli, short ziti, or *cavatappi*

2 cups (2 oz/60 g) loosely packed arugula (rocket) leaves

1 tablespoon olive oil

2 cups (12 oz/375 g) cherry tomatoes

1 clove garlic, minced

¼ cup (1 oz/30 g) crumbled fresh goat cheese

Freshly ground pepper

Salads and Side Dishes

About Salads and Side Dishes

Sweet or savory, hot or chilled, these recipes Include choices for any menu. Serve a fruit salad with pancakes or waffles, or partner a soup or side dish with eggs. A substantial seafood or vegetable salad makes an ideal main dish, accompanied by homemade or fresh bread.

In addition to the diversity of options in this chapter, you'll appreciate the ease with which the recipes can be prepared or assembled. Preparation also goes smoothly when you are familiar with basic techniques. Individual recipes provide detailed instructions for many specific procedures, such as cutting oranges into sections, trimming fennel bulbs, peeling peaches, and toasting nuts. Here are others that will help speed your work and contribute to the success of each dish.

WASHING GREENS

Especially if a salad will stand on a buffet table, the greens need to remain crisp. Taking care when you wash the greens is the most important step for ensuring that a salad does not turn soggy shortly after being tossed with dressing. After discarding any damaged leaves, immerse the leaves in a bowl of cool water. Carefully lift them out, then repeat with a bowl of clean water until the water is clear when the leaves are removed. Dark greens such as spinach and escarole tend to hold sand and dirt and therefore may require several rinsings.

Greens need to be dried thoroughly—but also carefully to avoid crushing or bruising them. A salad spinner, if you have one, works best. Another option is enclosing them in a clean kitchen towel and shaking the towel gently. If you are cleaning a large quantity of greens, do them in batches.

Parsley, mint, and other leafy herbs should be similarly washed and dried. Dry them well or they will stick to the knife when chopped.

PREPARING VEGETABLES

Before bell peppers (capsicums) can be chopped, diced, or otherwise cut, the unusable parts need to be removed so they don't affect the taste and texture of a dish. Cut the pepper in half lengthwise from stem to base. Once the interior is exposed, you can pull out the stem from each half with your fingers or cut it out with a small knife. Next, pull off the seeds and trim the white ribs.

Chiles are trimmed in the same way as peppers. It is important to remove the seeds and membranes, as these parts carry the most heat. Capsaicin, the compound responsible for this heat, can also irritate the skin. To protect your hands, wear gloves, and after you have finished, wash the cutting board and knife.

Shallots, which add a subtle onion flavor to recipes, are often minced into fine pieces. If the shallot has multiple parts, separate them. After peeling the shallot, trim each end, leaving some of the root end intact to facilitate cutting. With the shallot flat side down, make a series of thin lengthwise cuts, again leaving the root end intact. Make thin cuts horizontally and then crosswise. Discard the root end. Gather the pieces and chop them until very fine.

Asparagus spears must be trimmed before cooking, as the bases tend to be woody. Hold the spear in both hands and bend until it breaks, which is always where the tough base meets the tender section. Depending on the spear's thickness, the skin can be tough. If this is the case, use a vegetable peeler to remove the skin to within 2 inches (5 cm) of the tip.

COOKING AND PURÉEING POTATOES

Potatoes of many varieties are often cooked for use in salads or prior to being incorporated into another recipe. Whether cooked whole or in pieces, they should be tender throughout but not falling apart. You should be able to pierce the potatoes with a table fork or a long metal skewer.

Potatoes made into a richly textured soup (page 235) or baked into a gratin (page 240) are mashed or puréed. If you want to preserve some texture in the finished dish, press the potatoes against the side of the pan with a table fork. For a smoother consistency, use a potato masher. If you prefer a still finer texture, pass the cooked potatoes through a food mill or potato ricer.

READYING FRUITS

Strawberries require minimal preparation, but you want to be sure to remove the white center cores along with the leaves. A strawberry huller, a tool resembling a wide pair of tweezers, will do both with one motion. You can also cut out the core with a small paring knife.

The fastest way to remove skin from an apple is with a vegetable peeler but a small paring knife will also work. You can cut out the core with a small knife, but using a melon baller is more efficient. After cutting the apple in half lengthwise, insert the baller in the center, turn it, and remove the core.

Apples and avocados quickly turn brown when exposed to air. After cutting, use them immediately, or place in a bowl and toss with a tablespoon or two of lemon juice to halt oxidation. Acidic ingredients, such as lemon juice and vinegar, will prevent other fruits and vegetables from discoloring as well, such as the artichokes in the salad on page 220.

Mango, Pineapple, and Papaya Salad

Fruit salad makes a refreshing side dish to a variety of breakfast and brunch classics, such as waffles, pancakes, and eggs and sausages or bacon. Here, tropical fruits, which are typically in the market year-round, are featured. When choosing mangoes and papayas, look for fruits that yield slightly to a gentle touch. A ripe pineapple will be fragrant, have deep green leaves, and give slightly when pressed.

Using a vegetable peeler, peel the papayas. Cut the papayas in half and scoop out and discard the seeds. Cut the flesh into 1/2-inch (12-mm) cubes. Place in a bowl.

Stand the mango on one of its narrow sides, with the stem end facing you. Position a sharp knife about 1 inch (2.5 cm) from the stem and cut down the length of the fruit, just missing the large pit. Repeat on the other side of the pit. Remove the peel from each half. Cut the flesh into 1/2-inch (12-mm) cubes. Add to the bowl.

If the leafy top is still on the pineapple half, lay the pineapple half on its side and cut off the top with the sharp knife. Stand the pineapple on its base and cut away the skin in long, vertical strips. Don't try to cut deeply enough to remove the brown "eyes" at the same time or you will remove too much flesh. Lay the pineapple on its side again and cut shallow furrows in the flesh to remove the eyes. Cut the pineapple half in half lengthwise, cut away the fibrous core, and cut the flesh into 1/2-inch (12-mm) cubes. Add to the bowl.

Pour the lime juice over the fruit and turn gently to coat. Serve at once. The salad may also be covered and refrigerated for up to 4 hours before serving.

2 papayas

1 mango

1/2 small pineapple, about 1 lb (500 g)

Juice of 3 limes

Grilled Fruit Salad

2 mangoes

½ small pineapple, about 1 lb (500 g)

2 nectarines

2 tablespoons lemon-infused olive oil

¼ cup (2 fl oz/60 ml) heavy (double) cream

1 teaspoon red wine vinegar

1 tablespoon sugar

Prepare a charcoal or gas grill for direct grilling over medium-high heat, or preheat a broiler (grill). Oil the grill rack.

Stand the mango on one of its narrow sides, with the stem end facing you. Using a sharp knife, cut slices 1 inch (2.5) thick on each side of the pit. Remove the peel from the slices. Place the slices in a bowl.

If the leafy top is still on the pineapple half, lay the pineapple half on its side and cut off the top with the sharp knife. Stand the pineapple on its base and cut away the skin in long, vertical strips. Don't try to cut deeply enough to remove the brown eyes at the same time or you will remove too much flesh. Lay the pineapple on its side again and cut shallow furrows in the flesh to remove the eyes. Cut the pineapple half in half lengthwise, cut away the fibrous core, and cut the flesh into ½-inch (12-mm) pieces. Add to the bowl.

Cut each nectarine in half and remove the pit. Cut each half in half again and add to the bowl. Drizzle the fruit with the 2 tablespoons olive oil and turn gently to coat evenly.

In a small bowl, whisk together the cream, vinegar, and sugar. Set aside.

BY GRILL: Arrange the fruit in a single layer in a grill basket. Place over the hottest part of the fire or directly over the heat elements and grill, turning once or twice, until the surface of the fruit begins to caramelize, about 5 minutes total.

BY BROILER: Arrange the fruit in a single layer on a baking sheet and place in the broiler about 6 inches (15 cm) from the heat source. Broil (grill), turning once or twice, until the surface of the fruit begins to caramelize, about 5 minutes total.

Arrange the fruit on a platter and drizzle with the cream mixture. Serve at once.

When fruit is grilled, the flesh softens and some of the natural sugars caramelize, creating an added layer of flavor that is reminiscent of the fruit in a deep-dish pie. Here, grilled fruits are combined in a warm salad drizzled with a creamy tart-sweet dressing. Almost any kind of fruit in season can be cubed, sliced, halved, and quartered, then grilled. If you can't find lemon-infused olive oil add a few drops of fresh lemon juice to 2 tablespoons olive oil.

Summer Fruit with Lime-Mint Sugar

The addition of lime zest to sugar adds a pleasant tartness to this refreshing salad. To prevent the mint leaves from discoloring when cut, snip them with scissors rather than mince them with a knife. Make the lime-mint sugar no more than an hour before serving the salad, as the aromatic oil in the zest quickly loses its potency.

In a small bowl, stir together the sugar, minced mint, and lime zest. Set aside.

In a bowl, combine the nectarines, peaches, and melon. Cut the grapes in half, and add to the bowl. Drizzle the fruit with the lime juice and stir gently to coat. Sprinkle with the sugar mixture and turn the fruit once or twice to coat evenly.

Transfer to a serving bowl and serve at once.

1/4 cup (2 oz/60 g) sugar

2 tablespoons minced fresh mint

2 teaspoons grated lime zest

2 *each* nectarines and peaches, halved, pitted, and cut into slices 1/2 inch (12 mm) thick

1/2 cantaloupe or other melon, seeded, peeled, and cut into 1/2-inch (12-mm) cubes

1 cup (6 oz/185 g) seedless grapes

Juice of 1 lime

Broiled Grapefruit
with Brown Sugar

3 grapefruits, halved

6 tablespoons (2½ oz/75 g) firmly packed light brown sugar

Preheat a broiler (grill). Line a baking sheet with aluminum foil.

Arrange the grapefruit halves, cut sides up, on the prepared sheet. Sprinkle each half with 1 tablespoon of the brown sugar. Place in the broiler about 4 inches (10 cm) from the heat source. Broil (grill) until the sugar has melted and is bubbling, 2–3 minutes. Transfer to a platter or individual bowls and serve at once.

Any grapefruit variety may be used for this old-fashioned dish. It was traditionally made with white grapefruits, which are slightly more tart than the currently popular pink and ruby grapefruits. If desired, use a serrated knife to separate the segments before broiling the fruit.

Strawberries and Kiwifruits
with Spinach

6 kiwifruits

2 teaspoons minced shallots

3 teaspoons white balsamic vinegar

1 teaspoon raspberry vinegar

2 teaspoons orange-infused or regular olive oil

2 cups (8 oz/250 g) strawberries, hulled and thinly sliced

1 cup (1 oz/30 g) baby spinach leaves

Peel and thinly slice the kiwifruits. Set aside.

Put the shallots in the bottom of a salad bowl. Add the balsamic and raspberry vinegars and the olive oil, and whisk to blend.

Add the strawberries and spinach and toss gently to coat. Add the kiwifruits and toss again. Serve at once.

Strawberries, kiwifruits, and spinach make a colorful combination. Red-leaf or green-leaf lettuce, or mixed salad greens, can be used instead of spinach. Other fruit pairings would work well, such as peaches, plums, melons, and figs. If using peaches or figs, choose fruits that are just slightly underripe.

Peaches and Raspberries in Almond Syrup

When fruit is macerated in syrup, they flavor each other, and the syrup takes on the color of the fruit. Here, the syrup becomes a lovely pale rose. Serve the peaches and raspberries on their own or spooned over waffles.

In a saucepan over medium-high heat, bring 2 cups (16 fl oz/500 ml) water and the sugar to a boil, stirring to dissolve the sugar. Cook until a thin syrup forms, about 5 minutes. Remove from the heat, stir in the almond extract, and set aside.

Bring a saucepan of water to a boil over high heat. Using a small, sharp knife, cut a shallow X in the blossom end of each peach. Immerse the peaches in the boiling water for 30 seconds. Lift out with a slotted spoon and let cool. Starting at the X, slip off the skins with your fingers or the knife. Cut each peach in half and remove the pit.

Place the peach halves in a large bowl. Add the raspberries. Pour the warm almond syrup over the fruit and let stand, turning gently several times, until the fruit is flavored with the syrup and the syrup is rosy red, about 3 hours. The fruit can be prepared up to 2 days ahead, covered, and stored in the refrigerator; bring to room temperature before serving.

Spoon the fruit into individual bowls. Add a little of the syrup and top with the toasted almonds, dividing them evenly. Place a dollop of Raspberry Whipped Cream (if using) on each serving. Serve at once.

1 cup (8 oz/250 g) sugar

2 teaspoons almond extract

4 peaches

4 cups (1 lb/500 g) raspberries

1/4 cup (1 oz/30 g) slivered blanched almonds, toasted (page 277)

Raspberry Whipped Cream (page 276), optional

Beet, Orange, and Fennel Salad

4 red or golden beets, about ¹/₂ lb (250 g) total weight

2 teaspoons olive oil

2 oranges

1 fennel bulb

2 tablespoons orange-infused olive oil

1 teaspoon red wine vinegar

1 teaspoon balsamic vinegar

¹/₂ teaspoon salt

¹/₄ teaspoon freshly ground pepper

8–12 red-leaf or other delicate lettuce leaves

¹/₂ cup (2 oz/36 g) grated pecorino cheese

¹/₄ cup (1 oz/30 g) slivered almonds, toasted (page 277)

Position a rack in the middle of the oven, and preheat to 350°F (180°C). If the beet greens are still attached, cut them off, leaving ¹/₂ inch (12 mm) of the stems attached. Place in a single layer in a shallow baking dish. Drizzle with the olive oil and turn to coat. Roast, turning occasionally, until tender when pierced with a fork, about 1¹/₄ hours. When cool enough to handle, remove the skins with your fingers. Cut each beet into quarters.

Cut a thick slice off the top and bottom of each orange. Stand the orange upright and, following the contour of the fruit, carefully slice downward to remove the peel, pith, and membrane. Holding the orange over a bowl, cut along each section of the membrane, letting each freed section drop into the bowl. Strain the oranges, reserving 2 teaspoons of the juice.

Cut off the stems and feathery leaves from the fennel bulb. Discard the outer layer of the bulb if it is tough. Quarter the bulb lengthwise and cut away any tough base portions. Cut the fennel into slices about ¹/₄ inch (6 mm) thick. Add to the bowl.

Add the beets to the bowl with the reserved orange juice, the orange-infused olive oil, red wine and balsamic vinegars, salt, and pepper. Turn to coat.

Place 2 lettuce leaves on each individual plate. Top with the beet mixture, dividing it evenly, and spoon some of the juices from the bowl over the salad. Sprinkle with the cheese and toasted almonds, again dividing evenly. Serve at once.

The combination of beet, orange, and fennel is perfect for a wintertime brunch. Any type of beet can be used, but keep in mind that red beets can color your fingers. To avoid stains, wear rubber gloves when peeling them. Chioggia beets, with their concentric red and white rings, bleed only slightly, and golden beets not at all. The flavors are quite similar, with golden beets slightly milder than the other two varieties.

Goat Cheese and Mesclun Salad

This classic salad, with its crisp goat cheese rounds, is a longtime restaurant standard. Look for a log-shaped fresh goat cheese, often simply labeled chèvre, and use a sharp, thin-bladed knife to ensure neat rounds.

To make the vinaigrette, in a small bowl, whisk together the olive oil, vinegar, and shallot. Season with salt and pepper. Let the vinaigrette stand for 30 minutes.

Meanwhile, position a rack in the middle of the oven and preheat to 325°F (165°C). Spread the walnuts in a single layer in a pie pan. Toast, stirring occasionally, until the nuts are fragrant and their color deepens, about 5 minutes. Remove from the oven and let cool, then coarsely chop.

Spread the bread crumbs on a plate. Using a thin-bladed knife, cut the goat cheese into 4 rounds of uniform thickness. Brush each round with 1 teaspoon of the olive oil. Place in the bread crumbs and turn to coat evenly.

In a large bowl, combine the mesclun and the walnuts. Add the vinaigrette and toss to coat evenly. Divide among individual plates.

In a frying pan over medium heat, warm the remaining 4 teaspoons olive oil. Add the goat cheese rounds and cook until nicely browned, 45–60 seconds. Turn and cook until nicely browned on the second sides, 45–60 seconds longer. Do not allow the cheese to burn or melt.

Place 1 round on each plate. Season with pepper and serve at once.

For the vinaigrette

3 tablespoons extra-virgin olive oil

1 tablespoon Champagne vinegar

1 shallot, finely minced

Salt and freshly ground pepper

½ cup (2 oz/60 g) walnuts

¼ cup (1 oz/30 g) fine dried bread crumbs

½ lb (250 g) fresh goat cheese without rind

8 teaspoons extra-virgin olive oil

6 cups (6 oz/185 g) mesclun greens

Hearts of Romaine with Garlic Croutons

Hearts of romaine, the small, paler yellow leaves in the center of the large heads, are crunchy and tender, with a distinctive flavor that stands up well to assertive flavors, such as the blue cheese in the dressing and the garlic in the croutons here. Escarole (Batavian endive) and frisée, lightly bitter members of the chicory family, can be substituted for the romaine.

To make the croutons, position a rack in the middle of the oven, and preheat to 350°F (180°C).

Place the baguette slices on a baking sheet. Drizzle with half of the olive oil. Turn and drizzle with the remaining oil. Bake until golden, about 10 minutes. Turn and bake until golden on the second sides, 5–7 minutes. Remove from the oven and use a fork or your fingers to rub both sides with the garlic. Break each slice into several pieces, making rough croutons. Set aside.

In a bowl, combine the olive oil and blue cheese. Using a fork, mash the blue cheese into the oil to make a creamy dressing. Stir in the vinegar.

Cut each romaine heart lengthwise into quarters. Place on a platter or on individual plates. Drizzle generously with the dressing, dividing it evenly over the salad. Sprinkle with the parsley and top with the garlic croutons. Serve at once.

For the croutons

8 slices baguette, about ½ inch (12 mm) thick, crusts trimmed

1½ tablespoons extra-virgin olive oil

3 cloves garlic

¼ cup (2 fl oz/60 ml) extra-virgin olive oil

2 oz (60 g) blue cheese, crumbled

1½ tablespoons red wine vinegar

2 large hearts of romaine (cos) lettuce

¼ cup (⅓ oz/10 g) minced fresh flat-leaf (Italian) parsley

Smoked Trout Salad

The use of almond oil and lemon juice in the vinaigrette for this salad echoes the flavors of trout amandine, a classic dish of sautéed trout topped with lightly browned almonds and lemon. Smoked trout is available in most well-stocked supermarkets, sometimes with added seasoning such as dill or lemon, either of which would work here. If you can't find white balsamic vinegar, regular may be substituted.

Using a small knife and working from the base of each Belgian endive head, cut out the core. Cut each head lengthwise into slices ¼ inch (6 mm) thick. Set aside.

Remove the tough stems from the watercress, reserving the leaves and tender stem clusters. Set aside several sprigs for use as a garnish.

In a bowl, whisk together the almond oil, lemon juice, white balsamic vinegar, pepper, and salt. Add the Belgian endives, watercress, and tarragon and toss gently to coat.

Mound the Belgian endive mixture on individual plates or a platter and top with the smoked trout. Garnish with the watercress sprigs and serve at once.

2 heads Belgian endive (chicory/whitloof)

2½ bunches watercress

1½ tablespoons almond oil

2 teaspoons fresh lemon juice

1 teaspoon white balsamic vinegar

½ teaspoon freshly ground white pepper

¼ teaspoon salt

¼ cup (⅓ oz/10 g) chopped fresh tarragon

4 or 5 smoked trout fillets, about 1 lb (500 g) total weight, torn into bite-sized pieces

Crab Salad with Tarragon Vinaigrette

2 bunches watercress

3 tablespoons extra-virgin olive oil

2 tablespoons white wine vinegar

3 teaspoons minced fresh tarragon

½ teaspoon salt

½ teaspoon freshly ground white pepper

Juice of ½ lemon

½ Granny Smith apple, peeled and cored

¾ lb (375 g) cooked lump crabmeat, picked over for shell fragments

2½ tablespoons snipped fresh chives

4 large red-leaf lettuce leaves

Remove the tough stems from the watercress, reserving the leaves and tender stem clusters. Set aside several sprigs for use as a garnish.

In a large bowl, whisk together the olive oil, vinegar, tarragon, salt, and pepper until blended. Set aside.

Fill a bowl with water and add the lemon juice. Cut the apple into strips ½ inch (12 mm) thick and 2 inches (5 cm) long. Place the strips in the lemon water.

Place the crabmeat in a bowl and, using a fork or your fingers, separate it into pieces a little smaller than bite-size. Drizzle with the vinaigrette and add the chives. Drain the apple strips and pat dry. Add them to the crab mixture and toss gently to combine. Add the watercress and toss again.

Place 1 lettuce leaf on each individual plate. Top with the crab mixture, dividing it evenly. Garnish with the watercress sprigs and serve at once.

The small amount of apple in this salad adds a hint of sweetness that mirrors the sweetness of the crab and also contributes a subtly crunchy texture. Peppery watercress spices up the salad, but mixed salad greens or butter (Boston) lettuce can be used for a milder version. The tarragon vinaigrette, with its hint of citrus, pairs well with almost any green.

Cannellini Bean Salad with Grilled Radicchio and Tuna

In this Italian-inspired salad, bitter radicchio, softened slightly by grilling, is paired with the small white beans popular in Tuscan cooking. Another Italian bean, borlotti, may be substituted. If you don't have time to soak the beans in cold water, bring the beans and water to a boil and simmer for 2 minutes, then remove from the heat, cover, and let stand for 1 hour. Alternatively, 3 cups (18 oz/560 g) canned beans, rinsed and warmed over medium-low heat, can be used.

To prepare the beans, pick over them and discard any misshapen beans or grit. Rinse the beans, put them in a bowl, add water to cover by about 3 inches (7.5 cm), and let soak for at least 4 hours or for up to overnight.

Drain the beans. Place them in a saucepan and add water to cover. Bring to a boil over high heat. Add the olive oil, garlic, and sage, cover, reduce the heat to low, and simmer gently until the beans are tender but not falling apart, about 1 hour. Remove from the heat and let stand for 10 minutes.

Prepare a charcoal or gas grill for direct grilling over medium-high heat, or preheat a broiler (grill). Oil the grill rack.

Cut each radicchio head into 4–6 wedges through the core, so that the wedges will keep their shape. Brush with olive oil and season with salt and pepper.

BY GRILL: Using tongs, place the radicchio wedges over the hottest part of the fire or directly over the heat elements and grill, turning once, until wilted and lightly browned, about 5 minutes total.

BY BROILER: Arrange the radicchio wedges in a single layer on a rimmed baking sheet and place in the broiler about 6 inches (15 cm) from the heat source. Broil (grill), turning once, until wilted and lightly browned, about 5 minutes total

Drain the beans well and place in a bowl. Add the celery, onion, oregano, 2 tablespoons olive oil, and 1 tablespoon of the lemon juice. Season with salt and pepper. Toss well. Taste and adjust the seasoning with more lemon juice, salt, and pepper.

Arrange the radicchio wedges on a platter. Spoon the beans in the center and top with the tuna. Serve at once.

For the beans

1 rounded cup (8 oz/250 g) dried cannellini beans

2 tablespoons olive oil

1 or 2 cloves garlic

1 fresh sage sprig

2 small heads radicchio

2 tablespoons olive oil, plus extra for brushing

Salt and freshly ground pepper

1 cup (5 oz/155 g) chopped celery, including some leaves

½ small red onion, chopped

Pinch of dried oregano

1–2 tablespoons fresh lemon juice

1 can (7 oz/220 g) olive oil-packed tuna, drained and separated into chunks

Niçoise Salad

6 small, waxy potatoes

20–24 baby green beans

½ lemon

6 baby artichokes (optional)

15–18 young fava (broad) beans, (optional)

½ lb (250 g) fresh tuna, or 1 can (7 oz/220 g) olive oil–packed tuna

3 tablespoons olive oil, for cooking fresh tuna

1 head butter (Boston) lettuce, leaves separated

9 small tomatoes, cut into wedges

1 red bell pepper (capsicum), seeded and cut into strips

1 small English (hothouse) cucumber, sliced

12 olive oil-packed anchovy fillets, halved lengthwise

⅔ cup (3 oz/90 g) Niçoise olives

12 fresh basil leaves, torn

For the vinaigrette

¾ cup (6 fl oz/180 ml) extra-virgin olive oil

3–4 tablespoons fresh lemon juice or red wine vinegar

2 cloves garlic, crushed

Salt and freshly ground pepper

6 hard-boiled eggs, quartered

Bring a saucepan three-fourths full of water to a boil. Add the potatoes and cook until tender, about 10 minutes. Drain, place under cold running water until cool, and drain again. Cut into slices ¼ inch (6 mm) thick. Set aside.

Refill the saucepan three-fourths full of water and bring to a boil. Trim the green beans, add them to the boiling water, and cook until tender, 2–3 minutes. Drain, place under cold running water until cool, and drain again. Set aside.

Squeeze the juice from the lemon half into a bowl of cold water. If using artichokes, working with 1 artichoke at a time, and using a sharp knife, slice off the top half or so of the leaves. Starting at the base, pull off and discard the tough outer leaves. Then pull off the outside leaves until you reach the pale green inner leaves. Cut off the stem and trim the base, and then cut the artichoke in half lengthwise. Using a small spoon, scrape out the prickly fibers, or choke, from the center, and then drop the halves into the lemon water.

Bring a saucepan three-fourths full of water to a boil. Drain the artichokes, add them to the boiling water, reduce the heat so the water is at a gentle boil, cover, and cook until the artichokes are tender when pierced with the tip of a knife, 10–15 minutes, depending on their size. Drain, place under cold running water until cool, and drain again. Set aside.

If using fava beans, bring a saucepan three-fourths full of water to a boil. Add the fava beans and blanch for 1 minute. Drain, place under cold running water until cool, and drain again. Using a small knife or your fingertips, slit the skin of each bean and squeeze to remove the bean from the skin. Set aside.

If using fresh tuna, cut into 1-inch (2.5-cm) chunks. In a large frying pan over high heat, warm the olive oil. Add the tuna slices and cook, turning once, until seared lightly, about 2 minutes total. Let cool and cut into 2-inch (5-cm) pieces. If using canned tuna, drain and separate into large flakes.

Line a large, wide bowl or platter with the lettuce. Arrange the potatoes, green beans, tomatoes, bell pepper, cucumber, anchovies, and tuna on the lettuce. Add the artichokes, and fava beans, if using. Garnish with the olives and basil.

To make the vinaigrette, in a bowl, whisk together the olive oil, lemon juice to taste, and garlic. Season with salt and pepper.

Pour the vinaigrette over the salad. Top with the eggs and serve at once.

The versions of this renowned French salad are infinite, but nearly all include lettuce, tomatoes, potatoes, green beans, eggs, anchovies, and Niçoise olives. Tuna is another typical addition, and this recipe offers the option of using fresh tuna, if it is available, or canned tuna in olive oil, a preference in many traditional salads.

Lobster with Grapefruit and Avocado

The grapefruit juice in the vinaigrette, along with the grapefruit sections in the salad, accent the sweetness of the succulent lobster. Smooth, creamy avocado adds a hint of richness. If using frozen lobster tails, allow enough time to thaw them overnight in the refrigerator.

If using frozen lobster tails, bring a large pot three-fourths full of water to a boil over high heat. Meanwhile, fill a large bowl with ice. Add the 1 tablespoon salt and lobster tails and boil until the shells are bright red and the meat is almost opaque throughout, about 8 minutes. Using tongs, transfer the lobster tails to a large colander, cover with ice, and let stand for 30 minutes. The quick cooling causes the flesh to pull away from the shells, making it easier to remove the meat.

Remove the lobster meat from the shells. Cut the cooked, frozen or fresh lobster meat into generous bite-sized pieces. Set aside.

Meanwhile, cut a thick slice off the top and bottom of the grapefruit. Stand the grapefruit upright and, following the contour of the fruit, slice downward to remove the peel, pith, and membrane. Holding the grapefruit over a bowl, cut along each section of the membrane, letting each freed section drop into the bowl. Strain the grapefruit, reserving 2 teaspoons of the juice.

In a large bowl, whisk together the 2 teaspoons grapefruit juice, 2 tablespoons of the vinegar, 2 tablespoons of the olive oil, the $\frac{1}{2}$ teaspoon salt, pepper, shallot, and 3 teaspoons of the chives. Add the lobster meat and turn gently until well coated.

Divide the greens among individual plates or shallow bowls. Arrange the grapefruit sections on the greens, dividing them evenly. Top with the lobster mixture and then with the avocado. Add the remaining $1\frac{1}{2}$ tablespoons olive oil and remaining $\frac{1}{2}$ tablespoon vinegar to the bowl, mix well, and drizzle over the salads. Garnish with the remaining 2 teaspoons chives and serve at once.

1 tablespoon salt, plus $\frac{1}{2}$ teaspoon

$1\frac{1}{2}$ lb (750 g) cooked lobster meat, picked over for shell fragments, or 5 frozen lobster tails, thawed and halved lengthwise

Ice

1 grapefruit

$2\frac{1}{2}$ tablespoons Champagne vinegar

$3\frac{1}{2}$ tablespoons extra-virgin olive oil

$\frac{1}{2}$ teaspoon freshly ground pepper

2 teaspoons minced shallot (about $\frac{1}{2}$ small shallot)

5 teaspoons snipped fresh chives

2–$2\frac{1}{2}$ cups (2–3 oz/60–90 g) mixed young greens

1 avocado, halved, pitted, peeled, and cut into $\frac{1}{2}$-inch (12-mm) cubes

Warm Escarole, Egg, and Bacon Salad

2 heads escarole (Batavian endive)

3 tablespoons extra-virgin olive oil

2 tablespoons red wine vinegar

½ teaspoon salt

½ teaspoon freshly ground pepper

6 slices bacon, cut into ½-inch (12-mm) pieces

1 teaspoon fresh lemon juice

4 large eggs

Remove the outer dark green leaves from each head of escarole and reserve for another use. Separate the inner pale yellow leaves. You should have 5 cups (15 oz/470 g). Tear the leaves into bite-sized pieces.

In a large bowl, whisk together the olive oil, vinegar, salt, and pepper. Add the escarole, but do not toss.

In a frying pan over medium heat, fry the bacon, stirring, until crisp, 4–5 minutes. Using a slotted spoon, transfer to paper towels to drain.

Add the bacon pieces to the bowl, toss the salad, and divide among 4 individual plates or shallow bowls.

Pour water to a depth of 2 inches (5 cm) into a large saucepan and add the lemon juice. Place over medium heat and bring to a gentle simmer. Break 1 egg into a small bowl. Hold the bowl so it is just touching the simmering water and slide the egg into the water. Quickly repeat with the remaining eggs, one at a time, spacing them about 1 inch (2.5 cm) apart. Adjust the heat to keep the water at a gentle simmer. Cook until the whites are set and the yolks are glazed over but still soft, 4–5 minutes. Using a slotted spoon, lift each egg from the simmering water, letting the excess water drain into the pan. Drain briefly on paper towels. Trim any ragged edges of egg white with kitchen scissors.

Top each salad with a poached egg and serve at once.

This is a classic French bistro dish, perfect for brunch. The eggs are poached until the whites are firm. The yolks are just barely cooked, so that, when broken, they run over the escarole (Batavian endive) leaves and combine with the vinaigrette. Frisée, the curly-leafed relative of escarole, may be substituted for the escarole. Or you can use a mixture of the two. For a bit of spice, add some arugula (rocket).

Curried Chicken Salad

The addition of spices, such as cayenne pepper and turmeric, bring an Asian flavor to this chicken salad. For a spicier curry, add a little more cayenne pepper. The salad can be served as is or used as a filling for halved avocados.

Season the chicken breasts with ¹/₂ teaspoon of the salt and ¹/₂ teaspoon of the pepper. In a frying pan over medium-high heat, warm the olive oil. Add the chicken breasts, skin sides down, and cook until golden, about 5 minutes. Add the rosemary, turn the chicken breasts over, and cook until brown on the second sides, 4–5 minutes longer. Pour in the wine and stir, scraping up any browned bits from the pan bottom. Add ¹/₄ cup (2 fl oz/60 ml) water, cover, reduce the heat to low, and cook, adding more water if necessary, until the chicken is opaque throughout, about 35 minutes. Set aside and let cool. The chicken can be cooked ahead, covered, and refrigerated overnight. Remove the skin from the chicken breasts and discard. Remove the meat from the bones and cut into ¹/₂-inch (12-mm) cubes. Set aside.

In a bowl, whisk together the mayonnaise, yogurt, crème fraîche, cumin, cayenne, turmeric, the remaining ¹/₂ teaspoon salt, and the remaining ¹/₂ teaspoon pepper. Add the chicken, celery, onion, chopped parsley, and nuts (if using). Turn to coat with the mayonnaise mixture.

Transfer the salad to a serving bowl or platter and garnish with the parsley sprigs. Serve at once.

3 skin-on, bone-in chicken breast halves, about 1¹/₂ lb (750 g) total weight

1 teaspoon salt

1 teaspoon freshly ground black pepper

2 teaspoons olive oil

3 fresh rosemary sprigs, each 2 inches (5 cm) long

¹/₂ cup (4 fl oz/125 ml) dry white wine such as Sauvignon Blanc or Pinot Grigio

¹/₄ cup (2 fl oz/60 ml) mayonnaise

¹/₄ cup (2 oz/60 g) plain nonfat yogurt

3 tablespoons crème fraîche (page 276)

1 teaspoon ground cumin

¹/₄ teaspoon cayenne pepper

¹/₂ teaspoon ground turmeric

5 celery stalks, finely chopped

¹/₂ small yellow onion, finely chopped

¹/₄ cup (¹/₃ oz/10 g) chopped fresh flat-leaf (Italian) parsley, plus sprigs for garnish

¹/₄ cup (1 oz/30 g) chopped almonds or cashews (optional)

Peas with Pancetta, Mint, and Ricotta Salata

5 lb (2.5 kg) English peas, shelled

1½ teaspoons salt

2 thin slices pancetta, chopped

1 tablespoon extra-virgin olive oil

1 teaspoon raspberry vinegar

½ teaspoon freshly ground pepper

2 tablespoons finely chopped fresh mint, plus sprigs for garnish

¼ lb (125 g) ricotta salata cheese, crumbled

Bring a large pot three-fourths full of water to a boil over high heat. Add the peas and 1 teaspoon of the salt and cook until the peas are barely tender, about 2 minutes. Drain, place under cold running water until cool, and drain again. Set aside.

In a frying pan over medium heat, cook the pancetta, stirring, until lightly crisped, 4–5 minutes. Using a slotted spoon, transfer to paper towels to drain.

In a large bowl, whisk together the olive oil, vinegar, pepper, and the remaining ½ teaspoon salt. Add the peas, pancetta, and mint and turn to coat. Stir in half of the ricotta salata cheese.

Transfer the salad to a serving bowl. Garnish with the remaining ricotta salata cheese and the mint sprigs. Serve at once.

Fresh English peas, full of natural sugars, are a specialty of spring. This simple salad showcases them with fried pancetta, aromatic mint, and ricotta salata, juxtaposing sweet and salty flavors without overpowering the peas. Look for young, tender pods that are plump with whole peas that will need only brief cooking.

Carrot Soup with Crème Fraîche Toasts

Brioche is a light, airy bread often used to make toasts and croutons for refined dishes, such as this puréed carrot soup. Look for brioche in a well-stocked market or bakery. Or, if you like, you can make your own (page 119). The soup and toasts can be prepared a day ahead. Store the soup, covered, in the refrigerator, then reheat before serving. Keep the toasts in an airtight container at room temperature. While the soup reheats, top the toasts with the crème fraîche.

Position a rack in the middle of the oven, and preheat to 350°F (180°C).

Cut each bread slice on the diagonal to make 8 triangles. Place in a single layer on a baking sheet. Bake until golden brown, 12–15 minutes, turning halfway through baking. Remove and set aside.

In a large saucepan over medium-high heat, warm the olive oil. Add the shallots and cook, stirring, until translucent, about 2 minutes. Stir in the carrots, pour in the stock, and bring to a boil. Reduce the heat to low, cover, and cook until the carrots are tender, about 20 minutes. Remove from the heat, uncover, and let the soup stand for 15 minutes to cool slightly.

Using an immersion blender, purée the soup in the pan until smooth. Alternatively, working in batches, purée the soup in a standing blender or food processor until smooth. Reheat the soup over medium heat. Season with salt and pepper.

Spoon the crème fraîche on each toast triangle, dividing it evenly. Ladle the soup into warmed bowls and float 2 toasts on each serving. Serve at once.

4 slices brioche or other firm, slightly sweet bread, about ¼ inch (6 mm) thick, crusts trimmed

1 tablespoon olive oil

2 large shallots, minced

1½ lb (750 g) carrots, peeled and coarsely chopped

6 cups (48 fl oz/1.5 l) chicken stock

Salt and freshly ground pepper

4 teaspoons crème fraîche (page 276)

Gazpacho with Serrano Chiles

4 large red bell peppers (capsicums), about 1½ lb (750 g) total weight

1¼ lb (625 g) tomatoes

½ English (hothouse) cucumber, peeled and cut into large chunks

½ yellow bell pepper (capsicum), seeded and cut into ¼-inch (6-mm) dice

2 serrano chiles, seeded and minced

1 small red onion, finely chopped

1 clove garlic, minced

2 tablespoons extra-virgin olive oil, plus extra for drizzling

1 tablespoon sherry vinegar

1 teaspoon salt

1 avocado, halved, pitted, peeled, and cut into ¼-inch (6-mm) cubes

1 tablespoon snipped fresh chives

½ teaspoon dried oregano

Preheat a broiler (grill). Arrange the red bell peppers on a baking sheet and place in the broiler about 6 inches (15 cm) from the heat source. Broil (grill), turning with tongs, until the skin is blistered and charred black on all sides, about 15 minutes. Place the peppers in a paper bag and let stand until cool enough to handle. Remove the stem from each pepper and discard. Slit the pepper open, then remove and discard the seeds and ribs. Remove the blackened skin with a small knife.

Cut the tomatoes in half crosswise. Using the largest holes on a box grater placed over a bowl, grate the tomato halves. Discard the skins. In a food processor, pulse the cucumber chunks until coarsely puréed. Add to the bowl. Process the roasted peppers until coarsely puréed. Add to the bowl. Stir in the yellow bell pepper, chiles, onion, garlic, 2 tablespoons olive oil, vinegar, and salt. Cover and refrigerate until slightly chilled.

Ladle the chilled gazpacho into individual glasses or bowls and garnish with the avocado, dividing it evenly. Sprinkle with the chives and oregano, and drizzle with olive oil. Serve at once.

Gazpacho is a thick, flavorful soup from the Andalusia region of Spain. It usually has a tomato base, is thickened with bread crumbs, and is always served cold. Here, it is spiced up with hot serrano chiles. Serve with a simple mixed green salad and pour a cold Spanish white wine, such as an Albariño or a Verdejo.

Potato-Rosemary Soup

Crushing the cooked potatoes instead of puréeing them gives the soup an interesting texture. There is no milk or cream in this soup, but it is no less flavorful. Fresh thyme can be substituted for the rosemary. To add sweetness, cook the minced white and light green parts of a leek or two with the shallot.

In a large saucepan over medium heat, warm the olive oil. Add the shallot and cook, stirring, until translucent, 1–2 minutes. Pour in the broth and bring to a boil. Add the potatoes, half of the minced rosemary, the bay leaf, and pepper. Cover partially, reduce the heat to low, and simmer until the potatoes are tender when pierced with a fork, 15–20 minutes.

Remove the pan from the heat and discard the bay leaf. Using a fork or potato masher, crush the potatoes into small chunks. Season with salt.

Ladle the soup into warmed bowls. Sprinkle with the remaining minced rosemary, dividing it evenly. Serve at once.

2 teaspoons olive oil

½ small shallot, minced

6 cups (48 fl oz/1.5 l) chicken broth

1 lb (500 g) Yukon gold or other potatoes, peeled and cut into large pieces

1 teaspoon minced fresh rosemary, plus sprigs for garnish

1 bay leaf

¼ teaspoon freshly ground pepper

Salt

Herb-Roasted Red Potatoes

12–15 small red potatoes, about 2 inches (5 cm) in diameter

3 tablespoons olive oil

1 teaspoon salt

½ teaspoon freshly ground pepper

4 or 5 fresh rosemary sprigs, about 3 inches (7.5 cm) long

6 fresh sage sprigs

In this dish, the potatoes are roasted long enough for the skins to wrinkle slightly, indicating that they are smooth and creamy on the inside. The rosemary sprigs and the sage sprigs, even if very dark and crisp, can be presented with the potatoes as a crunchy, edible garnish. Served at room temperature, the potatoes are a good choice for a buffet.

Position a rack in the middle of the oven, and preheat to 350°F (180°C).

Place the potatoes in a shallow baking dish just large enough to hold them snugly in a single layer. Pour the olive oil over the potatoes and turn several times to coat well. Sprinkle evenly with the salt and pepper and turn again. Tuck the rosemary and sage sprigs under the potatoes.

Roast the potatoes until the skins are slightly wrinkled and the potatoes are tender when pierced with a fork, about 1¼ hours.

Transfer to a serving bowl and serve hot or at room temperature.

Potatoes Lyonnaîse

This is a takeoff on the classic French dish of browned potato slices, caramelized onion slices, butter, and parsley. Here, the butter is mixed with olive oil for a slightly lighter result. Serve these potatoes with nearly any dish.

Place the potatoes in a large pot and add water to cover by 3 inches (7.5 cm). Add 1 tablespoon of the salt, bring to a boil, cover, reduce the heat to medium-low, and cook until tender when pierced with a fork, about 30–35 minutes. Drain, place under cold running water until cool, and drain again. Let cool completely. Cut the potatoes into slices ½ inch (12 mm) thick. Refrigerate until ready to do the second cooking.

In a large frying pan over medium-high heat, melt 2 tablespoons of the butter with 3 tablespoons of the olive oil. Add the sliced potatoes in a single layer, sprinkle with 1½ teaspoons of the salt, and cook until golden, 7–8 minutes. Turn, sprinkle with the remaining 1½ teaspoons salt, and cook until golden on the second side, about 5 minutes. Transfer to paper towels to drain.

In another frying pan over medium-high heat, melt the remaining 3 tablespoons butter with the remaining 2 tablespoons olive oil. Add the onions and cook, stirring, until soft and browned, about 15 minutes. Add the potatoes and stir gently just to combine the two.

Transfer the potatoes and onions to a warmed platter or bowl. Serve at once.

8–10 medium-sized Yukon gold or white potatoes, about 2½ lb (1.25 kg) total weight

2 tablespoons salt

5 tablespoons (2½ oz/75 g) unsalted butter

5 tablespoons (2½ fl oz/ 75 ml) olive oil

1 lb (500 g) yellow onions, thinly sliced

Sweet Potato Gratin with Pecans

⅓ cup (3 oz/90 g) pecan halves

4 thin slices prosciutto, about 2 oz (60 g) total weight, cut into ½-inch (12-mm) strips

4 sweet potatoes, 1½–2 lb (750 g–1 kg) total weight, cut into slices about 1 inch (2.5 cm) thick

2 tablespoons unsalted butter

¼ cup (2 fl oz/60 ml) crème fraîche (page 276)

½ teaspoon salt

½ teaspoon freshly ground pepper

Position a rack in the middle of the oven, and preheat to 350°F (180°C). Spread the pecans in a single layer in a pie pan. Toast, stirring occasionally, until the nuts are fragrant and barely golden, 10–12 minutes. Remove from the oven and let cool. Raise the oven temperature to 400°F (200°C).

In a frying pan over medium-high heat, cook the prosciutto, stirring, until crisp, 2–3 minutes. Set aside.

Place the sweet potato slices in a single layer in the top of a double boiler set over boiling water. Cover and steam the potatoes until tender when pierced with a fork, 10–15 minutes. When the slices are cool enough to handle, peel them and transfer to a bowl. Using a fork or potato masher, mash the potatoes until nearly smooth. Add 1 tablespoon of the butter, crème fraîche, salt, and pepper and stir to blend. Stir in the prosciutto. Spread the sweet potato mixture in a shallow 1–1½ qt (1–1.5 l) baking dish.

Coarsely chop the pecans. Sprinkle the chopped pecans over the sweet potato mixture. Cut the remaining 1 tablespoon butter into bits and dot the top.

Bake until the butter has melted, the top has formed a lightly golden crust, and the sweet potatoes are hot throughout, about 20 minutes. Serve at once.

Either type of sweet potato—the red-skinned, orange-fleshed variety and the tan-skinned, meaty yellow ones sometimes sold as yams—can be used to make this gratin. The latter will produce a thicker, denser dish than the former, which will be thinner and creamier. Serve as part of a breakfast buffet or alongside eggs and bacon.

Roasted Asparagus with Balsamic Glaze and Lemon Zest

Roasting asparagus spears with a little balsamic vinegar and lemon zest gives them a deep, almost smoky flavor and an attractive mahogany glaze. Serve the asparagus as a side dish for Ham and Cheddar Omelet (page 69), Ham, Leek, and Gruyère Quiches (page 61), or sausages and eggs. They can also be included on the menu for any breakfast or brunch buffet.

Position a rack in the middle of the oven, and preheat to 450°F (225°C).

Spread the asparagus in a baking dish large enough to hold them in a single layer. Drizzle with the balsamic vinegar and olive oil and sprinkle with the salt and pepper. Turn the asparagus spears several times to coat them evenly.

Roast the asparagus for 10 minutes, turning from time to time. Remove from the oven, sprinkle with the lemon zest, and turn the spears several times. Return to the oven and continue to roast the asparagus until the spears are tender-crisp and the color has darkened slightly, about 5–7 minutes longer.

Transfer the asparagus to a platter and serve at once. The asparagus can also be allowed to cool, covered with aluminum foil, and left at room temperature for up to 1 hour before serving.

20–25 asparagus spears, tough ends removed

⅓ cup (3 fl oz/80 ml) balsamic vinegar

1 tablespoon olive oil

½ teaspoon salt

½ teaspoon freshly ground pepper

2 teaspoons grated lemon zest

Herbed Sausage with Spicy Mustard

For the spicy mustard

1 cup (8 oz/250 g) Dijon mustard

2 tablespoons snipped fresh chives

1 teaspoon hot brown mustard

For the sausage

1¾ lb (875 g) boneless pork butt, cut into large chunks

3 tablespoons minced fresh sage

¼ cup (⅓ oz/10 g) minced fresh flat-leaf (Italian) parsley

2 tablespoons minced yellow onion

2 tablespoons Dijon mustard

2 teaspoons peppercorns

1 teaspoon mustard seed

1½ teaspoons salt

1½ tablespoons olive oil

To make the spicy mustard, in a small bowl, stir together the Dijon mustard, chives, and brown mustard. Cover and set aside.

To prepare the sausage, working in batches, pulse the pork in a food processor until coarsely ground. Transfer to a large bowl. Add the sage, parsley, onion, and Dijon mustard. Using a spice grinder or a mortar with a pestle, grind the peppercorns and mustard seed to a fine to medium texture. Add the ground spices and salt to the pork mixture. Using a wooden spoon, mix well to combine. Shape the mixture into patties about 4 inches (10 cm) in diameter and ½ inch (12 mm) thick. You will have 10–12 patties.

In a large frying pan over medium-high heat, warm the olive oil. Add the sausage patties and cook until browned, 3–4 minutes. Turn and cook until browned on the second sides, 3–4 minutes longer. Using a slotted spatula, transfer to paper towels to drain briefly.

Arrange the sausage patties on a warmed platter. Serve at once, accompanied by the spicy mustard.

A food processor is handy for grinding meat in small amounts for making sausage. Here, the pork is flavored with sage and parsley, two common sausage seasonings, but you can vary the herbs according to what you like, such as basil, thyme, or tarragon. You can also select a different mustard. These sausages are especially good with sliced heirloom tomatoes and Scrambled Eggs with Spinach and White Cheddar Cheese (page 53).

Fennel Sausage Patties

Fennel seed is a traditional spice in Italian sausages, which are made with pork. These patties, made with chicken, include both minced fresh fennel as well as fennel seeds for added flavor and texture. Chicken breast meat is quite lean, so bacon is added to provide the fat needed for moisture and so the patties will hold together when they are shaped and cooked.

Cut off the stems and feathery leaves from the fennel bulb. Discard the outer layer of the bulb if it is tough, and cut away any discolored areas. Quarter the bulb lengthwise and cut away any tough base portions. Mince the fennel.

In a frying pan over medium-high heat, warm the 2 teaspoons olive oil. Add the fennel, sprinkle with the pinch of salt, and cook, stirring, until translucent and soft, 3–4 minutes. Remove from the heat. When the fennel is cool enough to handle, transfer to a paper towel and squeeze out the moisture. Place in a large bowl.

Using a box grater set over a bowl, grate the apples. Working in batches, place the grated apples on a paper towel and squeeze out the moisture. Set aside.

Working in batches, pulse the chicken in a food processor until coarsely ground. Add to the fennel. Pulse the bacon until coarsely ground and add to the chicken-fennel mixture. Using your hands or a wooden spoon, mix well to combine. Using a spice grinder or a mortar with a pestle, grind the fennel seed, coriander seed, peppercorns, 1 1/2 teaspoons salt, and nutmeg until finely ground. Add the ground spices, cayenne, and grated apples to the mixture. Mix well until combined. Shape the mixture into patties about 4 inches (10 cm) in diameter and 1/2 inch (12 mm) thick. You will have 10–12 patties.

In a large frying pan over medium-high heat, warm the 2 tablespoons olive oil. Add the sausage patties and cook until browned, 3–4 minutes. Turn and cook until browned on the second sides, 3–4 minutes longer. Using a slotted spatula, transfer to paper towels to drain briefly.

Arrange the patties on a warmed platter and serve at once.

1 small fennel bulb

**2 teaspoons plus
2 tablespoons olive oil**

**Pinch of salt, plus
1 1/2 teaspoons**

**2 Granny Smith apples,
peeled and cored**

**1 1/2 lb (750 g) skinless,
boneless chicken breasts,
cut into large chunks**

1/4 lb (125 g) bacon

2 teaspoons fennel seed

1 teaspoon coriander seed

2 teaspoons peppercorns

**1/2 teaspoon freshly ground
nutmeg**

1/2 teaspoon cayenne pepper

Bacon with Brown Sugar and Cardamom

2 lb (1 kg) thick-sliced lean bacon

³⁄₄ cup (6 oz/185 g) firmly packed golden brown sugar

¹⁄₂ teaspoon ground cardamom

¹⁄₂ teaspoon freshly ground pepper

Position a rack in the upper third of the oven and another rack in the lower third, and preheat to 350°F (180°C). Line the bottom and sides of 2 rimmed baking sheets with aluminum foil.

Arrange the bacon slices in a single layer on the prepared pans. In a small bowl, toss together the brown sugar, cardamom, and pepper. Sprinkle the mixture evenly over the bacon slices.

Place 1 pan on the upper rack and the other pan on the lower rack. Bake the bacon, without turning, for 25 minutes. Switch the position of the pans and rotate them 180 degrees. Continue to bake the bacon, without turning, until dark brown but not quite crisp, 10–15 minutes longer. Using tongs, lift the bacon slices from the pans, gently shaking off the excess drippings, and transfer them to paper towels to drain briefly.

Arrange the bacon on a warmed platter and serve at once.

Almost everyone likes bacon, but seasoning it with brown sugar and fragrant cardamom and baking it in the oven puts this breakfast mainstay over the top. These flavorful slices are the perfect accompaniment to nearly any egg dish.

Cider-Glazed Sausage

Pork and apple are a traditional pairing. Here, a mixture of apple cider and honey is brushed on pork sausages during the final minutes of cooking to create a sweet glaze. If applied sooner, the sugar in the cider and the honey might burn. Hard cider is the first choice, but sweet cider may be substituted. Serve the sausages with eggs, Herb-Roasted Red Potatoes (page 236), or Sweet Potato Gratin with Pecans (page 240). They also make a tasty breakfast sandwich.

Position a rack in the middle of the oven, and preheat to 350°F (180°C). In a small bowl, stir together the cider and honey. Set aside.

In a large ovenproof frying pan over medium-high heat, melt the butter. When the butter foams, add the sausages and cook, turning occasionally, until browned, 7–8 minutes.

Brush the sausages with about one-third of the cider-honey mixture and place the pan in the oven. Bake, turning once at the midpoint, until the juices run nearly clear when a sausage is pierced with a fork, about 10 minutes. Brush the sausages with half of the remaining cider-honey mixture and continue to bake until a glaze forms, about 2 minutes. Brush with the remaining cider-honey mixture and bake for 2 minutes longer.

Transfer the sausages to a warmed platter and serve at once.

½ cup (4 fl oz/125 ml) hard or regular apple cider

2 tablespoons light honey

2 teaspoons unsalted butter

1½ lb (750 g) pork sausages

Sandwiches and Panini

About Sandwiches and Panini

Why not start the morning with a sandwich? Several fillings layered between bread slices make a complete dish in a handheld package. Two breakfast standards come together in a fried egg and ham sandwich. For a meal timed closer to lunch, serve slow-cooked pork tucked in a roll.

Sandwiches and panini are also suitable for any occasion. Tea sandwiches, small bites with salmon, cucumber, or chicken, are perfect for an elegant brunch. If you're holding your event outdoors, consider one of the sandwiches in this chapter with fillings cooked on the grill. Here are some tips for successful grilling and for making other sandwich components.

GRILLING BY TEMPERATURE

Cooking foods over a charcoal or gas grill gives them an irresistibly smoky flavor and succulent texture. On the following pages, hamburgers (page 269) and the fillings for two sandwiches—chicken (page 266) and vegetables (page 256)—are grilled. Even the rolls or bread slices for sandwiches can be toasted over hot coals.

All three recipes call for direct grilling over medium-high heat. The foods cook quickly, some as fast as just a few minutes per side. The key to achieving chicken breasts that are golden brown on the outside and succulent on the inside, or hamburgers that are lightly charred on the outside and medium-rare on the inside, is the careful monitoring of both the food and the heat level.

To prevent foods from drying out or burning, you can create different heat zones and move the food if you sense it is cooking too fast. For a charcoal grill, vary the depth of the coals when you distribute them on the grate. You can also raise or lower the grill rack, if it is adjustable. As a general guide for cooking over medium-high heat, arrange the coals

in 2 layers and place the rack 5 to 6 inches (13 to 15 cm) above them. Reserve part of the grate for a single layer of coals, and transfer the food to this lower-temperature area if it is cooking too fast. You can also create a low-heat area for keeping cooked foods warm.

If you don't have a special grill thermometer for checking the heat level, here is an easy way to gauge temperature: Carefully hold your hand about 4 inches (10 cm) over the fire. If you can keep your hand in place comfortably for 2 or 3 seconds, the fire is medium-hot.

For cooking over medium-high heat on a gas grill, heat zones are easily established by preheating all the elements to high and then adjusting one element to medium-high and another to low. If there is a third element, turn it off. Most gas grills have thermometers. Medium-high heat is 375°F (190°C). The same hand test above applies.

MAKING THE PERFECT AIOLI

Mayonnaise, horseradish, mustards, and other condiments add spark and richness to sandwich fillings. In this chapter, aioli, the French garlic-infused mayonnaise, is prepared with a slight variation—incorporating roasted red bell pepper (capsicum)—as a condiment for grilled chicken sandwiches (page 266).

Aioli is easy to make, providing you proceed slowly so that the finished sauce has the right consistency. The aim is to create an emulsion, a uniform blend of two or more liquids and other ingredients that remains stable and

does not separate. Emulsions must have an agent to help hold the ingredients together. For aioli, egg yolks act as the emulsifier.

The egg yolks, aromatics such as garlic, and seasonings such as herbs, are first combined in a blender and puréed. With the blender motor running, the liquid—extra-virgin olive oil—initially should be added drop by drop. Once the mixture begins to emulsify, you can start adding the oil in a slow, thin, steady stream. Be sure to avoid rushing the process by pouring in the remaining oil all at once, or the emulsion may break down.

TOASTED SANDWICHES

Panini, the diminutive of the Italian word *pan* or "bread," and translated as "little breads," refers to sandwiches in general and most often to cooked sandwiches that are compressed as they are grilled. Pressing a panino creates a crisp exterior and helps fuse the layers of filling, which often include melted cheese (pages 263 and 264).

After brushing them lightly on the outside with olive oil, the panini are placed in a preheated frying pan or grill pan. To press them using equipment you have on hand, select a frying pan of about the same diameter and set it on top of the panini. Then weight the pan with 2 or 3 cans of food, spacing them evenly so the pan won't be off-balance.

You can also purchase a cast-iron press. This roughly square plate, with a handle in the center, is preheated on the stove top, then is placed on top of the panini. Because the press is heavy, there's no need to weight it.

If you will be cooking panini regularly, you might appreciate an electric press, a countertop appliance that can be adjusted to hold panini of different thicknesses. Some models have nonstick surfaces for easy cleanup.

Tea Sandwiches

An array of delicate sandwiches makes an impressive presentation. The three sandwiches here, each with a distinctive filling, are easy to pick up with fingers and enjoy with a cup of tea or coffee. Accompany them with a selection of muffins, scones, and toast with butter and an assortment of jams. Shortbread and tea cookies are also good accompaniments.

SMOKED SALMON AND HORSERADISH–CREAM CHEESE SANDWICHES Set out the cream cheese and let soften. In a bowl, stir together the cream cheese and horseradish until thoroughly blended. Season with salt and pepper. Brush the salmon slices with the lemon juice and season with a little pepper.

Trim the crusts from 20 of the bread slices. Spread each of the bread slices with the cream cheese mixture. Divide the salmon evenly among the cheese-topped slices. Put the remaining bread slices on top and press gently. Cut each sandwich in half on the diagonal. Arrange the sandwiches on a platter and serve at once.

CUCUMBER-RADISH-CHIVE SANDWICHES In a large bowl, whisk together the vinegar, and olive oil. Season with salt and pepper. Add the cucumber and radishes and toss to coat. In a small bowl, stir together the butter and chives until thoroughly blended. Season with salt and pepper.

Trim the crusts from 20 of the bread slices. Spread each of the bread slices with the butter mixture. Divide the cucumbers and radishes evenly among the buttered slices. Put the remaining bread slices on top and press gently. Cut each sandwich in half on the diagonal. Arrange the sandwiches on a platter and serve at once.

LEMON-CHICKEN SALAD SANDWICHES Place the chicken in a small frying pan with cold water to cover. Season lightly with salt and pepper. Bring to a boil over high heat, reduce the heat to medium, and simmer the chicken until opaque throughout, 7–10 minutes. Using a slotted spoon, transfer to a plate and let cool. Use your fingers or 2 forks to pull the chicken into shreds.

In a bowl, whisk together the mayonnaise, lemon juice, celery, and green onion until blended and smooth. Fold in the chicken.

Trim the crusts from 20 of the bread slices. Spread each of the bread slices with mayonnaise. Divide the chicken mixture among 10 of the slices. Put the remaining bread slices on top and press gently. Cut each sandwich in half on the diagonal. Arrange the sandwiches on a platter and serve at once.

60 thin slices sandwich bread

Smoked Salmon and Horseradish–Cream Cheese

½ lb (250 g) cream cheese

2 tablespoons horseradish

Salt and freshly ground pepper

¾ lb (375 g) thinly sliced smoked salmon

2 teaspoons fresh lemon juice

Cucumber-Radish-Chive Spread

2 tablespoons *each* red wine vinegar and extra-virgin olive oil

Salt and freshly ground pepper

1 large cucumber, peeled and thinly sliced

10–12 radishes, thinly sliced

½ cup (4 oz/125 g) unsalted butter, softened

2 tablespoons snipped chives

Lemon-Chicken Salad

2 skinless, boneless chicken breast halves, 6 oz (185 g) each

Salt and freshly ground pepper

½ cup (4 fl oz/125 ml) mayonnaise

2 teaspoons fresh lemon juice

2 celery stalks, thinly sliced

3 green (spring) onions, white

Grilled Eggplant, Red Pepper, and Herbed Goat Cheese Sandwiches

2 tablespoons red wine vinegar

2 tablespoons olive oil

1 teaspoon chopped fresh thyme

1 teaspoon chopped fresh rosemary

1 clove garlic, minced

½ teaspoon salt

¼ teaspoon freshly ground pepper, plus extra for serving

½ large eggplant (aubergine), about ¾ lb (375 g), cut crosswise into slices ¼ inch (6 mm) thick

1 red bell pepper (capsicum)

4 large ciabatta rolls or crusty French rolls, split

¼ lb (125 g) herbed fresh goat cheese, softened

8–12 large fresh basil leaves

In a large bowl, whisk together the vinegar, olive oil, thyme, rosemary, garlic, salt, and pepper. Add the eggplant slices and turn to coat. Let marinate at room temperature for 1 hour.

Prepare a charcoal or gas grill for direct grilling over medium-high heat, or preheat a broiler (grill). Oil the grill rack.

BY GRILL: Using tongs, set the bell pepper over the hottest part of the fire or directly over the heat elements and grill, turning with the tongs, until the skin is blistered and charred black on all sides, about 15 minutes. Enclose the pepper in a paper bag and let stand until cool enough to handle. Remove the eggplant slices from the marinade and place over the hottest part of the fire or directly over the heat elements and grill, turning once, until softened, about 10 minutes total. Transfer to a plate and keep warm. Place the rolls, cut side down, over the hottest part of the fire or directly over the heat elements and grill until toasted, 1–2 minutes.

BY BROILER: Set the bell pepper on a baking sheet and place in the broiler about 6 inches (15 cm) from the heat source. Broil (grill), turning with tongs, until the skin is blistered and charred black on all sides, about 15 minutes. Enclose the pepper in a paper bag and let stand until cool enough to handle. Remove the eggplant slices from the marinade and arrange in a single layer on the baking sheet. Broil, turning once, until softened, about 10 minutes total. Transfer to a plate and keep warm. Place the rolls, cut sides up, on the baking sheet and broil until toasted, 1–2 minutes.

Remove the stem from the pepper and discard. Slit the pepper open, then cut away and discard the ribs and seeds. Remove the blackened skin with a small knife or your fingers. Cut lengthwise into ¼-inch (6-mm) strips.

Spread the bottom halves of the rolls with the goat cheese. Divide the eggplant slices among the rolls and top with the bell pepper strips. Season with salt and pepper. Lay 2 or 3 basil leaves on each sandwich. Put the tops of the rolls in place. Cut each sandwich in half or into quarters. Arrange on individual plates and serve at once.

Use any type of herbed fresh goat cheese you like. Or, you can make your own by mixing 3 tablespoons minced fresh chives, parsley, chervil, thyme, or basil, or a mixture, into plain goat cheese.

Albacore Tuna, Hard-Boiled Egg, and Tapenade Sandwiches

The combination of tuna, eggs, anchovies, and olives recalls *pain bagna,* a sandwich sold on the streets of Nice in the south of France. The sandwiches are best when made at least an hour ahead, so the flavors can meld and infuse the bread.

To make the tapenade, in a food processor, combine the olives, anchovies, capers, and garlic. With the motor running, drizzle in the olive oil. Continue to process, stopping to scrape down the sides of the bowl as necessary, until the tapenade is puréed but still coarse. Transfer to a small bowl and season with pepper.

In a bowl, stir together the tuna, vinegar, and olive oil. Season lightly with salt and pepper.

Cut the baguette crosswise into 4 equal sections and then split each section horizontally. Scoop out some of the soft interior from both sides.

Spread the tops and bottoms of the baguette sections evenly with the tapenade. Divide the tuna mixture among the bottoms, and top with the egg slices. Season to taste with salt and pepper. Put the tops of the baguette sections in place. Wrap each sandwich tightly in plastic wrap and let sit at room temperature for 1 hour to allow the flavors to blend. (The sandwiches can be made up to a day ahead, wrapped, and refrigerated, and then brought to room temperature before serving.)

Unwrap the sandwiches, place on individual plates, and serve at once.

For the tapenade

³/₄ cup (4 oz/125 g) pitted black olives such as Niçoise or Kalamata

6 olive oil-packed anchovy fillets, rinsed and patted dry

¹/₄ cup (2 oz/60 g) capers, drained and rinsed

1 clove garlic, chopped

¹/₃ cup (3 fl oz/80 ml) extra-virgin olive oil

Freshly ground pepper

2 cans (6 oz/185 g each) albacore tuna, preferably olive-oil packed

3 tablespoons red wine vinegar

2 teaspoons extra-virgin olive oil

Salt and freshly ground pepper

1 baguette, 22–24 inches (54–56 cm) long

3 hard-boiled eggs, peeled and thinly sliced

Crab, Peppered Bacon, and Tomato Sandwiches

1 red bell pepper (capsicum)

½ cup (4 fl oz/125 ml) mayonnaise or Aioli (page 277)

1 tablespoon chopped fresh tarragon

4 thick slices peppered bacon, about 6 oz (185 g) total weight

4 sandwich rolls or buns, split

2 tomatoes, cut into slices ¼ inch (6 mm) thick

1 small head butter (Boston) or Bibb lettuce, leaves separated

½ lb (250 g) cooked Dungeness crabmeat (about 1½ cups), picked over for shell fragments

Preheat the broiler (grill). Set the bell pepper on a rimmed baking sheet and place in the broiler about 6 inches (15 cm) from the heat source. Broil (grill), turning with tongs, until the skin is blistered and charred black on all sides, about 15 minutes. Enclose the pepper in a paper bag and let stand until cool enough to handle. Remove the stem from the pepper and discard. Slit the pepper open, then remove and discard the seeds and ribs. Remove the blackened skin with a small knife or your fingers. Finely chop the pepper and place in a small bowl. Add the mayonnaise and tarragon and stir to blend.

In a large frying pan over medium-high heat, fry the bacon until crisp, about 10 minutes. Spread the cut sides of the tops and bottoms of the rolls with the roasted pepper mixture, dividing it evenly. Top the bottom halves with the tomato slices and then the lettuce leaves. Divide the crabmeat evenly among the sandwiches, and then divide the bacon. Put the tops of the rolls in place.

The sweetness of crabmeat and the tomatoes complement the saltiness of the bacon in this summery sandwich. Purchase freshly cooked crabmeat, rather than canned or frozen, for the best flavor. If Dungeness is not available, look for lump blue crabmeat.

Turkey, Smoked Mozzarella, and Arugula Panini

Smoked mozzarella complements the mild turkey and tangy mustard in this takeoff on the Italian tradition of pressed sandwiches. If you have a panini press or a panini grill, use it as directed in the manufacturer's instructions. If not, you can easily weight these tasty sandwiches with a heavy pan and a couple of heavy objects, as described here.

Cut the loaf of bread crosswise into 4 equal sections and then split each section horizontally. Brush the cut sides with some of the olive oil. Spread the 4 bottoms with the mustard. Divide the turkey among the bottoms. Top with the mozzarella and then with the arugula. Put the top sections of bread in place.

Heat a grill pan or heavy frying pan over medium-high heat. Lightly brush the outside of the sandwiches with the olive oil. When the pan is hot, place 2 sandwiches in the center. Set another heavy pan on top of the sandwiches and place 2 or 3 heavy cans in the pan to weight it down evenly. Cook the sandwiches until lightly browned, about 3 minutes. Turn the sandwiches, weight them again, and cook until the sandwiches are browned on the second sides and the cheese is melting, about 3 minutes longer. Remove from the pan and keep warm while cooking the remaining 2 sandwiches the same way.

Place the sandwiches on individual plates and serve at once.

1 loaf Italian or French bread, about ³⁄₄ lb (375 g)

¹⁄₂ cup (4 fl oz/125 ml) olive oil

¹⁄₂ cup (4 oz/125 g) whole-grain mustard, or more to taste

¹⁄₂ lb (250 g) thinly sliced roasted turkey

¹⁄₂ lb (250 g) smoked mozzarella cheese, thinly sliced

1 small bunch arugula (rocket), stems removed, torn into large pieces

Smoked Ham, Cheddar Cheese, and Pear Panini

8 thick slices multigrain bread

½ cup (4 oz/125 g) whole-grain mustard

½ lb (250 g) thinly sliced smoked ham

1 Bartlett (Williams') pear, peeled, cored and cut into slices about ¼ inch (6 mm) thick

½ lb (250 g) medium-sharp cheddar cheese, thinly sliced

½ cup (4 fl oz/125 ml) olive oil

Brush the bread slices on one side with the mustard. Divide the ham evenly among 4 of the slices. Top with the pear slices and then with cheese. Top with the remaining bread slices, mustard side down.

Heat a grill pan or heavy frying pan over medium-high heat. Brush the outsides of the sandwiches with the olive oil. When the pan is hot, place 2 sandwiches in the center. Set another heavy pan on top of the sandwiches and place 2 or 3 heavy cans in the pan to weight it down evenly. Cook the sandwiches until lightly browned on the first sides, about 3 minutes. Turn the sandwiches, weight them again, and cook until browned on the second sides and the cheese is melting, about 3 minutes longer. Remove from the pan and keep warm while cooking the remaining 2 sandwiches the same way.

Cut the sandwiches in half, place on individual plates, and serve at once.

Here, the flavors of salty ham and sweet pears are nicely balanced by pungent mustard and a full-flavored cheddar cheese. If you can't find a Bartlett pear, a Comice or Anjou is a good substitute. Accompany the sandwiches with a simple tossed green salad. If you have a panini grill, use it as directed in the manufacturer's directions.

Grilled Chicken Sandwiches with Roasted Pepper Aioli

4 skinless, split boneless chicken breast halves, about 6 oz (185 g) each

Salt and freshly ground pepper

1 tablespoon fresh lemon juice

2 tablespoons extra-virgin olive oil

2 teaspoons chopped fresh thyme

For the aioli

1 small red bell pepper (capsicum)

1 large egg yolk

2 cloves garlic, minced

1 tablespoon fresh lemon juice

2 teaspoons Dijon mustard

1 teaspoon tomato paste

2 tablespoons chopped fresh flat-leaf (Italian) parsley

½ teaspoon salt

¼ teaspoon freshly ground pepper

¾ cup (6 fl oz/100 ml) extra-virgin olive oil

8 thick slices coarse country bread

Working with 1 chicken breast half at a time, place it between 2 sheets of waxed paper and, using a meat pounder, pound to an even thickness of ¾ inch (2 cm) thick. Season on both sides with salt and pepper. Place the breasts in a nonreactive dish large enough to hold them in a single layer. Add the lemon juice, olive oil, and thyme. Turn the breasts over several times to coat. Cover loosely with plastic wrap and let marinate at room temperature for 1 hour or in the refrigerator overnight.

To make the aioli, preheat a broiler (grill). Set the bell pepper on a baking sheet and place in the broiler about 6 inches (15 cm) from the heat source. Broil (grill), turning with tongs, until the skin is blistered and charred black on all sides, about 15 minutes. Enclose the pepper in a paper bag and let cool completely.

If broiling the chicken, leave the broiler on. If grilling the chicken, prepare a charcoal or gas grill for direct grilling over medium-high heat. Oil the grill rack.

Remove the stem from the pepper and discard. Slit the pepper open, then remove and discard the seeds and ribs. Remove the blackened skin with a small knife or your fingers. Coarsely chop the pepper. In a blender or food processor, combine the roasted pepper, egg yolk, garlic, lemon juice, mustard, tomato paste, parsley, salt and pepper. Process until puréed. With the motor running, add the olive oil drop by drop. As the mixture begins to emulsify, add the oil in a slow, steady stream. Continue to process until the aioli is thick and has the consistency of mayonnaise. The aioli can be made a day ahead and stored in an airtight container in the refrigerator.

BY BROILER: Remove the chicken breasts from the marinade and arrange in a single layer on a rimmed baking sheet. Broil until lightly browned, 3–5 minutes. Turn and broil until lightly browned on the second sides and firm to the touch, 3–5 minutes. Transfer to a plate. Place the bread on the baking sheet and toast, turning once, until golden, 3–5 minutes total.

BY GRILL: Remove the chicken breasts from the marinade and place over the hottest part of the fire or directly over the heat elements and grill until lightly browned, 3–5 minutes. Turn and grill until lightly browned on the second sides and firm to the touch, 3–5 minutes. Transfer to a plate. Place the bread slices on the grill rack and toast, turning once, until golden, about 2 minutes total.

Spread the bread slices with the aioli. Place the chicken breasts on 4 of the slices. Put the remaining bread slices on top. Halve the sandwiches and serve at once.

Traditional garlic-laced aioli is given a boost of color and flavor with the addition of smoky roasted bell pepper, tomato paste, and parsley. If you like, add avocado or tomato slices or curly lettuce leaves to the sandwiches. Any leftover aioli will keep, tightly covered, in the refrigerator for up to 3 days.

Fried Egg Sandwiches with Ham and Dijon Mustard

Ham and eggs are a classic breakfast combination, whether you are seated at the counter at the local diner or at your kitchen table. Here, this familiar pair is slipped between slices of bread spread with tangy Dijon mustard. You can use English muffins or soft rolls in place of the sandwich bread.

Spread the 8 bread slices with 2 tablespoons of the butter. Spread 4 of the butter-covered slices with the mustard. Divide the ham among the slices.

In a large frying pan over medium-high heat, melt the remaining 2 tablespoons butter. When the butter foams, break the eggs into the pan, spacing them about 2 inches (5 cm) apart. Reduce the heat to low and season the eggs with salt and pepper. Cover the pan and cook until the whites are set and the yolks begin to firm around the edges, 5–7 minutes. For eggs over easy, cook for $2^1/2$ minutes, then, using a slotted spatula, carefully turn the eggs over and cook the second sides for $2^1/2$ minutes.

Divide the eggs among the sandwiches, setting them on top of the ham. Put the remaining bread slices in place. Cut the sandwiches in half, arrange on individual plates, and serve at once.

8 thick slices sandwich bread

4 tablespoons (2 oz/60 g) unsalted butter, softened

2 tablespoons Dijon mustard, or to taste

$1/2$ lb (250 g) sliced ham

4 large eggs

Salt and freshly ground pepper

Hamburgers with Fried Eggs

In this version of "eggs on horseback," fried eggs top grilled hamburgers. The soft egg yolk in each sandwich breaks and seeps into the beef, making a heavenly combination of tastes and textures. Serve with Potatoes Lyonnaïse (page 239), simple fried potatoes, or seasoned tomatoes for a special morning treat.

In a bowl, combine the beef, salt, and pepper. Gently toss with a fork. Wet your hands and form 4 patties about ¾ inch (2 cm) thick. Place on a plate, cover, and refrigerate until ready to cook. The burgers can be prepared a day in advance, wrapped tightly, and kept in the coldest part of the refrigerator.

Prepare a charcoal or gas grill for direct grilling over medium-high heat, or preheat a broiler (grill). Oil the grill rack.

BY GRILL: Using tongs, place the hamburgers over the hottest part of the fire or directly over the heat elements and grill, turning once, until done to your liking, 5–7 minutes per side for medium-rare.

BY BROILER: Arrange the patties in a single layer on a rimmed baking sheet and place in the broiler about 6 inches (15 cm) from the heat source. Broil (grill), turning once, until done to your liking, 5–7 minutes per side for medium-rare.

Meanwhile, in a large frying pan over medium-high heat, melt the butter. When the butter foams, break the eggs into the pan, spacing them about 2 inches (5 cm) apart. Reduce the heat to low and season the eggs with salt and pepper. Cover the pan and cook until the whites are set and the yolks are just beginning to firm around the edge, about 5 minutes.

If desired, spread each bun or roll with aioli. Place the burgers on the bottoms of the warmed buns or rolls and set an egg on top of each burger. Sprinkle with salt and pepper. Put the tops of the rolls or buns in place. Arrange on individual plates and serve at once.

1½ lb (750 g) ground (minced) beef, preferably chuck

1 teaspoon salt

½ teaspoon freshly ground pepper

2 tablespoons unsalted butter

4 large eggs

Salt and freshly ground pepper

4 large rolls or hamburger buns, split and warmed

Aioli (page 277) or mayonnaise for topping the buns

Classic Reuben

For the dressing

1 cup (8 fl oz/250 ml) mayonnaise or Aioli (page 277)

¼ cup (2 fl oz/60 ml) ketchup

1 tablespoon chopped fresh flat-leaf (Italian) parsley

2 tablespoons green pickle relish

1 tablespoon grated yellow onion

1 teaspoon Worcestershire sauce, or to taste

Salt and freshly ground pepper

8 slices rye bread with caraway seeds

2 tablespoons unsalted butter, softened

1 lb (500 g) sliced corned beef

1 cup (8 oz/250 g) drained sauerkraut

4–8 slices Gruyère cheese

Stories about the invention of this iconic American sandwich vary. Some trace it to a grocer in Omaha, others to a restaurateur in New York. Although the exact origin cannot be verified, the inventor left his name on an enduringly popular combination of corned beef, sauerkraut, and cheese on rye bread moistened with Russian dressing and then grilled to a perfect finish. Any leftover dressing can be tightly covered and stored in the refrigerator for up to 5 days.

To make the dressing, in a bowl, stir together the mayonnaise, ketchup, parsley, relish, onion, and Worcestershire sauce until blended. Season to taste with salt and pepper. Cover and refrigerate until ready to serve.

Position a rack in the middle of the oven, and preheat to 425°F (220°C). Line a rimmed baking sheet with aluminum foil. Arrange the bread slices in a single layer on the prepared sheet. Toast, turning once or twice, until the slices are lightly browned, about 5 minutes total. While the toasted bread is still warm, spread each slice with butter.

Spread a generous amount of the dressing on the buttered sides of 4 bread slices. Divide the corned beef and sauerkraut evenly among the slices. Top evenly with the cheese. Put the remaining bread slices in place, buttered sides down, and press down gently.

Arrange the sandwiches on the baking sheet and bake until they are heated through and the cheese starts to melt, 5–7 minutes. If the tops are not sufficiently browned, turn on the broiler (grill) and briefly broil (grill) the sandwiches. Cut the sandwiches in half, place on individual plates, and serve at once.

Pulled Pork Sandwiches

Pulled pork, a specialty of North Carolina, calls for cooking the pork until the fibers break down and the meat is tender and easy to shred. The shredded pork is always simmered in a sauce before serving. Some cooks swear that the best sauce is vinegar based, while others contend that tomato sauce is better. The recipe here, using purchased barbecue sauce, is almost as good as the authentic hickory-smoked version but is much easier to prepare. You can ask the butcher to trim the pork shoulder and tie it for you. Traditional accompaniments are coleslaw, baked beans, potato salad, and lots of pickles.

In a large pot over medium-high heat, melt the butter with the canola oil. Add the pork and cook, turning frequently, until browned on all sides, 5–10 minutes. Transfer to a platter. Pour off all but 2 tablespoons of the fat. Return the pot to medium-high heat, add the onion and garlic, and cook, stirring, until the onion is slightly softened, about 2 minutes. Return the pork to the pot, add the broth, and season with salt and pepper. Cover, reduce the heat to medium, and cook the pork, turning occasionally, until very tender, about 2 hours. Transfer to a clean platter and let cool. Using clean hands or 2 forks, pull the meat apart into thin shreds. Remove and discard all the fat and gristle.

To make the sauce, in a large saucepan over medium-high heat, stir together the barbecue sauce, mustard, honey, soy sauce, salt, and pepper.

Add the pork to the sauce and cook uncovered, stirring frequently, until the pork is very soft and the flavors are blended, about 45 minutes.

Place the rolls, cut sides up, on individual plates. Divide the pork among the rolls, spooning it on the bottom halves. Put the tops of the buns or rolls in place and serve at once.

2 tablespoons unsalted butter

2 tablespoons canola oil

1 boneless pork shoulder, about 3 lb (1.5 kg), trimmed and tied

1 yellow onion, chopped

1 clove garlic, minced

1/2 cup (4 fl oz/125 ml) chicken broth

Salt and freshly ground pepper

For the sauce

2 cups (16 fl oz/500 ml) barbecue sauce

2 tablespoons Dijon mustard

2 tablespoons honey

1 tablespoon soy sauce

1/2 teaspoon salt

1/4 teaspoon freshly ground pepper

6 hamburger buns or large rolls, split and warmed

Basic Recipes

This collection of basics offers a wide variety of options such as flavored butters, syrups, jam, marmalade, and lemon curd to serve alongside your favorite breakfast and brunch recipes. Also included are staple recipes, such as pizza dough, and instructions for toasting nuts.

Orange Blossom Maple Syrup

1 cup (11 fl oz/345 ml) maple syrup

1½ teaspoons orange flower water

½ teaspoon vanilla extract

In a small saucepan over low heat, warm the maple syrup. Pour into a small bowl or pitcher and stir in the orange flower water and vanilla until well blended. Serve warm. Or, store in an airtight container in the refrigerator for up to 3 days. Warm over low heat before serving.

Makes 1 cup (8 fl oz/250 ml)

Blueberry Syrup

1¼ cups (5 oz/150 g) fresh or frozen blueberries

1½ teaspoons fresh lemon juice

1¼ cups (10 oz/315 g) sugar

Put the blueberries in a large bowl. Using a fork, crush them into a coarse purée. Transfer the crushed berries to a small, nonaluminum pan and place over medium-high heat. Stir in the lemon juice and sugar and bring to a boil, stirring occasionally. Boil for about 1 minute. Let cool, then strain through a fine-mesh sieve. Discard the pulp. Line the sieve with cheesecloth (muslin) and strain again. Pour into a small bowl or pitcher and serve at room temperature. Or, store in an airtight container in the refrigerator for up to 3 days.

Makes 1 cup (8 fl oz/250 ml)

Honey Butter

½ cup (4 oz/125 g) unsalted butter, at room temperature

¼ cup (3 fl oz/90 ml) honey

Pinch of salt

In a bowl, using a large spoon, vigorously stir together the butter, honey, and salt until blended smoothly. Transfer to a small bowl or to small individual ramekins and serve at room temperature. Or, store in an airtight container in the refrigerator for up to 5 days. Bring to room temperature before serving.

Makes ¾ cup (7 oz/220 g)

Orange Butter

½ cup (4 oz/125 g) unsalted butter, at room temperature

1 teaspoon finely grated orange zest

Pinch of salt

In a bowl, using a large spoon, vigorously stir together the butter, orange zest, and salt until blended smoothly. Transfer to a small bowl or to small individual ramekins and serve at room temperature. Or, store in an airtight container in the refrigerator for up to 5 days. Bring to room temperature before serving.

Makes ½ cup (4 oz/125 g)

Cinnamon Butter

½ cup (4 oz/125 g) unsalted butter, at room temperature

1 teaspoon ground cinnamon

Pinch of salt

In a bowl, using a large spoon, vigorously stir together the butter, cinnamon, and salt until blended smoothly. Transfer to a small bowl or to small individual ramekins and serve at room temperature. Or, store in an airtight container in the refrigerator for up to 5 days. Bring to room temperature before serving.

Makes ½ cup (4 oz/125 g)

Maple Butter

½ cup (4 oz/125 g) unsalted butter, at room temperature

¼ cup (3 fl oz/90 ml) maple syrup

Pinch of salt

In a bowl, using a large spoon, vigorously stir together the butter, maple syrup, and salt until blended smoothly. Transfer to a small bowl or to small individual ramekins and serve at room temperature. Or, store in an airtight container in the refrigerator for up to 5 days. Bring to room temperature before serving.

Makes ¾ cup (7 oz/220 g)

Brandy Butter

½ cup (4 oz/125 g) unsalted butter, at room temperature

2 tablespoons brandy

Pinch of salt

In a bowl, using a large spoon, vigorously stir together the butter, brandy, and salt until blended smoothly. Transfer to a small bowl or to small individual ramekins and serve at room temperature. Or, store in an airtight container in the refrigerator for up to 5 days. Bring to room temperature before serving.

Makes ¹/₂ cup (4 oz/125 g)

Berry Jam

2 teaspoons cornstarch (cornflour) dissolved in 3 tablespoons water

1 cup (4 oz/125 g) blueberries

1 cup (4 oz/125 g) blackberries

1 cup (4 oz/125 g) raspberries

3 tablespoons sugar

3-inch (7.5-cm) cinnamon stick

In a nonaluminum saucepan over medium heat, combine the dissolved cornstarch, blueberries, blackberries, raspberries, sugar, and cinnamon. Bring to a gentle boil and cook, stirring gently, until the jam thickens slightly and the liquid becomes clear, about 1 minute. Cover, reduce the heat to low, and cook at a gentle simmer for 3 minutes, adjusting the heat as necessary to maintain a simmer. Uncover and continue to simmer, stirring occasionally, for 2 minutes. Remove and discard the cinnamon stick. Serve warm. Or, the jam can be stored in an airtight container in the refrigerator for up to 3 days. Warm over low heat before serving.

Makes 2 cups (16 fl oz/500 ml)

Orange Marmalade

3 large Seville or navel oranges, quartered

1 lemon, quartered

3¹/₂–4 cups (28–32 oz/875 g–1 kg) sugar

Place the oranges and lemon in a nonaluminum pot, add 5¹/₂ cups (44 fl oz/1.25 l) water, and soak overnight. Remove the fruit and cut into

slices about ¹/₈ inch (3 mm) thick. Return the fruit to the pot and bring to a boil over high heat. Reduce the heat to medium-high and simmer uncovered, stirring occasionally, for 1 hour. Add the sugar, stirring until dissolved, and continue to boil until the fruit is tender. After about 20 minutes, the color will deepen to amber, and as the temperature rises, the bubbles will become smaller. Serve warm. Or, store in an airtight container in the refrigerator for up to 3 days. Warm over low heat before serving.

Makes about 4 cups (32 fl oz/1 l)

Strawberry-Rhubarb Compote

4 cups (1¹/₂ lb/750 g) coarsely chopped rhubarb stalks

¹/₄ cup (2 oz/60 g) sugar

1¹/₂ cups (6 oz/185 g) strawberries, hulled and halved

In a nonreactive saucepan over medium heat, combine the rhubarb, sugar, and ¹/₄ cup (2 fl oz/60 ml) water. Cook until the mixture begins to simmer and release liquid, about 10 minutes. Uncover and stir in the strawberries. Cook at a gentle simmer until the rhubarb is soft when pierced with a fork, about 10 minutes. Skim any foam from the top and discard. Serve warm. Or, store in an airtight container in the refrigerator for up to 3 days. Warm over low heat before serving.

Makes 1 cup (8 fl oz/250 ml)

Cranberry-Apple Compote

2 apples such as Granny Smith or Baldwin, peeled, cored, and cut into ³/₄-inch (2-cm) pieces

1 cup (4 oz/125 g) fresh or thawed, frozen cranberries

2 tablespoons sugar

¹/₂ cup (4 fl oz/125 ml) fresh orange juice

2 slices fresh ginger, about ¹/₄ inch (6 mm) thick

In a nonaluminum saucepan over medium heat, combine the apples, cranberries, sugar, orange juice, and ginger. Cover, bring to a simmer, and cook, stirring occasionally, until the apples are soft when pierced with a fork, about 15 minutes. Serve the compote warm, or chill in the refrigerator and serve cold. Or, store in an airtight container in the refrigerator for up to 3 days.

Makes 2 cups (16 fl oz/500 ml)

Raspberry Compote

¹/₂ cup (4 oz/125 g) sugar

2 teaspoons fresh lemon juice

¹/₄ teaspoon almond extract

1 cup (4 oz/125 g) raspberries

In a small saucepan over low heat, combine ¹/₂ cup (4 fl oz/125 ml) water and the sugar and cook, stirring, until the sugar dissolves. Remove from the heat and pour the sugar syrup into a bowl. Stir in the lemon juice and almond extract. Cover and let the syrup cool to room temperature, or refrigerate for up to 3 days, letting the syrup come to room temperature before serving. Gently stir in the raspberries. Set aside.

Makes 2 cups (16 fl oz/500 ml)

Lemon Curd

2 large eggs

2 large egg yolks

Juice of 2 lemons (about 1/3 cup/3 fl oz/80 ml), strained

1 cup (8 oz/250 g) sugar

6 tablespoons (3 oz/90 g) unsalted butter, cut into pieces

1 teaspoon finely grated lemon zest

In the top of a double boiler, combine the eggs, egg yolks, lemon juice, sugar, and butter. Place over (not touching) gently simmering water and whisk steadily until the sugar dissolves and the butter melts. Continue to whisk until the curd coats the back of a spoon, about 8 minutes. Do not let the curd boil.

Strain the curd through a medium-mesh sieve into a clean, dry bowl. Stir in the lemon zest. Cover with plastic wrap, pressing it gently onto the surface of the curd to prevent a skin from forming. Poke a few holes in the plastic with the tip of a knife to let steam escape. Let cool, then refrigerate until well chilled, about 3 hours, or for up to 3 days.

Makes 1 1/4 cups (10 fl oz/310 ml)

Caramel Glaze

4 tablespoons (2 oz/60 g) unsalted butter

1/2 cup (3 1/2 oz/105 g) firmly packed dark brown sugar

1/8 teaspoon salt

2 tablespoons corn syrup

1/3 cup (3 fl oz/80 ml) heavy (double) cream

1/2 teaspoon vanilla extract

In a large, heavy saucepan over low heat, melt the butter with the brown sugar, salt, and corn syrup. Cook, stirring, until the sugar dissolves. Raise the heat to medium and bring the mixture

to a boil, stirring frequently. Remove from the heat and stir in the cream and vanilla. Be careful, as the mixture may bubble up. Use immediately, or let cool, cover, and refrigerate for up to 5 days. Warm over low heat before using.

Makes 1 cup (8 fl oz/250 ml)

Whipped Cream

1 cup (8 fl oz/250 ml) heavy (double) cream

2 tablespoons confectioners' (icing) sugar

1 teaspoon vanilla extract

BY HAND: In a large bowl, combine the cream, sugar, and vanilla. Using a balloon whisk, beat until medium peaks form.

BY MIXER: In a large bowl, combine the cream, sugar, and vanilla. Using a stand mixer fitted with the whip attachment or a hand mixer, beat on medium-high speed until medium peaks form.

Use immediately, or cover and refrigerate for up to 3 hours.

Makes 2 cups (16 fl oz/500 ml)

Raspberry Whipped Cream

1 cup (8 fl oz/250 ml) heavy (double) cream

2 tablespoons seedless raspberry preserves

2 teaspoons framboise

BY HAND: In a large bowl, combine the cream, preserves, and framboise. Using a balloon whisk, beat until soft peaks form.

BY MIXER: In a large bowl, combine the cream, preserves, and framboise. Using a stand mixer fitted with the whip attachment or a hand mixer, beat on medium-high speed until soft peaks form.

Use immediately, or cover and refrigerate for up to 3 hours.

Makes 2 cups (16 fl oz/500 ml)

Pastry Cream

1 1/2 cups (12 fl oz/375 ml) whole milk

4 large egg yolks

1/2 cup (3 1/2 oz/105 g) firmly packed light brown sugar

2 tablespoons cornstarch (cornflour)

1 teaspoon vanilla extract

In a saucepan over medium heat, warm the milk until small bubbles appear along the edge. Meanwhile, in a bowl, whisk together the egg yolks, brown sugar, and cornstarch until smooth. Slowly whisk in the hot milk until blended. Return the mixture to the saucepan. Cook over medium-low heat, whisking constantly, until the mixture comes to a boil and thickens. Continue cooking, whisking constantly, for 1 minute longer. Pour through a fine-mesh sieve into a clean bowl. Stir in the vanilla. Gently press a piece of plastic wrap directly onto the surface to prevent a skin from forming. Poke a few holes in the plastic with the tip of a knife to let steam escape and let cool.

Makes about 1 1/4 cups (10 fl oz/310 ml)

Crème Fraîche

1 cup (8 fl oz/250 ml) heavy (double) cream

2 tablespoons buttermilk

Spoon the heavy cream into a plastic or glass container. Stir in the buttermilk until blended. Cover with a tight-fitting lid and let stand in a warm spot, shaking once or twice, until thickened, 24–48 hours. The crème fraîche can be stored in the refrigerator for up to 3 days.

Makes 1 cup (8 oz/250 g)

Applesauce

4 or 5 large, sweet apples such as Rome Beauty or Baldwin, 2–3 lb (2–2.5 kg) total weight, peeled, quartered, and cored

¾ cup (6 fl oz/180 ml) apple cider or water

¼ teaspoon ground cinnamon

¼–½ cup (2–4 oz/60–125 g) sugar

Fresh lemon juice

In a large, heavy nonaluminum saucepan over low heat, combine the apples and cider. Cook, stirring once or twice, until the apples are very tender, 20–30 minutes.

Drain the apples, reserving the liquid. Pass the apples through a food mill into a bowl. Alternatively, purée the apples in a food processor and transfer to a bowl. Stir in the cinnamon, sugar, lemon juice to taste, and about ¼ cup (2 fl oz/60 ml) of the cooking liquid, or as needed to achieve a good consistency. Transfer to a bowl and serve. The applesauce can be stored in an airtight container in the refrigerator for up to 3 days.

Makes 2 cups (16 fl oz/500 ml)

Aioli

½ cup (4 fl oz/125 ml) low-fat mayonnaise

4 cloves garlic, chopped

2 teaspoons fresh lemon juice

½ teaspoon extra-virgin olive oil

Kosher salt and freshly ground white pepper

Place the mayonnaise and garlic in a food processor or blender. Process until blended, about 1 minute, stopping 3 or 4 times to scrape down the sides of the bowl. Add the lemon juice, olive oil, ¼ teaspoon salt, and ⅛ teaspoon pepper. Process until smooth and creamy, about 1 minute.

Use the aioli immediately, or refrigerate, tightly covered, for up to 1 hour before using, to allow the flavors to meld.

Makes ½ cup (4 fl oz/125 ml)

Bread Crumbs

4 slices white bread

Pinch of salt

Pinch of freshly ground pepper

¼ teaspoon thyme or rosemary, finely chopped

Cut the crusts off the bread and discard. Tear the bread into pieces. In a food processor, combine the pieces of bread, salt, and pepper. Process to form coarse crumbs.

Add the thyme or rosemary and pulse a few times, just until well mixed. Use immediately, or store in an airtight container in the freezer for up to 6 months.

Makes about 1 cup (2 oz/60 g)

Pizza Dough

1 package (2½ teaspoons) active dry yeast

¾ cup (6 fl oz/180 ml) lukewarm water (110°F/43°C)

2 cups (10 oz/315 g) all-purpose (plain) flour

¾ teaspoon salt

2 tablespoons olive oil, plus extra for brushing

BY HAND: In a large bowl, dissolve the yeast in the lukewarm water and let stand until foamy, about 5 minutes. Using a wooden spoon, stir in the flour, salt, and the 2 tablespoons olive oil to make a soft dough. Turn the dough out onto a lightly floured work surface and knead until smooth and shiny, about 10 minutes.

BY STAND MIXER: In the 5-qt (5-l) bowl of a stand mixer, dissolve the yeast in the lukewarm water and let stand until foamy, about 5 minutes. Add the flour, the salt, and the 2 tablespoons olive oil. Place the bowl on the mixer, attach the dough hook, and knead on medium speed until the dough pulls away from the sides of the bowl and is smooth and shiny, about 10 minutes.

Form the dough into a ball, transfer to a lightly oiled bowl, turn to coat with the oil, and loosely cover with a damp kitchen towel. Let the dough rise in a warm, draft-free spot until it doubles in bulk, about 1 hour. Alternatively, cover with plastic wrap and refrigerate for up to 24 hours. Punch down and use as directed in the recipe.

Makes four 6- to 8- inch (15- to 20-cm) crusts

Toasting Nuts

Position a rack in the middle of the oven and preheat to 325°F (165°C). Spread the nuts in a single layer on a rimmed baking sheet or a pie pan. Toast, stirring occasionally, until the nuts are fragrant and their color deepens, 5 to 20 minutes, depending on the type of nut and the size of the pieces. For example, sliced (flaked) almonds will toast quickly, while hazelnuts (filberts) will take much longer.

Glossary

AIOLI A garlic-flavored mayonnaise popular in the south of France. The word derives from a combination of the Provençal words for garlic, *aïl,* and oil, *oli.* Typically used as a dipping sauce or as a sandwich spread.

ALMOND PASTE A smooth paste made from ground almonds, sugar, glycerine, and sometimes almond extract. Similar to marzipan but not as sweet, almond paste is used to flavor a variety of baked goods.

ANGOSTURA BITTERS An elixir made of herbs and angostura bark with a strongly bitter taste. Originally created as a tonic to improve digestion and heighten appetite, it is most commonly used today as a flavoring in cocktails.

AQUAVIT A distilled liquor from Scandinavia that is either sipped slowly like whiskey or downed in a single gulp. Like vodka, it is distilled from potato or grain, and is usually flavored with herbs such as anise, dill, fennel, or coriander. Aquavit is used to cure salmon for gravlax (page 170).

ARBORIO RICE A northern Italian variety of medium-grain rice. The plump, oval grains are rich in surface starch, which produces the creamy texture characteristic of a good risotto.

ARUGULA This slender, leafy green, also known as rocket, is a member of the mustard family. Tender, young arugula leaves have a pleasing delicacy. Older specimens have a more peppery, slightly bitter taste.

BAKING POWDER A mixture of an acid and an alkaline that gives a lift to quick breads like muffins and coffee cakes. Cornstarch (cornflour), a typical ingredient of baking powder, absorbs moisture, keeping the powder dry and preventing its activation until liquid is added.

BAKING SODA Another chemical leavener, similar to baking powder. Baking soda, also known as bicarbonate of soda, releases carbon dioxide gas when it comes into contact with an acidic ingredient such as sour cream, buttermilk, or citrus juice.

BALSAMIC VINEGAR This aged vinegar, a specialty of the Italian region of Emilia-Romagna, makes an excellent salad dressing. It is produced from the unfermented juice of Trebbiano grapes. Authentic balsamic vinegar is designated by the word *tradizionale* or an Italian consortium seal on the label, and can be aged for just 1 year to more than 75 years.

BELL PEPPERS Sweet-fleshed, bell-shaped members of the pepper family, also known as sweet peppers and capsicums. Green bell peppers are usually more sharply flavored than red ones, the latter being a sweeter and more mature stage of the former. Orange and yellow bell peppers are separate varieties.

BUTTER, UNSALTED Also labeled "sweet butter," unsalted butter is preferred by many cooks because salted butter adds to the total amount of salt in a recipe, which can interfere with taste. Unsalted butter is likely to be fresher, since salt acts as a preservative and prolongs shelf life.

BUTTERMILK To produce buttermilk, live cultures are added to low-fat or nonfat milk, thickening the milk and giving it a creamy, tangy flavor. Buttermilk contributes moisture and flavor to baked goods. It should not be substituted for regular milk.

CELERY SALT A blend of celery seed and salt. Celery salt can be found in the spice section of most grocery stores.

CHAI A popular beverage in India. Chai is a blend of tea, milk, sugar, and ground spices, usually cardamom, cinnamon, cloves, ginger, and nutmeg.

CHEESES A versatile ingredient in many breakfast and brunch dishes, cheese is typically baked with other ingredients or used as a flavoring or topping.

Cheddar This cow's milk cheese ranges from mild to sharp, with the sharpest cheeses aged 1 year or longer. American cheddars, except for Vermont cheddar, are typically colored orange by annatto seeds. Most other cheddars are white.

Farmer A white, fresh cheese that is a form of cottage cheese from which most of the liquid has been removed. It is mild and slightly tangy, and is sold in a fairly solid loaf shape.

Fresh goat Made from pure goat's milk or a blend of goat's and cow's milk. Fresh goat cheese is mild, creamy, and only slightly tangy. As goat cheeses age, they harden, and their flavor sharpens.

Gruyère Firm, smooth-textured cow's milk cheese produced in Switzerland and France, noted for its mild, nutty flavor.

Mascarpone A rich, fresh Italian cheese made from cream, with a soft, smooth texture reminiscent of sour cream. It is sold in plastic tubs, found in most upscale markets.

Monterey Jack Made from cow's milk, this mild, soft, white cheese originated in California and is ideal for melting in sandwiches, omelets, and baked dishes.

Mozzarella A mild, creamy, fresh cheese that melts easily. Many versions are made from cow's milk. A prized Italian variety is made from buffalo's milk.

Parmesan Trademarked as Parmigiano-Reggiano, this cheese comes from the

Emilia-Romagna region of northern Italy. Made from partially skimmed cow's milk, the aged, firm cheese is mild, salty, and fragrant. One of the most prized grating cheeses.

Pecorino Romano Italian grating cheese made from sheep's milk. It has a grainy texture and is pleasantly salty. Sometimes called simply romano, originates in the area around Rome.

Queso Fresco A crumbly, soft fresh Mexican cheese made from cow's milk and similar in flavor to farmer cheese.

Ricotta A whey-based Italian cheese produced by heating the whey left over from sheep's, goat's, or cow's milk cheese. Most of the ricotta available outside Italy is made from cow's milk, either whole or part skim, and is sold packed into plastic containers.

Ricotta Salata Aged Italian sheep's milk cheese. It is lightly salted and low in fat, with a firm texture ideal for grating.

CHICKEN BROTH A stock made by cooking chicken in water. In this book, it is used as a base for soups. Low-sodium versions are now available and are recommended because they allow more control of the flavoring in a recipe.

CHOCOLATE Made from the tropical cacao bean, chocolate flavors many drinks and desserts, and is popularly eaten out of hand. In this book, it appears in Spicy Hot Cocoa (page 26) and Bittersweet Café Mocha (page 26). Always purchase the best-quality chocolate you can afford. Many excellent U.S. and South American artisanal brands and high-quality European chocolates are now on the market.

Bittersweet A lightly sweetened eating, baking, or melting chocolate with a full, rich flavor. Look for bittersweet chocolate that contains at least 61 percent cacao (percentage by weight of cacao bean, with the balance primarily sugar). The higher the percentage, the more bitter the taste.

Cocoa Powder Made by removing nearly all of the cocoa butter from chocolate liquor and then grinding it to an unsweetened powder. Not as high in fat as other chocolate, it still contains about 22 percent cocoa butter. Dutch-processed cocoa powder is treated with an alkali to make it milder and more soluble than nonalkalized cocoa powder. Nonalkalized or natural cocoa powder is lighter in color but bolder in flavor. Either type can be used when a recipe calls for cocoa powder.

CLOTTED CREAM A specialty of Devonshire, England, this extra-rich cream is traditionally made by gently heating milk until a crust develops on the surface and the liquid beneath it thickens. High in milk fat, it is an English teatime staple for topping bread or scones.

CORNMEAL Dried corn kernels that have been ground to a fine, medium, or coarse consistency. The color of the corn determines the color of the cornmeal. Yellow and white cornmeal can be used interchangeably, but the yellow variety contains more vitamin A. Look for cornmeal labeled "water ground" or "stone ground," which contains the nutritious germ of the corn and has a slightly nutty flavor. More perishable than degerminated cornmeal, stone-ground cornmeal should be stored in the refrigerator. It will keep for up to 4 months.

CRÈME FRAÎCHE This rich, cultured cream product makes a luxurious topping and can be purchased or made at home. To make crème fraîche, see page 276.

CURRANTS, DRIED Dried currants are added to baked goods, such as scones and muffins. They are actually a seedless grape that has been dried and resemble a small raisin.

FENNEL This popular Mediterranean vegetable has the flavor of anise and is celerylike in appearance, with stalks, feathery leaves, and

a thick, rounded base. Its distinctive taste and crunchy texture enhance salads and other dishes. Also known as sweet fennel, Italian fennel, and *finocchio*.

FLOUR Made primarily by milling grains, seeds, or nuts, flour is an essential ingredient in most baked goods and in pancakes, waffles, and crepes, providing structure, flavor, and texture.

All-purpose Flour made from both soft and hard wheat, from which the bran and germ have been removed. It is available both unbleached and regular, the latter chemically treated to whiten it. The former, in the opinion of some cooks, has a better flavor. Also called plain flour, all-purpose flour is highly versatile, making it suitable for use in a wide range of recipes.

Bread An unbleached hard-wheat flour. Its high protein content creates an elastic dough for a higher rise and more structure in breads and pizza crusts.

Buckwheat A dark flour with a nutty, slightly sweet flavor and firm texture. Popular for making pancakes and crepes.

Cake Milled from soft wheat and containing cornstarch (cornflour), cake flour is low in protein and high in starch and yields a light crumb. Cake flour has undergone a bleaching process that increases its ability to hold water and sugar, so baked goods made with cake flour are less likely to fall. Also called soft-wheat flour.

Whole-wheat Flour ground from whole-wheat berries. Also known as wholemeal flour, it contains more vitamins, minerals, starch, and fiber than all-purpose (plain) flour. Baked goods using whole-wheat flour are dense and have a nutty, sweet flavor.

GIN This grain-based liquor gets its flavor from juniper berries and is often enjoyed in mixed drinks, such as Ramos Gin Fizz (page 41).

GRITS Also known as hominy grits, this ground meal of yellow or white corn is cooked to a thick porridge, a popular breakfast dish in the American South.

HAM A portion of the lean hind leg of a pig that has been cured, or preserved, and flavored, often by smoking. The curing is done by various methods, depending on the style of ham. Traditional European hams, like Italian prosciutto, are dry-cured in salt and air-dried. In the United States, the hind leg of the pig is traditionally dry-cured or cured in brine, then smoked and aged for months to become country ham; the best-known version is the Smithfield ham of Virginia.

HERBS An important source of flavor for many dishes, herbs are typically easy to grow at home or can be purchased at farmers' markets and many grocery stores.

Basil One of the world's best-loved herbs, basil is related to mint but tastes faintly of anise and cloves. It is often paired with tomatoes, as in Tomato Tarts with Basil and Fresh Goat Cheese (page 131), and is also an excellent addition to scrambled eggs.

Cilantro Also called fresh coriander and Chinese parsley, cilantro is a distinctly flavored herb. It is best to use at the end of cooking, as its flavor disappears during long exposure to heat.

Chervil A springtime herb with a taste reminiscent of parsley and anise, chervil is customarily used to flavor vegetables.

Chives Slender, bright green stems used to impart an onionlike flavor without the bite. Chives make an excellent garnish for all kinds of cooked eggs. They lose their flavor, color, and texture during long exposure to heat, however, so add them at the end of cooking

Dill Fine, feathery leaves with a distinct aromatic flavor. It complements savory foods, such as fish (page 170), and is used in the making of pickles.

Lemon verbena A strongly lemon-scented herb native to South America. It pairs well with fruits and makes a good infusion for herbal teas.

Mint Refreshing herb available in many varieties, with spearmint the most common. Used fresh to flavor a broad range of savory dishes, drinks, and desserts.

Parsley Adds vibrant color and pleasing flavor to almost any savory dish. The two most popular varieties are curly-leaf and flat-leaf (also called Italian parsley). Both have a refreshing and faintly peppery flavor, but flat-leaf parsley is stronger and more complex.

Oregano Aromatic, pungent, and spicy, oregano, also known as wild marjoram, is used fresh or dried to season a variety of savory dishes. It is especially compatible with tomatoes and other vegetables.

Tarragon A distinctively sweet herb with a flavor similar to anise. Tarragon is a good seasoning for egg and vegetable dishes.

Rosemary A member of the mint family, this Mediterranean herb, used both fresh and dried, has a strong, fragrant flavor well suited for eggs, meats, poultry, seafood, and vegetables.

Sage Soft, gray-green sage leaves are sweet and aromatic. Used fresh or dried, they pair well with poultry, vegetables, and pork.

Thyme One of the most important culinary herbs of Europe, thyme delivers a floral, earthy flavor to all types of food, including vegetables and poultry. One variety, lemon thyme, adds a subtle citrus note.

HONEY A natural sweetener made when honey bees extract syrupy nectar from flowers. Its flavor and color—from off-white to dark brown—depend on the source of the nectar. Honeys are usually named after their source, such as orange blossom or wildflower. Many types of honeys are flavored with herbs such

as rosemary or lavender. To reliquefy honey that has crystallized, remove the lid and set the jar in a pan of very hot water for 1–15 minutes, or microwave it in 30-second intervals, stirring after each interval, until melted.

HORSERADISH This spicy, bright-tasting root is used raw. It is commonly grated, mixed with vinegar, and then sold in jars labeled "prepared horseradish." Using fresh horseradish, which is becoming more widely available, ensures a purer flavor. Wash, peel, and trim any green areas of the root. Cut into slices and purée in a food processor. Add white vinegar to taste and pulse to make a paste. Refrigerate until ready to use.

LEEKS The mildest member of the onion family, the leek, which resembles a giant green (spring) onion, has a bright white stalk and long, overlapping green leaves. Native to the Mediterranean region, leeks bring a hint of both garlic and onion to the dishes they flavor. Choose smaller leeks with dark green leaves that are crisp, firm, and free of blemishes.

MAPLE SYRUP Pure maple syrup is made from the boiled sap of the sugar maple tree. Blended maple syrups contain only 2 to 15 percent real maple syrup. Pure maple syrup is expensive, but is so flavorful that less is needed to impart a maple flavor. Maple syrup is graded according to its quality and color. In general, the lighter the color, the milder tasting the syrup.

MEYER LEMONS A popular lemon that is slightly smaller, sweeter, and more fragrant than regular Eureka or Lisbon lemons. Meyer lemons also have a looser skin, making them easier to peel and handle.

MOLASSES This thick, sweet syrup is a by-product of sugar refinement, a process that requires repeated boiling of cane syrup. Molasses comes in three basic types: light, dark, and blackstrap. It is used to top many breakfast dishes and to sweeten many recipes such as Gingerbread Pancakes (page 141).

OILS Used for cooking and flavoring, oils are fats that are liquid at room temperature. A recipe's other ingredients and its heat requirements usually suggest which oil is most appropriate to use.

Asian sesame Deep amber-colored oil pressed from toasted sesame seeds. Used sparingly to add a rich, nutty flavor to recipes.

Canola Pressed from rapeseed, a relative of the mustard plant. High in healthful monounsaturated fat, this bland oil is recommended for general cooking and baking.

Corn Deep golden, relatively flavorless all-purpose oil primarily used for general cooking and deep-frying.

Olive Pressed from the fruit of the olive tree and high in monounsaturated fat. Extra-virgin olive oil is produced from the first press of the olives without the use of heat or chemicals. It has a clear green or brownish hue and a fruity, even slightly peppery flavor. Olive oils labeled "mild," "light," "pure," or simply "olive oil" are not as fragrant as extra-virgin.

ORANGE FLOWER WATER A fragrant extract made from orange blossoms, typically used as a flavoring in baked goods and cocktails. Look for it in specialty-food stores.

PANCETTA The name of this flavorful unsmoked bacon is derived from *pancia,* Italian for "belly." This flat cut of belly pork is first cured with salt and sometimes a selection of spices and then is rolled into a tight cylinder for air drying. When the cylinder is cut, the slices display a distinctive spiral of lean, satiny meat and pure, white fat.

PANKO Japanese bread crumbs made from wheat flour. The coarse flakes are used to coat foods before cooking, giving them a light, crunchy coating.

POLENTA Refers to both a milled grain (Italian cornmeal) and the cooked dish made from the grain. For brunch, it is served soft like oatmeal or in a form that can be cut and grilled.

PROSCIUTTO Unsmoked, uncooked Italian ham that is seasoned, cured with salt, and air-dried. The most prized prosciutto is aged up to 2 years. It is typically sliced paper thin and is best when served raw or only lightly cooked, since longer cooking can toughen the meat.

RHUBARB Although technically a vegetable, rhubarb is treated like a fruit in the kitchen. Its long, celerylike stalks range in color from cherry red to pale pink. Rhubarb usually is cooked with a good dose of sugar to balance its tartness. It is often paired with strawberries, which appear in the same season and whose sweetness provides a nice contrast. When buying rhubarb, look for crisp, firm stalks without blemishes or cuts and with good color. Avoid stalks that are turning from red or pink to green.

SALT The most basic and ancient of seasonings. Varieties include table salt, sea salt, and kosher salt. Table salt usually contains iodine along with additives that prevent it from caking so that it flows freely. Sea salt, by contrast, rarely has additives and contains more minerals than table salt. It is produced naturally by evaporation, with the taste of each variety reflecting the location where it was made. Available in coarse or fine grains that are shaped like hollow, flaky pyramids, sea salt adheres better to foods and dissolves more quickly than table salt. Many cooks prefer kosher salt. Its large, coarse flakes are easy to handle, and it is usually free of additives or preservatives. Kosher salt can be

used more liberally since it does not taste as salty as regular table salt.

TOMATOES A member of the nightshade family and native to South America, tomatoes have become an important part of many cuisines, especially those of the Mediterranean. For the best tomatoes, visit a farmers' market in the summertime.

To Peel Tomatoes: Fill a large saucepan three-fourths full with water and bring to a boil over high heat. Using a slotted spoon, lower the tomatoes into the boiling water for 30 seconds. Transfer the tomatoes to a colander. When the tomatoes are cool enough to handle, use a paring knife to slip off the skin. Then core, and use as directed in individual recipes.

TRIPLE SEC An orange-flavored liqueur primarily used as an ingredient in cocktails such as Blackberry Champagne Cocktail (page 42).

VODKA Originally made from potatoes, vodka is now usually produced from grain. Unaged and clear, vodka has little taste, making it a good candidate for mixing with a wide variety of other liquids.

YEAST A leavening agent used in many baked goods such as pizza dough, focaccia, and brioche. Doughs made with quick-rise yeast rise in half the time of those leavened with active dry yeast. Quick-rise yeast, also called instant yeast, does not need to be dissolved in a warm liquid but can be combined with other dry ingredients in a recipe to which a warm liquid is added.

YOGURT Produced from milk fermented with friendly bacterial cultures, yogurt is thick and tart with a custardlike texture. Available plain or sweetened and flavored, yogurt is made from cow's, goat's, or sheep's milk, and can be full fat, low fat, or nonfat.

Index

OXMOOR HOUSE INC.

Oxmoor
House®

Oxmoor House books are distributed by Sunset Books
80 Willow Road, Menlo Park, CA 94025
Telephone: 650-321-3600 Fax: 650-324-1532
VP and Associate Publisher Jim Childs
Director of Sales Brad Moses

Oxmoor House and Sunset Books are divisions of
Southern Progress Corporation

WILLIAMS-SONOMA, INC.
Founder & Vice-Chairman: Chuck Williams

WELDON OWEN INC.
CEO, Weldon Owen Group John Owen
CEO and President Terry Newell
Chief Financial Officer Simon Fraser
Senior VP, International Sales Stuart Laurence
VP Sales and New Business Development Amy Kaneko
VP and Creative Director Gaye Allen
VP and Publisher Hannah Rahill
Associate Publisher Amy Marr
Senior Designer and Photo Director Andrea Stephany
Designer Rachel Lopez Metzger
Associate Editor Donita Boles
Production Director Chris Hemesath
Color Manager Teri Bell
Production Manager Michelle Duggan
Photographers Tucker + Hossler
Food Stylist Jen Straus
Food Stylist's Assistant Alexa Hyman
Text Writers Judith Dunham, Stephanie Rosenbaum

ACKNOWLEDGMENTS
Weldon Owen would like to thank the following individuals for
their generous support in producing this book: Ken DellaPenta,
Peggy Fallon, Carolyn Keating, Lesli Neilson, Danielle Parker, and
Sharon Silva.

THE ESSENTIALS SERIES
Conceived and produced by
WELDON OWEN INC.
814 Montgomery Street, San Francisco, CA 94133
Telephone: 415-291-0100 Fax: 415-291-8841

In Collaboration with Williams-Sonoma, Inc.
3250 Van Ness Avenue, San Francisco, CA 94109

A WELDON OWEN PRODUCTION
Copyright © 2007 Weldon Owen Inc.
and Williams-Sonoma, Inc.

First printed in 2007
10 9 8 7 6 5 4 3 2 1

ISBN 13: 978-0-8487-3192-2
ISBN 10: 0-8487-3192-1

Printed by Midas Printing Limited
Printed in China